In Good Conscience

"Humanity faces two big and escalating challenges: climate change and social inequality. In their book, *In Good Conscience*, Professors Ind and Iglesias argue that it's time for business to transcend corporate social responsibility and to step up and play key role in addressing these major global challenges. Moreover, their timely and practical guide demonstrates convincingly that doing the right thing also happens to be good business."

— Alan Jope, *CEO Unilever*

"This is the first book to take a serious look at the role of conscience in business ethics. It will stimulate much conversation about the role of individuals and organizations in creating ethical businesses."

—R Edward Freeman, Professor, *The Darden School, University of Virginia*

"The gravity of the intertwined environmental and social crisis demands that we emerge from what Veblen described as the "predatory phase" of our development into a new era, in which we make use of our capacities to recognize reality and cooperate to address its challenges. *In Good Conscience* is timely and on the mark, recognizing both the necessity for business to earn its operating license and the power of conscience to help us plant the seeds of change that can yield a thriving planet and human culture."

—Vincent Stanley, Director, *Patagonia Philosophy*

Nicholas Ind • Oriol Iglesias

In Good Conscience

Do the Right Thing While Building a Profitable Business

Nicholas Ind
Kristiania University College
Oslo, Norway

Oriol Iglesias
Universitat Ramon Llull
ESADE Business School
Barcelona, Spain

This work contains media enhancements, which are displayed with a "play" icon. Material in the print book can be viewed on a mobile device by downloading the Springer Nature "More Media" app available in the major app stores. The media enhancements in the online version of the work can be accessed directly by authorized users.

ISBN 978-3-031-09337-1 ISBN 978-3-031-09338-8 (eBook)
https://doi.org/10.1007/978-3-031-09338-8

This Palgrave Macmillan imprint is published by the registered company Springer Nature Switzerland AG.
The registered company address is: Gewerbestrasse 11, 6330 Cham, Switzerland

Springer Nature More Media App

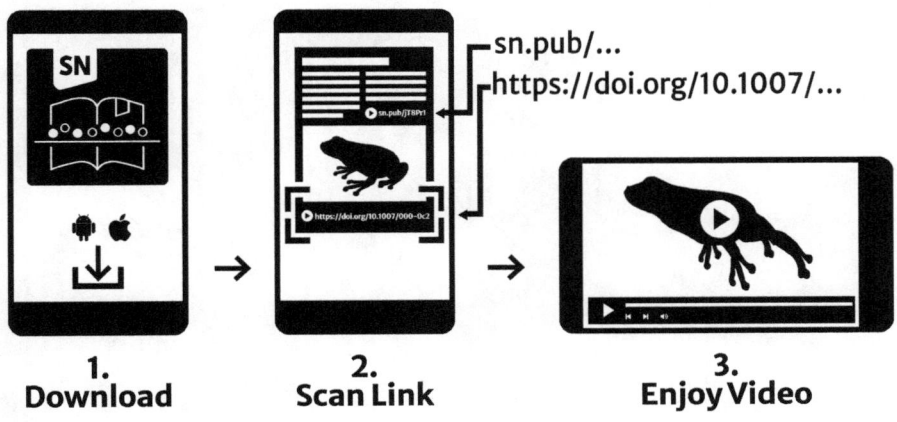

sn.pub/...
https://doi.org/10.1007/...

1.
Download

2.
Scan Link

3.
Enjoy Video

Support: customerservice@springernature.com

Acknowledgements

Researching and writing *In Good Conscience* has been an adventure; a journey into the concept of conscience and how organizations can use it to steer their thoughts and actions. While we started with some preconceptions based on the research we have done over the years, as we read, discussed ideas and conducted additional research, we both affirmed some of our beliefs and also found new insights. So, the journey we have been on has been a shared one with our interviewees, guest writers and discussants, all of whom have helped to enrich the content of the book. Our interviewees include Vincent Stanley at Patagonia; Sonu Shivdasani, Bruce Bromley, Carissa Nimah and Remon Alphenaar at Soneva; NK Chaudhary at Jaipur Rugs; August Bard Bringéus at Asket; Sergi Capell at La Casa de Carlota; Louise Fuchs, Regi Turid Pettersen and Aurora Vildskog at Oda; Kené Umeasiegbu at Tesco; Sarah Gillard at John Lewis Partnership; Wiebe Draijer, Isabelle O. Garcia van Gool and Tanja Kliphuis at Rabobank; Carolina Alvarez-Ossorio at Ecoalf; Toni Ballabriga at BBVA; and many managers at Unilever. Thanks also to Ana Palencia and Annick Boyen at Unilever for their invaluable support; to Iolanda Montserrat at HP; to Patrik Karlsson at Zettle; and to Ine Stulthens at Royal Auping.

Our guest writers whom we found through their inspirational writing are Chris Kersbergen, Marianne Waite, Sandro Kaulartz, Liz Sweigart and Brian Berkey. Our research discussants with whom we have been investigating conscience and its components in a series of studies are Stefan Markovic at Copenhagen Business School; Michela Mingione at Università degli Studi di Roma Tor Vergata; Christof Backhaus, Nathalia Tjandra and Alessandro Feri at Edinburgh Napier University; and David Woisetschläger and Barbara Seegebarth at the Technical University of Braunschweig.

Thanks to our friends at the Medinge Group think tank who have been working with conscience since 2005 and have provided an invaluable sounding board as we developed our ideas. Also, many thanks to Pål Rokke, Nick Coates and Steven Round for their thoughts and advice on content; Patrick Ind for the design of the charts and models; Maite Martin for her logistic support and Liz Barlow at Palgrave Macmillan for her guidance as an editor in helping to shape the book. Finally, thanks to the Spanish State Research Agency for the Grant PID2020-117315GB-I00 funded by MCIN/AEI/ 10.13039/501100011033.

Contents

About the Authors

Nicholas Ind is an author, academic and consultant. He has written 16 books which have been published in 9 different languages and articles in a wide variety of journals. He has been a consultant to adidas, Telia, Telenor, *The Economist*, The Foreign and Commonwealth Office and Greenpeace International, amongst others. He is a professor at Kristiania University College, Norway, and a visiting professor at Universitat Ramon Llull, ESADE Business School, Spain, and Edinburgh Napier University.

Oriol Iglesias is an author, academic, consultant and entrepreneur. He is an associate professor and head of the Marketing Department at Universitat Ramon Llull, ESADE Business School, Spain. Oriol has consulted and/or developed custom in-company training for leadings firms worldwide such as Porsche, Audi, Volkswagen, Telefónica, HP, Nestlé, Sara Lee, Banco de Santander, PwC, Ogilvy and Meliá Hotels, among others. He was a founder and partner in three companies in the entertainment, logistics and consultancy industries. He has written four books and many academic articles. He also teaches at China Europe International Business School (CEIBS), China; Rotterdam School of Management, The Netherlands; and WU Vienna, Austria.

List of Figures

1

Introducing Conscience: The Structure of the Book

In the famous opening line from *A Tale of Two Cities* (1859), Charles Dickens writes, 'It was the best of times, it was the worst of times'. He then goes on to counterpoint the best with the worst—the age of wisdom versus the age of foolishness, the spring of hope versus the winter of despair, and so on. The quote is often used, perhaps over-used, because it appears to apply to many eras. It captures the sense that good and bad co-exist and that there is always uncertainty and fluidity. The writing of this book on conscience and business also sits on certain dualities: the rapid development of new business models that reduce impacts and a core model that fuels climate change, biodiversity loss and inequality; the emergence of pioneering conscientious companies that do the right thing and those that are reluctant to change well-established profitable practices; companies with a balanced stakeholder model with a long-term perspective and those that believe in shareholder primacy with its short-term temptations. The challenge is how to get more of the best and less of the worst. This means companies using their conscience and their authority, their knowledge and their power to effect positive change. This is the theme of *In Good Conscience* and as the sub-title suggests, to do this, while being profitable.

The background to the book is that often businesses are not responding to the crises we face adequately. Not surprisingly, there is much heated discussion on corporate social responsibility (CSR) and sustainability and growing expectations of business from government, investors, employees, consumers and citizens. This creates pressure on organizations to devise strategies and take actions on environmental and social issues. Yet—as we will see in this book—some companies ignore the pressure or provide a response that is skin

© The Author(s), under exclusive license to Springer Nature Switzerland AG 2022
N. Ind, O. Iglesias, *In Good Conscience*, https://doi.org/10.1007/978-3-031-09338-8_1

deep. It's easier for a company to make gestures and tempting for a company to gloss over current failings. The key problem is that such actions are not rooted in conscience, which reduces commitment. When difficulties emerge then expediency or evasion tends to get the better of good intentions. Our argument is that environmental and social strategies are only sustainable when they are driven by a strong organizational conscience. As one of our interviewees in this book, Wiebe Draijer, CEO of Rabobank, argues about the role of the bank in the world, 'conscience has led to the conviction we have an opportunity, but also an obligation to sometimes bring about system change'.

The power of conscience is evident in many of the businesses that feature in this book. It shows how companies can transform themselves and others through their commitment, but we also see how some damage people and the environment. For example, the accelerating loss of biodiversity means that since 1970 the global wildlife population has fallen by 68% and currently one million species are threatened by extinction because of activities, such as forestry and the production of cattle feed, soybean and palm oil. In spite of the urgency, 43% of the 500 most influential commodity supply chains have no commitment on deforestation.[1] It doesn't have to be this way. Our belief is that the regenerative power of capitalist enterprise can help to identify our most urgent and substantive problems and find solutions that change the way we see and do things. We have been here before. If we take a step into the past and the practices of the Atlantic slave trade, some argued that there was nothing wrong with the trade itself, it just needed adjustment, while others, driven by conscience, argued the system itself was wrong. From our vantage point we can see there was undoubtedly the 'worst' in the iniquities of the trade itself and the willingness of businesses to see people as objects and to justify their actions in terms of self-interest. For the 'best', we can see how conscientious, impassioned people and some companies promoted and effected significant change.

The Power of Conscience: From Wedgwood to Chocolonely

In 1781, the British slave ship Zong set sail from Ghana for Jamaica with more than 400 African slaves onboard, 17 crew and an inexperienced captain. Even by the standards of slave ships, the Zong was over-crowded and under-manned. When the ship arrived in Caribbean waters, it got lost and sailed

---

[1] Citi GPS (2021) Biodiversity: the ecosystem at the heart of business. July 2021.

some 300 miles past Jamaica. The sailors then decided to discard some of their cargo and threw 132 slaves overboard. They later claimed they had done this because there was insufficient drinking water, although this was later disputed as they eventually arrived in Jamaica with a good supply. The real benefit of discarding the slaves was that the insurers would pay out if some people were thrown overboard to save the rest of the cargo, to the tune of £30 per slave. However, the insurers sensed fraud and refused to pay. The claim ended up in court in London where the verdict was that the killing of slaves was legal in certain circumstances. Undeterred, the insurers appealed the verdict and argued that the owner's arguments could not justify the killing of innocent people, which was tantamount to murder. The insurers won their appeal, but no trial followed.

The idea that human beings could be treated as a commodity, like cotton or sugar, is shocking. It's hard to imagine how one could think like that and how conscience could allow such actions. At the time some were also deeply troubled by what had happened. The murder of the slaves was seen as a stain on the conscience of the nation and an indication of the moral dangers of elevating economic conditions above humanity. As the historian, Bronwen Everill notes, it demonstrated the anxiety that 'the financial accounting of everything, the transformation of not only things and then time, but also people into commodities with a monetary value had gone too far'.[2] The sense of morality and capitalism in conflict impacted not only the perceptions of the tainted slave owners and traders but also the attitudes of government, companies and consumers. The story of the Zong galvanized those involved in the incipient abolitionist movement in its confrontation with the widespread acceptance of slavery as a 'legitimate social institution'.[3]

Following the Zong case, things slowly began to shift. In 1807, due to the growing power of the abolitionist movement the slave trade came to an end. The period between the Zong and abolition saw the emergence of companies and consumers using their power to challenge the institution of slavery. In a foretaste of companies acting on their conscience while at the same time building equity, the pottery company, Wedgwood, developed products featuring an illustration of a kneeling slave in chains with the line 'Am I not a man and a brother?'—it became the logo of the abolitionists.

Wedgwood and others aimed to appeal to a new class of ethically aware citizens who wanted to demonstrate their commitment to abolition and to

---

[2] Everill, B. (2020). *Not Made by Slaves. Ethical capitalism in the age of abolition*. Cambridge Mass: Harvard University Press, p. 42.
[3] Drescher S, (2012) 'The Shocking Birth of British Abolitionism', *Slavery & Abolition* 33, no. 4: 571–93.

communicate their identity through consumption: 'Differentiation through political values was another means of "virtue signalling" to other middle-class consumers by turning morality into fashion'.[4] Such consumers boycotted the sugar produced by slave owners in the West Indies in favour of alternative sources. These products though often came at a premium, which led to woke-washing *avant la lettre*, as unscrupulous companies played on the conscience of consumers with spurious claims. In response credible companies worked to verify supply chains, ensure slave/free labour produce was not mixed together and demonstrate provenance through ethical labelling.

The story of the Zong might seem distant history, but given that today, some 25 million workers worldwide are estimated to be modern slaves, this is still a live issue.[5] The slave trade had profound implications at the time and it foreshadows many of the themes that we will be exploring in this book, from how a company can opt to do the right thing and be successful, to the power of consumers when they act as conscientious citizens, to the importance of authentic principles. Underlying these themes is the overarching importance of conscience—that which guides individuals and corporations in making good choices. In echoes of Wedgwood and other conscientious organizations from the early nineteenth century, we will be visiting and learning from companies such as Tony's Chocolonely (confronting modern slavery in West Africa), Unilever (tackling environmental and social challenges), Asket (meeting the problem of supply chain transparency), Rabobank (integrating conscience into strategic decisions and creating systemic change) and Patagonia (enabling consumers to be advocates for environmentalism). And we'll also try to understand why some companies still see people as objects and seem to lack conscience.

Becoming Conscientious

Our interest in conscience comes from a belief that business can be a force for good. This does not argue that companies always do good things. Inevitably they are inconsistent. But they do have the resources and the intellectual capital to deliver positive change—if they are committed. The question we have considered for many years is, what drives that commitment? And the answer is a belief system that is rooted in conscience. The context to this is that we are

[4] Everill, B. (2020) op cit., p. 89.
[5] Gold, S., Trautrims, A., & Trodd, Z. (2015). Modern slavery challenges to supply chain management. *Supply chain management: an international journal*; ILO (2017) https://www.ilo.org/wcmsp5/groups/public/@dgreports/@dcomm/documents/publication/wcms_575479.pdf.

both part of a think tank, called Medinge (after the location in Sweden where it was founded), which from 2005 ran a project, celebrating those brands that were deemed to be highly conscientious. In 2016, we wrote a book, *Brands with a Conscience,* which featured 18 case histories. Since then, we have conducted research projects into the attitudes and behaviour of company managers, marketing agency managers and consumers and conducted a detailed case history of Unilever and its supply chain partners.[6] These studies consistently show a set of common attributes of conscientious companies and brands that form the basis of *In Good Conscience.* However, we not only draw on the theory we have developed through research but on our experience of consulting for companies, conducting executive programmes and the interviews conducted specifically for this book. Our aim is to not only provide you with insights into both already conscientious and becoming conscientious companies and their practices but to provide inspiration as to how you can work to help transform your organization and meet the needs of society and the environment. Additional to our research, insights and inspirations also come from the valuable inputs of five guest writers—Chris Kersbergen, Marianne Waite, Sandro Kaulartz, Liz Sweigart and Brian Berkey—who have produced sections in the book that develop, extend and sometimes challenge the ideas we put forward.

A final point to note before we look at the content of the book is language. Especially when discussing this book with those whose first language is not English, 'conscience' often gets conflated with 'conscious'. In his book on *Moral Conscience Through the Ages,* Richard Sorabji shows how the terms inter-link and details how the idea of conscience changes over time. What should be noted here is that conscience does include consciousness (awareness), but is different in that it specifically concerns action as well as belief. Also, in the book we interweave the use of 'conscience' and 'conscientious', depending on the way we phrase an argument. To be clear when we use the word 'conscientious', it means relating to a person's or a company's conscience, not the sense of the word which is concerned with being dutiful and thorough.

---

[6] Iglesias, O. & Ind, N. (2016). How to be a brand with a conscience. In Ind, N. & Horlings, S., *Brands with a conscience: How to build a successful and responsible brand* (pp. 203–211). London: Kogan Page; Iglesias, O., & Ind, N. (2020). Towards a theory of conscientious corporate brand co-creation: the next key challenge in brand management. *Journal of Brand Management, 27*(6), 710–720; Ind, N., Iglesias, O., & Markovic, S. (2020). Conscientious Organizations: How Business is Accelerating Toward a Fairer Future. *California Management Review.*; Holmes L and Ind N. (2022) *Brands with a Conscience: a Research Study into How Business Can Do the Right Thing and Be Profitable.* https://medinge.org/brands-with-a-conscience-a-research-study-into-how-business-can-do-the-right-thing-and-be--profitable/.

The Content

In Chap. 2, we delve into the nature of conscience and in Chap. 3, how it works in organizations. Conscience is a complex idea with a long history, but at its simplest it is a belief system rooted in experience, knowledge and reflection that involves awareness of others, which drives morally good acts.[7] It is both a guide for future intentions and a point of accountability for choices made—which is why we can be troubled by our conscience when we fail to live up to our own expectations. The playwright, dissident and eventual statesman, Václav Havel, who referred to his conscience as 'this intimate universal partner of mine', was keenly aware of this. During imprisonment in 1977 for his role as a dissident spokesperson, he was outfoxed by his interrogator and agreed to step aside in his role in return for early release. Reflecting on this moral failing he went through years of 'silent desperation, self-castigation, shame, inner humiliation, reproach and uncomprehending questioning'. He noted in one of his letters to his wife that while it was not hard to stand behind one's successes, it was devilishly hard 'to accept responsibility for one's failures'.[8]

While most discussions of conscience focus on the individual, what we do here is shift perspective. We build on the work of certain writers and researchers to argue that conscience can be seen from an organization's viewpoint and used to guide strategies, business models, innovations, processes, partnerships, communications and sustainability practices. Contrary to CSR approaches, which are all too often tangential, conscience should be core to the way a company operates. Many of the businesses, both small and large, new and old, that you will meet in this book demonstrate that conscience, properly and consistently exercised, can be the foundation of activities and deliver profound and enduring outcomes. You'll also read about companies that are becoming conscientious and the challenges they face in making the transformation.

A challenge though with moving from an individual perspective to a collective, corporate perspective is that conscience becomes hard to pin down. When we think of our own conscience, we have a sense of what we believe is right and wrong, even if it is only when we confront a moral dilemma and have to choose a course of action, that we become fully aware of it. However, where do we find the organizational conscience? Somewhere in the office

---

[7] Sorabji R. (2014). *Moral Conscience through the Ages: fifth century BCE to the Present.* Chicago: Chicago University Press.

[8] Ignatieff M. (2021) *On Consolation: finding solace in dark times.* London: Picador, p. 237.

building there might be a door with CSR, but there is no place labelled conscience. It lives in the ideas and actions of people and in the organizational culture. To make conscience explicit and usable, a company will often put its belief system into words, by using such concepts as purpose (its raison d'être) and principles (the fundamental tenets that guide acts). This is not exactly conscience, which is irreducible and ineffable, but is rather a proxy for it. Conscience comes to life when purpose and principles are used to adapt to the specific contexts in which choices can be made. This means that although we try to think of conscience in words, its precise meaning is always in flux as beliefs meet events. Our guest writer in Chap. 3, **Brian Berkey,** reminds us that this sometimes means making difficult choices.

In Chap. 4, we look at the process of articulating conscience and then in Chap. 5, how companies can curate and embed it in their everyday work. Curation indicates that companies must choose where they are going to focus their resources. Some companies, especially smaller ones, have a very defined purpose and they concentrate on delivering that. For example, Dutch chocolate brand, Tony's Chocolonely has a strong social cause which is to make the production of chocolate slave fee, whereas Spanish fashion brand, Ecoalf, is focused on textile innovation and promoting recycling. However, larger companies such as software company, SAP and Unilever, while stressing the centrality of purpose, often align activities with the UN's 17 Sustainable Development Goals and try to deliver on a broader range of environmental, social and governance issues not only within the boundaries of their organization but together with their business-to-business partners and suppliers in their ecosystems. Increasingly, there is an expectation that even if a company is an exemplar in an area such as environmentalism, it should also address other factors, such as racial justice, wellbeing, inequality and, as **Marianne Waite** eloquently argues, disability.

When it comes to embedding conscience, companies have to make it meaningful. In this context, we bring in a concept called 'power *with*', created by the pioneering management thinker, Mary Parker Follett. She persuasively argues that if you want to build commitment you can't impose it, but instead you need a jointly developed, co-active power. Follett conceived of this idea with a focus on the company, but as the example of UK Supermarket chain Tesco, and others show, the application of power *with*, should be extended beyond the boundaries of the company. In practice, this means using conscience to reflect on, and discuss, the choices that confront an organization. For example, should Tesco help suppliers to make their own systems more sustainable? Should it encourage consumers to eat more vegetables and less meat? Should it move to using sustainable energy sources? These questions could simply be answered in terms of their potential economic consequences. And if we were adhering to the beliefs of shareholder primacy, which elevates the needs of shareholders above all others, that is what we would do. So, from this view, we would say 'no' to more vegetables and 'no' to less (high margin) meat. Yet, when we introduce a stakeholder perspective and think more in terms of what is the right thing to do for suppliers, farmers, consumers and citizens, we are starting to consider bigger, longer-term, human-centric issues connected to fairness and responsibility. For these decisions we need more data and we need to work together with stakeholders to find solutions that address the need to do the right thing and to be profitable. So, 'yes' we should try to persuade consumers to eat less meat because of the health and environmental implications of meat production and consumption,[9] but then we need to think innovatively together with suppliers, farmers and start-ups, to create new higher value vegetable meals and introduce new vegetable variants. This grounding of conscience in specifics demonstrates how we can move from theory, which generalizes, to critically reflect on practice.

Many of the organizations we have researched for this book have conscientious roots. Companies like Ecoalf, Tony's Chocolonely and John Lewis Partnership were founded on a cause. Yet, others, such as Britain's largest supermarket, Tesco, have little in their pasts that indicate anything other than a whole-hearted pursuit of profitability. The motto of Tesco's founder, Jack Cohen, and indeed the title of his authorized biography, was 'pile it high, sell it cheap'. Yet, Tesco makes a fascinating case, because it is typical of the commercial business landscape in its faltering journey from shareholder primacy and a focus on weekly sales figures to a more conscientious and longer-term approach. Look at media commentary and you can find plenty of criticism of its environmental and social policies, but you can also see that the same energy that drove Tesco's rapid business expansion is now being used to transform its approach to sustainability. Directing this dynamism gives us some sense of 'how' an organization can make conscience live. This is the theme that we develop in Chap. 6 on innovation, Chap. 7 on communication and Chap. 8 on leadership.

In Chap. 6 we show how companies are using their powers of innovation to address some of the problems of over-consumption of goods and a disposable mindset that pays little attention to what happens after we discard things. In a previous book we wrote, titled *Brand Desire*, we opened with a quote by the psychoanalyst, Jacques Lacan, *Desidero ergo sum* ('I desire, therefore I am').

---

[9] Kong B. (2021) Why have I heard that eating meat is bad for the climate? MIT Climate Portal. https://climate.mit.edu/ask-mit/why-have-i-heard-eating-meat-bad-climate.

Lacan's aphorism is a statement of an essential drive, without which, people become 'listless, passive and indifferent to the world'.[10] In *Brand Desire* we go on to outline the five sources that drive this love of desire: meaningfulness, surprise, authenticity, social identity and sensuality. These sources drive our feeling that we must have that new Apple iPhone, replacement Patagonia jacket or that long longed-for Porsche car. Our argument in this book is that companies should recognize the importance of desire, but instead of satiating it through new products to instead focus on new positive experiences. While there are some consumers who are deliberately trying to minimize their footprint, for most a hairshirt approach isn't desirable. Therefore, conscientious companies look to meet consumers' desires, but to do so through different strategies that generate less impact, which we categorize as slowing down (better management of supply and demand and longer product life cycles), circularity (recycling, upcycling and servicification) and extending (reselling, renting and repair). In this chapter, **Sandro Kaulartz** uses his experience to develop these arguments and show how challenger brands are rethinking established markets with products that address the rising value-based, conscientious consumer with innovations that bring guilt-free products, carbon-neutrality and a transparent sustainability agenda.

Chapter 7 builds on the ideas in the previous chapter by showing how conscientious companies help consumers to make good choices. Various writers have noted that people struggle to identify virtuous organizations. Amidst all the claims and corporate bragging about environmental and social initiatives, and the surfeit of labels and schemes, how do consumers know who to trust?.[11] To tackle this problem, conscientious companies are explicit and transparent in their communications. They not only ensure that claims are backed by hard evidence, but they also avoid over-claiming. Instead of being distant and shouting about themselves, they work to bring their stakeholders into the dialogue. Such companies as Patagonia, Tony's Chocolonely and Rabobank (which **Chris Kersbergen** describes for us) are engaged in building movements of change that challenge assumptions and dissipate organizational barriers. These transformative companies are doing the right thing, but they also reap the rewards of a stronger relationship with their consumers and other stakeholders. Vincent Stanley, Patagonia's Director of Philosophy, argues that taking a stance on important societal issues that matter to people has

---

[10] Ind N and Iglesias O (2016) *Brand Desire: how to create consumer involvement and inspiration*. London: Bloomsbury, p. 10.

[11] Lacey N & Long J. (2020). The Sustainability Imperative: the case for building sustainable businesses has never been stronger. *Ipsos Views*. November 2020.

become an important part of their business model: 'our relationship to the customer is becoming less transactional, more engaged by this idea of being in common cause'.

Leaders of conscientious companies and those becoming conscientious have to work in new ways. Leaders of already conscientious companies are often impassioned individuals such as Yvon Chouinard at Patagonia, Sonu Shivdasani at Soneva and Javier Goyeneche at Ecoalf. Their individual consciences strongly influence the corporate conscience. The leaders of companies that are becoming conscientious have a more fundamental task in that they need to listen to internal and external stakeholders, be aware of environmental, social and governance requirements and act as the conduit to the corporate conscience. This requires empathy and humility as well as the ability to execute effectively. It is a role that has been likened to that of a conductor.[12] Yet, whatever the accuracy of that analogy, the challenges that leaders face are manifold. Often their backgrounds make them ill equipped to meet the ever more strident demands of investors, customers and government to deliver on environmental and social issues, to meet the needs of ever more activist employees, to overcome the uncertainty as to the best course of action and to know what can be publicly said without fear of criticism. In this chapter, **Liz Sweigart** illuminates the dilemmas of leadership and the requirement for a new ethical approach of leaders as moral integrators.

In the final chapter of the book, we move from the actions of leaders to the way all of us can contribute to improving the organizations we have a stake in. We invite readers to make a difference. The essential ingredient here is that we have to care. If we care enough we can contribute, but we also need to be willing to take responsibility—some organizations make that easier for us to do than others—encourage transparency and be consistently human-centric. Of course, it is one thing to analyse the dilemmas that confront business and another to outline recipes for change. And yet another for it to happen. Should we be optimistic about this? This takes us back to our opening quote from Dickens. The pessimistic view is that talk outruns actions, while in the optimist corner, there is a strong groundswell of activism in support of a more sustainable approach coming from investors, employees and consumers, which should give us hope for the future.

---

[12] Michel, G. 2017. From brand identity to polysemous brands: Commentary on "Performing identities: Processes of brand and stakeholder identity co-construction". *Journal of Business Research* 70: 453–455.

2

What Is Conscience? And Why Does It Matter?

Should a pharmacy retailer sell tobacco? In 2014, the US pharmacy chain CVS decided that the sale of tobacco was inconsistent with its purpose: *helping people on their path to better health*. Larry Merlo, Group President and CEO, stated that it was 'simply the right thing to do for the good of our customers and our company'.[1] If we wanted to be churlish, we might argue that CVS were a bit slow in taking the initiative. More than 40 years earlier the American Pharmaceutical Association had recommended that pharmacies stop selling tobacco as being antithetical with their public role, but faced with the loss of revenue, pharmacies didn't take action. For CVS, with some 7600 retail outlets, the hit was some $2 billion, but a study showed the benefit to public health in that smokers who bought tobacco exclusively at CVS were 38% less likely to buy tobacco afterwards.[2] Also, CVS seemed to realize an immediate benefit both in terms of reputation—President Barack Obama applauded the move—and in terms of valuation, with CVS shares closing at their highest value in 34 years on the news.[3] However, CVS's competitors were critical, arguing that it would do little to reduce tobacco consumption. Competitor, Walgreens, for example, countered the pressure by arguing that selling tobacco was an issue of consumer choice and that they were simply meeting those desires. CEO of Walgreens Boots Alliance, Stefano Pessina,

---

[1] www.cvshealth.com/news-and-insights/articles/cvs-quits-a-message-from-larry-merlo-president-and-ceo.

[2] Polinski, J. M., Howell, B., Gagnon, M. A., Kymes, S. M., Brennan, T. A., & Shrank, W. H. (2017). Impact of CVS pharmacy's discontinuance of tobacco sales on cigarette purchasing (2012–2014). *American journal of public health, 107*(4), 556–562.

[3] https://www.bbc.com/news/business-29057840.

N. Ind, O. Iglesias, *In Good Conscience*, https://doi.org/10.1007/978-3-031-09338-8_2

noted that there were a lot of negative reactions when they had tested removing tobacco from stores.[4]

Given the impact of tobacco consumption on public health (some 480,000 people over the age of 35 are estimated to die each year in the US from smoking),[5] it would seem that CVS has made the right choice. Yet others might counter, perhaps citing the libertarian philosopher, John Stuart Mill, that people should be free to do what they want as long as it doesn't harm others and that the market is not a moral space where judgements about doing the right thing should be made. As John Ladd argues, 'Thus, for logical reasons it is improper to expect organizational conduct to conform to the ordinary principles of morality. We cannot and must not expect formal organizations, or their representatives acting in their official capacities, to be honest, courageous, considerate, sympathetic, or to have any kind of moral integrity.'[6]

The free-market view (and that word 'free' is important) does not allow for the intrusions of conscience beyond the principle of freedom itself. This conception of freedom focuses on ensuring that people are not constrained from exercising their individual rights. In doing so it rejects such notions as equality and fairness, because they are seen to inhibit liberty rather than enable it.[7] However, this approach to freedom ignores the problem as to whether those consumers that are addicted to tobacco are truly free to choose (it's a similar argument to the challenge of opioid addiction) both from a biological point of view and from the perspective of social convention and whether smokers owe a responsibility to the passive smokers who happen to share their social spaces.[8] In essence this perspective of freedom denies the importance of the other and runs counter to beliefs about inclusion and participation. It's the opposite of a belief in a social view of freedom, which recognizes our common humanity—a point made clearly by Nelson Mandela is his view that those who oppress and those who are oppressed are both unfree: 'For to be free is not merely to cast off one's chains, but to live in a way that respects and enhances the freedom of others'. [9] This debate about the role of business and

---

[4] https://www.wsj.com/articles/walgreens-isnt-ready-to-quit-cigarette-sales-yet-11554049495.

[5] https://www.cdc.gov/tobacco/data_statistics/fact_sheets/fast_facts/index.htm.

[6] Ladd J. Morality and the Ideal of Rationality in Formal Organizations, *The Monist*, October 1970, p. 499.

[7] De Dijn, A. (2020). *Freedom: an unruly history*. Cambridge, Mass: Harvard University Press.

[8] Kant argues that to act autonomously is to act in line with a law I give myself. We are not free if driven by uncontrolled desires. Kant I. (1998) Groundwork of the Metaphysics of Morals. Trans. M. Gregor. Cambridge: Cambridge University Press.

[9] https://www.nelsonmandela.org/content/page/a-selection-of-nelson-mandela-quotes.

moral responsibility has been played out in the divergent views of shareholder primacy versus stakeholders.

In broad terms, the distinction here is a view that sees the primacy of the shareholder as the key factor in corporate decision-making and that allows for choices to be made only as long as they benefit shareholders and a stakeholder-led view that recognizes that businesses have a broader responsibility to all their audiences and to society and the environment. In the case of the shareholder view the most visible advocate has been the economist, Milton Friedman, who in his polemic, *The social responsibility of business is to increase its profits* (*The New York Times*, 1970), railed against the 'fundamentally subversive doctrine' that organizations should be diverted from their primary responsibility to shareholders as 'pure and unadulterated socialism'. He argued that a company executive was beholden to his owners and that he should not be spending their funds on adjacencies to maximizing shareholder funds.[10] The only allowable context for spending company money on social responsibility, such as supporting a local community, is because there are business benefits. Friedman concludes with the assertion, 'there is one and only one social responsibility of business—to use its resources and engage in activities designed to increase its profits so long as it stays within the rules of the game, which is to say, engages in open and free competition without deception or fraud'. In other words, in this view, 'being profitable' is the *sine qua non* of business practice, while 'the right thing' is an occasional fortunate side effect.

However, over the years, the limitations of shareholder primacy have been questioned and challenged in terms of both morality and effectiveness. Friedman and his colleagues put forward three key arguments, which while appealing to the spirit of the times now look less robust. First, they argued that free markets are perfectly efficient and that this makes them a spectacular driver of economic prosperity. However, following the financial collapse of 2008, we now recognize (if we needed reminding) that markets are not perfectly efficient and are subject to biases and distortions. While it can be argued that competitive markets allocate resources effectively and efficiently, they need to be tempered by frameworks that ensure that there isn't a gap between value and values.[11] As the former central bank governor, Mark Carney, reminds, a market 'is a social construct whose effectiveness is determined partly by the rules of the state and partly by the values of society'.

The second argument rests on the normative primacy of individual freedoms; that personal, individual freedom is—or should be—the primary goal

---

[10] The use of 'his' and 'he' is in the original text.

[11] Carney M (2021) *Value(s): building a better world for all*. William Collins, p. 130.

of society and that an individual's ability to make decisions about the disposition of her resources and time should be one of society's highest goals. Here, Friedman's arguments are connected to those of the economist Friedrich Hayek's, in articulating an intellectual counterpoint to centralized planning and economic control as practiced in the Soviet Union. Freedom in this context is 'freedom from'—the ability to make decisions free from the interference of others, but as the sociologist Zygmunt Bauman notes, we not only seek freedom, but also safety and security in our lives: 'Promoting security always calls for the sacrifice of freedom, while freedom can only be expanded at the expense of security ... this circumstance gives philosophers a headache with no known cure. It also makes living together conflict-ridden, as security sacrificed in the name of freedom tends to be *other people's* security, and freedom sacrificed in the name of security tends to be *other people's* freedom.'[12]

Third, managers are agents for their investors. Acting as a trustworthy agent is a moral commitment on its own. This is a valid argument, but it should always recognize that investors can be interested in both short- and long-term gains and that value creation for investors is also dependent on other stakeholders. These arguments in favour of shareholder primacy and the maximization of freedom gained significant political support in the 1980s from US President Ronald Reagan and British Prime Minister Margaret Thatcher. Yet at the same time there was another emergent perspective which was stakeholder theory. This countered the pure focus on shareholders and argued that companies have a responsibility to meet the needs of employees, customers and communities. While companies may be accountable to shareholders, the stakeholder perspective indicates that businesses have a societal role. As Svensson and Wood note, business is 'allowed to exist because in capitalist societies it is deemed to have a central and pivotal role in the betterment of society'.[13] In adopting this view, benefits to non-shareholders are not a side effect, but the result of conscious and conscientious consideration of the needs of diverse stakeholders. Whereas the shareholder view encourages abstraction, the stakeholder view is human-centric and recognizes the responsibility we owe to others. It makes the interests of people an integral part of the decision-making process, because engaged and motivated employees are treated as individuals and suppliers are treated as productive partners in the co-creation of value together with customers.

---

[12] Bauman Z (2001) *Community: seeking safety in an insecure world*. Cambridge: Polity Press, p. 20.
[13] Svensson, G., & Wood, G. (2008). A model of business ethics. *Journal of Business Ethics, 77*(3), 303–322, p. 305.

The role that business plays matters, because companies exert a significant influence on the world in the way that they treat people, their actions on the environment and the impact on local communities. In terms of revenues, out of the 100 largest economic entities on our planet, 69 are corporations.[14] Comparing revenues to national GDP, Walmart is bigger than Argentina and Amazon is bigger than Greece. These entities have considerable influence on government and other institutions and directly affect the livelihoods of considerable numbers: Walmart alone employs some 2.2 million people, while Unilever sources ingredients from more than 1.5 million farmers. While some might advocate that business should not become embroiled in social and political issues, the centrality of business in our world makes this impossible. Increasingly this change is being recognized. Highly influential bodies that have long been wedded to shareholder primacy have changed their mind and become advocates for a stakeholder view. In August 2019, the Business Roundtable (an association of nearly 200 of the largest companies in the US) ditched its 1997 statement that 'The paramount duty of management and of boards of directors is to the corporation's stockholders' for a new commitment to 'An economy that serves all Americans' by creating 'value for customers', 'investing in employees', fostering 'diversity and inclusion', 'dealing fairly and ethically with suppliers', 'supporting the communities in which we work', and 'protect[ing] the environment'. Shareholders don't get a mention until word 250 of the 300 word statement. [15] Then, in December 2019 the World Economic Forum (which aims to improve the world through public-private co-operation) refreshed its 30-year old Manifesto to state: 'The purpose of a company is to engage all its stakeholders in shared and sustained value creation. … The best way to understand and harmonize the divergent interests of all stakeholders is through a shared commitment to policies and decisions that strengthen the long-term prosperity of a company.'

Whereas, not so long ago, business was perceived as a constraint on effecting positive environmental and social change, and kept at arm's length, by such bodies as the United Nations, with the launch of the United Nations Sustainable Development Goals in 2015, companies have become integral to the process of change: 'a new paradigm in development thinking is recognizing the centrality of private enterprise in pursuit of the development agenda' (UN Global Compact White Paper). Business can bring resources, innovative approaches and specific competences to the challenges that the world faces,

---

[14] https://www.globaljustice.org.uk/news/69-richest-100-entities-planet-are-corporations-not-governments-figures-show/.
[15] Business Roundtable, "Statement on the Purpose of a Corporation," Aug. 19, 2019, https://opportunity.businessroundtable.org.

that would be insurmountable without their commitment. However, before we get carried away with this changing spirit, we should also recognize the gap between rhetoric and action and the challenge of divergent motivations that lead companies to tinker with responsibility, rather than integrating it into the core of what they do—and to sometimes make grandiose claims, while doing little of substance.[16] This is an issue of conscience.

Defining Conscience

Conscience is something that guides us in our actions and contains the idea that we should be true to ourselves and be aware of the needs of others. Adam Smith in his 1759 book *The Theory of Moral Sentiments* connects conscience back to its Greek origins and the idea of the split individual, by arguing that we should imagine our choices being judged by an impartial spectator, who calls to us and makes us reflect on the impact on ourselves and on others.[17] In the opening of *The Theory of Moral Sentiments*, Smith writes: 'How selfish soever man may be supposed, there are evidently some principles in his nature, which interest him in the fortune of others, and render their happiness necessary to him, though he derives nothing from it except the pleasure of seeing it'.[18] Smith notes that we cannot truly experience the world as others do, but he asks us to imagine the experience of others and to apply that sense back on ourselves, so that we can conceive of what it would feel like to be in their situation. We might be tempted to think of conscience purely in terms of rationality, but as Smith reminds us it requires thoughtfulness and imagination. Before we choose, we must imagine the impact of our choice.

Similarly, Immanuel Kant sees conscience in terms of an inner court of judgement that encourages us to examine and reflect upon our decisions and to recognize our duty to act morally towards others; to be worthy of our common humanity.[19] In this view, conscience both warns us before we act and pronounces a verdict over actions already performed.[20] The key missing ingredient in these definitions is how we determine what is the right thing. Kant's

[16] Scheyvens, R., Banks, G., & Hughes, E. (2016). The Private Sector and the SDGs: The Need to Move Beyond 'Business as Usual.' *Sustainable Development*, *24*(6), 371–382. https://doi.org/10.1002/sd.1623.

[17] Smith, A. (2009). *The theory of moral sentiments*. First published (1759). Penguin Books.

[18] Smith, A. (2009) ibid., p. 13.

[19] Kant, I. (1998). *Groundwork of the Metaphysics of Morals*. First published as Grundlegungzur Metaphysik der Sitten, (1785). Trans. Mary Gregor. Cambridge: Cambridge University Press.

[20] Wood, A. (2006). Kant on conscience. *Kantovski Sbornik*, 1–17. https://web.stanford.edu/~allenw/webpapers/KantOnConscience.pdf.

formula for this is the categorical imperative—that we should 'act only according to that maxim whereby you can at the same time, will that it should become a universal law'.[21] This tells us what we ought to do, unconditionally, independently of societal norms or the law. Indeed, we are only free when our actions are not determined by something or someone outside of ourselves and we show an ability to empathize with others. The ideas of Smith and Kant require us to search within ourselves for the right moral choices, to engage in self-questioning and then to act with moral commitment. Of course, the easy option is to coast along without thinking about why we do what we do and ignoring difficult moral choices. However, if we ignore the voice of our conscience, then we may not only disappoint or injure others, but we also have to live with ourselves. As the political philosopher Hannah Arendt writes 'if I disagree with other people, I can walk away; but I cannot walk away from myself.'[22]

An interesting business example of someone who was not prepared to walk away from himself was Dave Lewis, CEO of the UK's largest retailer, Tesco. In July 2020, at the height of the COVID-19 pandemic, Lewis decided to write an opinion piece for the *Financial Times*, entitled, 'The UK's food strategy cannot be left to the market'.[23] Clearly, many free-marketers would argue that food should be left to the market and a number of people in business, in farming and within Tesco felt it was controversial, but Lewis was driven by his conscience and the belief that a lack of what he called a whole society approach to food, 'damages our health, education, economy and environment'. In stakeholder language he argues for a more resilient, sustainable and equitable system that benefits all and specifically says that people must eat less meat and dairy in the cause of climate change. He goes on to advocate the importance of ensuring sustainable supply chains, reporting requirements on food waste and switching energy to renewables. It's a measured but impassioned article that Lewis persuaded Tesco to support by setting a target to increase the sale of plant-based meat alternatives and by taking customers on the journey to a meat reduced diet. Even if there was discomfort with Lewis's opinions, it shows how an individual can listen to their conscience, especially when tensions have to be explored and choices made in pursuit of social and environmental benefits that go beyond self-interest.

Traditionally, writers have focused on individual conscience, which is important, not least because we should recognize that institutions cannot

---

[21] Kant I. (2004) *op cit.*, 31.

[22] Arendt H. (2003). *Responsibility and Judgment.* Schocken Books, p. 90.

[23] https://www.ft.com/content/acfd1251-24e9-478b-b8db-c6cc70d64b39.

improve themselves—that is the responsibility of the people that populate them.[24] However, the broader issue, and a much debated one, is whether organizations and brands can have a conscience. There are two opposing views here. One view is that while individuals can initiate and support conscientious action, organizations do not have moral agency as such, because they are not capable of behaving in a morally good or bad way.[25] Similarly, from a legal viewpoint it can be argued that corporate misbehaviour is the moral responsibility of particular individuals, who should be held responsible for their actions rather than the organization which does not have a unified consciousness and therefore cannot act intentionally.[26] When we have researched this issue and asked managers whether a brand can have a conscience, a minority reject the possibility and argue that conscience is an attribute of people not organizations or brands.

The other view, which most managers endorse, is that organizations and brands can have a conscience, because they have a unity that enables them to act with moral agency. The premise here is that organizations have an entitativity and a collective intelligence that goes beyond individual actions.[27] In a persuasive article Kenneth Goodpaster and John Matthews Jr argue that organizations can have a conscience in that the rationality and responsibility traits that we expect of individuals can also be found within corporations: 'thus attributing actions, strategies, decisions and moral responsibilities to corporations as entities distinguishable from those who hold offices in them poses no problem'.[28] In considering the nature of conscience in medical institutions, Daniel Sulmasy notes that these institutions possess the features of moral agents and act intentionally because they have an identity and purpose that is more than the sum of their constituent parts.[29] Similarly, the philosopher Bernard Williams writes, 'There are collective enterprises which not only bring together the virtues of various individuals, but which display collective virtues, the virtues of a team or a group who share a certain culture or outlook'.[30] In other words, to be moral we need others. Individuals bring their

---

[24] Popper K. (2002). *The open society and its enemies*. Routledge.

[25] Köllen, T. (2016). Acting out of compassion, egoism, and malice: A Schopenhauerian view on the moral worth of CSR and diversity management practices. *Journal of Business Ethics*, 138(2), 215–229.

[26] Velasquez, M. (2003). Debunking corporate moral responsibility. *Business Ethics Quarterly*, 13(4), 531–562.

[27] Holmes L & Ind N, (2022). Brands with a Conscience report. www.medinge.org.

[28] Goodpaster, K. E., & Matthews, J. B. (1982). Can a corporation have a conscience? *Harvard Business Review*, 60(1), 132–141.

[29] Sulmasy, D. P. (2008). What is conscience and why is respect for it so important? *Theoretical Medicine and Bioethics*, 29(3), 135–149.

[30] Williams B (2002). *Truth and Truthfulness*. Princeton University Press. p. 127.

own purposes and principles to organizations and the purpose and principles of the organization, together with its leadership, governance and culture, influence the moral life of individuals as part of their identity and strengthen their identification with the organization.[31] Our perspective aligns with those of Goodpaster, Matthews and Sulmasy in that we argue you can attribute conscience to individuals within organizations and to organizations—and their brands. Conscience then is both concerned with a truth to self (for organizations and people) and an awareness of the responsibility that this entails towards the wellbeing of others and the planet. However, we should stress that while there is a tendency to think of conscience as a faculty of knowing and judging right from wrong, it also requires people and organizations to act in accordance with their beliefs. Conscience is not passive but active.[32]

We will develop the definition of a company with a conscience in the next chapter, but to illustrate its essence, here is an example: the Spanish fashion brand, Ecoalf. Founded in Madrid in 2009, Ecoalf was the inspiration of Javier Goyeneche, whose conscience was troubled by the way fashion companies lacked any real sense of the emergent climate crisis and business models that encouraged over-consumption through multiple collections and wasteful habits by ignoring the use and after-life of products. Goyeneche set out to change behaviour. However, he faced two challenges. First, he wanted to ensure the use of recycled and recyclable materials, but consumer perceptions were that recycled fabrics were of lesser quality. Second, there was a lack of suppliers. The solution was to partner with different manufacturers to develop high-quality recycled fabrics, the first of which was Ecoalf 1.0—developed from recycled PET plastic bottles. By 2021 the company had developed more than 450 fabrics sold through 1500 outlets, using a variety of materials from discarded fishing nets to coffee grounds to used car tyres. Undoubtedly, Goyeneche's beliefs drive the company, but the collective conscience is evident in the culture of the company and the actions of individuals. What gives unity and direction is the clarity of purpose and consistency of commitment. The company is relentless in exploring new and better ways to generate fabrics, in encouraging its customers to buy less (e.g. with its recycling Black Friday campaign) while urging them to repair the clothes they own and to wash them less and at lower temperatures and in promoting a sustainability message through the line emblazoned on its clothing: 'Because there is no planet B'.

---

[31] Ellemers, N. and Van Der Toorn, J (2015). Groups as moral anchors. *Current opinion in psychology.* 6: 189–194; Henderson, R., and Van den Steen E. (2015). "Why Do Firms Have 'Purpose'? The Firm's Role as a Carrier of Identity and Reputation." *American Economic Review* 105 (5) (May): 326–330.

[32] Fuss P (1964) Conscience. *Ethics.* 74(2), 111–120.

Ecoalf typifies the idea of a company with a conscience in that it deliberately judges its impact on others and acts in line with its beliefs. As Head of Marketing and Communications, Carolina Alvarez-Ossorio Speith, notes 'we consider the brand DNA of Ecoalf to be around the commitment we have for people and the planet … we're concerned about the coherence between what we say and what we do'. The company is commercially successful, not least because of the way buying Ecoalf products contributes to consumers' sense of identity, but it is not driven by growth for its own sake. Rather, it sees an opportunity to influence consumer behaviour and the attitudes of its partners, government and competitors towards sustainability.

Thus, we can view conscience both from the perspective of people and their pronouncements and actions, such as in Dave Lewis's conscientious commitment to a specific view of the role of food, and from organizations, such as Ecoalf with its environmental advocacy, driven by a pellucid purpose and principles that help to unite its stakeholders. This centripetal force provides cohesion, but there can also be centrifugal forces at work in the organization that bring about heterogeneity. For example, individuals who represent the organization can also find that their conscience does not align with the business and that they feel a need to challenge existing norms and break rules. Even if some organizations support this in theory with the use of ethics committees and whistleblower policies, managing the tension between consent and dissent is complex and involves a nuanced insight into the nature of freedom and its constraints. In this book we will be exploring the tension (and also, opportunity), as to how organizations can best manage freedom so that people have the ability to be true to their conscience while also contributing to the organization. On the positive side, the interaction between individual and organization can help to ensure that good moral choices are made to the benefit of all stakeholders, while on the negative side conflicts such as divergent understandings of purpose and principles, misjudgements and occasional duplicity can all impair individual conscience and damage the organization.[33]

---

[33] Yagil, D., & Shultz, T. (2017). Service with a conscience: Moral dilemmas in customer service roles. *Journal of Service Theory and Practice*, 27(3), 689–711.

Where Conscience Goes Wrong

Companies, like people, don't always make good moral choices. Sometimes, they ignore what their inner voice is telling them. Sometimes, they struggle to reconcile competing interests. Sometimes, doing the right thing is difficult to judge. In a study of how we can drift ethically, Celia Moore and Francesca Gino explore how a moral compass can deviate due to intrapersonal reasons (caused by human cognitive limitations) and interpersonal reasons (caused by the influence of others). In the case of the former, failings occur because we lack objectivity, especially about our own weaknesses and failings, while in the case of the latter, social norms, amplified by social categorizations, weaken our moral commitment and encourage conformity.[34] These individual factors can be exacerbated by organizations in the way that they socialize people into unethical behaviour (it's just the way we do things round here), defining roles that incorporate moral blinders (don't pay attention to that) and goal setting (just hit the target no matter what). Yet, when managers ask their employees to be unethical, they not only do moral wrong, they also affect employees' motivation and performance—especially for those employees that find it hard to morally disengage.[35] Companies need to be aware of the power of the social norms they help to create and the cultural impact this can have. This is nowhere better illustrated than in the case of Wells Fargo.

In his narrative of the unravelling cross-selling scandal at Wells Fargo, Governance researcher, Brian Tayan, shows how norms can corrupt and how a seemingly good company can ignore its conscience.[36] Tayan notes that the Wells Fargo bank had a long-held reputation for sound management and that its Chair and CEO, John Stumpf had been awarded Banker of the Year in 2013 by *American Banker*. In 2015, it was ranked 7th on *Barron's List* of 'Most Respected Companies'. Its vision states that, 'Our vision has nothing to do with transactions, pushing products, or getting bigger for the sake of bigness. It's about building lifelong relationships one customer at a time.' The company claimed that their vision and values guided their collective decision-making approach and was vital in ensuring that proper practices were embedded in their divisions. From this outline, Wells Fargo sounds like an exemplar of good

---

[34] Moore, C., & Gino, F. (2013). Ethically adrift: How others pull our moral compass from true North, and how we can fix it. *Research in organizational behavior*, 33, 53–77.

[35] Smith I.H., Kouchaki M., & Wareham J, (2021). The price leaders pay for cutting ethical corners. *MIT Sloan Management Review*. 62(4): 18–20.

[36] Tayan, B., (2019) The Wells Fargo Cross-Selling Scandal. *Stanford Closer Look Series*. January 8, 2019. Topics, Issues and Controversies in Corporate Governance No. CGRP-62 Version 2, Stanford University Graduate School of Business Research Paper No. 17-1, Available at SSRN: https://ssrn.com/abstract=2879102.

governance and for many years it was listed in Gallup's 'Great Places to Work'. However, in 2013, rumours emerged that Wells Fargo employees in Southern California were aggressively cross-selling products. Some 30 employees were fired for opening new accounts for customers without their knowledge. At the time this was dismissed as a blip—the actions of a small group of rogue employees. In 2016, it transpired that the cross-selling practice was much wider as the company admitted employees had opened as many as 2 million accounts during a five-year period. During this time $2.6 million was refunded to customers and 5300 employees were dismissed. In 2017, Wells Fargo then increased its estimate of unauthorized consumer accounts to 3.5 million and issued an additional $2.8 million in refunds. However, these sums were small compared to the $1 billion settlement paid to the Consumer Financial Protection Bureau and Office of the Comptroller of the Currency, $480 million to settle a class action and $575 million to resolve civil claims in 50 states. There was also considerable reputational damage. In 2018 the Federal Reserve Board forbade the company growing any further until it had demonstrated an improvement in corporate controls. And here's Senator Elizabeth Warren of Massachusetts laying into John Stumpf in a US Senate hearing:

> You know, here's what really gets me about this, Mr. Stumpf. If one of your tellers took a handful of $20 bills out of the cash drawer, they'd probably be looking at criminal charges for theft. They could end up in prison. But you squeezed your employees to the breaking point so they would cheat customers and you could drive up the value of your stock and put hundreds of millions of dollars in your own pocket. And when it all blew up, you kept your job, you kept your multimillion dollar bonuses, and you went on television to blame thousands of $12-an-hour employees who were just trying to meet cross-sell quotas that made you rich. This is about accountability. You should resign. You should give back the money that you took while this scam was going on, and you should be criminally investigated by both the Department of Justice and the Securities and Exchange Commission.

So, what did go wrong at Wells Fargo? An independent investigation raised a slew of issues concerned with leadership, culture and operating practices, but at the heart of the scandal were the sales goals that led to employees feeling pressurized to perform and their resulting actions of opening false accounts. The fact that the problem was not dealt with seems to have been management myopia—a sense that there was nothing wrong systemically in the organization. In the narrative of the case people seem to objectify their audiences; employees don't see customers with needs, but rather targets, and managers don't see employees as humans with ambitions and anxieties, but as percentages. The tendency—exacerbated by the positives about the bank before the scandal broke—was to reject systemic mis-selling. Perhaps, if the bank's managers had paid more attention to conscience, and critically reflected on their actions, they would have been more challenging of their convictions and recognized their complicity in the scandal rather than making it the action of 'others'. As Serena Parekh observes, 'Judgment, then, does not depend only on my own experiences or perceptions, but on the way I am able to imagine things from the point of view of others'.[37]

Wells Fargo shows what happens when a moral compass drifts. In spite of companies and brands sometimes having inspirational purposes and principles that are meant to guide their moral choices, rhetoric and action become disconnected. This can be because the purpose and principles are superficial—a bit of burnish for internal and external stakeholders, but not truly lived and reflected upon, especially in times of moral crisis, when they should come to the fore. Or because of an imbalance in meeting the needs of their different stakeholders: shareholders seeking returns, employees and their need for economic security and job fulfilment and customers and their desire for a trusting relationship. When a company skews its attention towards one stakeholder group over another, it creates the potential for delinquent behaviour. Finally, actually identifying doing the right thing is often complex. While conscientious companies, such as Unilever and Patagonia, see an alignment between doing the right thing and being profitable, tensions can emerge between principle and profit. Then companies have to make a choice between what is morally correct and what is expedient; to listen to their inner voice, regardless of others, or to acquiesce and have to live with wrongdoing.

Doing the Right Thing

One problem is that there are no easy answers as to what constitutes good conscience. Spike Lee's 1989 film *Do the Right Thing* (we borrowed the film title for the sub-title of this book) makes this challenge explicit. Set in Brooklyn on a burning hot summer's day, the film lays out the everyday and barely suppressed irritations and racial tensions between Blacks and Whites. Emotions erupt into violence following an argument between Sal the local Italian pizza owner and a Black character called Radio Raheem. The police arrive—and in a prescient scene—use a chokehold that kills Raheem. The lead character in the film, Mookie, has been told to do the right thing, but it's not clear what that might mean. He initiates the destruction of the pizza restaurant after Raheem's death, but afterwards has, if not a reconciliation with Sal, at least an understanding. As the film ends, two quotations appear—Martin Luther King Jr arguing that violence is always self-defeating and Malcolm X saying that violence in self-defence may be necessary. These opposing quotations give way to a photo of the two civil rights leaders shaking hands. The inference is that conscience can lead us to different places and to different interpretations about the right thing, but that critical reflection and dialogue provide for better choices.

Why Conscience Matters

The story of Ecoalf provides an apt example of the benefits of conscience: its potential to provide direction, to guide moral choices, to inspire employees and to provide a point of accountability. Similarly, Wells Fargo illustrates the downsides of when conscience fails. It demonstrates in particular the reputational damage associated with bad choices and the way in which trust can be diminished and social capital destroyed. This in turn can lead to direct costs— in the US in 2021, a record $3.62 billion was paid out in class action workplace settlements.[38] However, beyond this, why should corporate conscience matter?

We might argue that it's simply better for people and for the world if companies reduce the negative impacts they have on society and the environment and enhance the positive: generating wealth for the many, being a responsible actor and supporting the aims of the UN Sustainable Development Goals. In this way, companies can become a force for good. This ought to be a sufficient argument in itself, because it is only through the responsible actions of business that we can address the most significant challenges of our times. But, we can also cloak the argument in self-interest. Conscientious organizations are more appealing places to work (e.g. 87% of millennials want to work for a company that engages in corporate responsibility),[39] are less prone to the risks associated with negative environmental and social factors (witness the need to phase out $480 billion in fossil fuel subsidies)[40] and provide consumers with good reasons to buy their products and services.[41]

Some have argued that the companies and brands that engage in virtuous activity, such as outdoor clothing brand, Patagonia, are essentially niche and only appeal to a coterie of virtuous consumers, while others see the orientation towards conscience and a multi-stakeholder approach as PR blather. Both these criticisms are worthy of discussion. Consumers certainly do use brands that contribute to their identity by associating with relevant cultural elements that reinforce their sense of self—such as wearing Ecoalf clothes with their bold statements. For consumers that want to do the right thing and

---

[38] Workplace Class Action Litigation Report (2022). https://www.workplaceclassactionreport.com.

[39] Fidelity Charitable (2020) The new definition of philanthropy includes any act of social good. https://www.fidelitycharitable.org/insights/2021-future-of-philanthropy/new-definition.html.

[40] Group of Thirty (2020) Mainstreaming the Transition to a Net-Zero Economy. https://group30.org/images/uploads/publications/G30_Mainstreaming_the_Transition_to_a_Net-Zero_Economy_2.pdf.

[41] NYU Stern (2020) CSB Sustainable Market Share Index. https://www.stern.nyu.edu/experience-stern/about/departments-centers-initiatives/centers-of-research/center-sustainable-business/research/research-initiatives/csb-sustainable-market-share-index.

to signal their commitment to others, a brand with a conscience has a clear appeal. However, it is no longer simply virtuous consumers that are engaging in these consumption behaviours. Increasingly mainstream consumers make sociopolitical statements as they become more aware of the impact of their choices on society and the environment. A large-scale diverse business such as Unilever, which was the highest rated sustainable brand globally in 2020 in an assessment by 700 experts in 71 countries (Patagonia was second and IKEA third), focuses more and more on developing socially relevant statements of purpose for the brands in its portfolio.[42] Notably, among Unilever's 400 plus brands, it is the ones that are designated purpose-led, Sustainable Living Brands that are the fastest growing and deliver the majority of the company's growth.[43] Nor is Unilever alone among larger companies in adopting this approach. Research by HSBC (2020) of over 10,000 companies demonstrates this growing commitment towards taking a stance on environmental (e.g. energy usage, recycling) and social (e.g. diversity, local community impacts) issues, not least because there is also a strong belief that this will benefit companies in terms of meeting consumer expectations and boosting growth. Many also anticipate that there are additional benefits in terms of boosting employee wellbeing (37%), recruiting talent (28%), attracting investment (30%) and enhancing corporate reputation (32%).[44]

The second argument is rooted in the judgement that companies are susceptible to the desire to be liked and loved by others. The results are gestures designed to enhance perceptions without really troubling the organization's conscience. Whereas the role of conscience should be to act in accordance with what one believes, these are disconnected actions. This is typified by the world of wokewashing and greenwashing where organizations take initiatives and create communications that suggest a commitment to a minority group or to environmentalism that goes beyond what they actually deliver.[45] An example of the former was Pepsi-Cola's 2017 advertisement featuring celebrity

---

[42] Globescan (2020) The 2020 Globescan/SustainAbility Leaders Survey, 12 August 2020. https://globescan.com/2020-sustainability-leaders-report/.

[43] Unilever. (2019). Brands with purpose grow—and here is the proof. *Unilever global company website*. https://www.unilever.com/news/news-and-features/Feature-article/2019/brands-with-purpose-grow-and-here-is-the-proof.html.

[44] HSBC. (2020). Navigator Report | Global Commercial Banking | HSBC. https://www.business.hsbc.com/navigator/report. Accessed 14 July 2021.

[45] Kim, E. H., & Lyon, T. P. (2015). Greenwash vs. Brownwash: Exaggeration and undue modesty in corporate sustainability disclosure. *Organization Science, 26*(3), 705–723, https://doi.org/10.1287/orsc.2014.0949; Lyon, T. P., & Montgomery, A. W. (2015). The Means and End of Greenwash. *Organization and Environment, 28*(2), 223–249. https://doi.org/10.1177/1086026615575332; Marquis, C., Toffel, M. W., & Zhou, Y. (2016). Scrutiny, norms, and selective disclosure: A global study of greenwashing. *Organization Science, 27*(2), 483–504. article. https://doi.org/10.1287/orsc.2015.1039.

endorser, Kendall Jenner, which used the context of political protests, to present the message that an ice-cold Pepsi delivered to a police officer by Jenner would somehow bring peace. The advertisement was ridiculed and then promptly withdrawn by Pepsi-Cola, both because it belittled real causes, such as Black Lives Matter, and because it lacked any visible commitment to the issue of racial injustice. In a comprehensive study of the issue during 2020, it was clear that people do believe that businesses can address racial injustice and can play a valuable role in promoting inclusivity and fairness, but with some exceptions, such as Target and Ben & Jerry's, they believed that most companies are tokenistic: 'including more Black people in advertisements, talking up diversity, profiting off the Black Lives Matter movement, and writing about future intentions without specific goals'.[46]

Conclusion

In this chapter, we have set out the core argument in support of conscience. This is based on the view that organizations and brands are an integral part of our worlds as consumers, employees, investors and citizens. Therefore, they have to be responsive and responsible. They cannot opt out of our lives and nor would we want them to. Companies have to make moral choices and reject the idea that they operate in a morally neutral world. This is easier to do when they are human-centric and focused on people's needs and wants rather than dealing in abstract ideas or numbers. Not all organizations and brands think this way of course, but our research shows (which we will share in this book) that increasingly managers understand the value of involving others in building brands and in a wider societal role for organizations. Sometimes conscientious behaviour is driven by the desire of the people that populate organizations simply to do the right thing, but it is also due to the pressure from consumers and others. Organizations feel this pressure—even if it is sometimes overstated in consumer research by the moral paradox of people's desire to want to appear moral in the eyes of others[47]—and they also see the business benefits of a conscientious approach.

---

[46] Ind, N., & Payton, K. (2021). Do the Right Thing : How Business Can Respond to the Challenge of Racial Injustice. *California Management Review.* https://cmr.berkeley.edu/2021/03/racial-injustice/. Accessed 14 July 2021.

[47] Ellemers, N., & Van der Toorn, J. (2015). Groups as moral anchors. *Current Opinion in Psychology, 6,* 189–194. https://doi.org/10.1016/J.COPSYC.2015.08.018.

3

The Business of Conscience

If businesses are going to be profitable and help tackle such crises as environ-mental degradation, climate change, racial justice and inequality, managers will have to think deeply and critically about the issues and then use their conscience as a spur to responsible action that meets the needs of all stake-holders and the planet. The challenge here is twofold. First, we can easily fail to think critically. As President John F Kennedy noted in an address at Yale University in 1962, 'too often we enjoy the comfort of opinion without the discomfort of thought'.[1] There is security in the rituals and myths that we use in daily life that support our psychological needs and interests. Issues are often viewed through an ideological lens, even if we are only dimly aware of it, and such perspectives are then reinforced in discussion, together with like-minded others and amplified in social media echo chambers.[2] As a consequence issues become conflated, difficult thinking is avoided and inaction justified. In the context of the crises that confront us, this means rejection of the imperative to change and an acceptance, or even endorsement, of things as they are. Yet, having a conscience means questioning taken for granted assumptions and using judgement that is rooted not only in one's own experiences and belief

---

[1] https://www.jfklibrary.org/archives/other-resources/john-f-kennedy-speeches/yale-university-19620611.

[2] Jost, J. T. (2017). Ideological asymmetries and the essence of political psychology. *Political psychology*, *38*(2), 167–208; Shepherd, S., Chartrand, T.L. and Fitzsimons, G.J. (2015), When brands reflect our ideal world: the values and brand preferences of consumers who support versus reject society's dominant ideology, *Journal of Consumer Research* 42(1), 76–92.; Barbera, P., Jost, J.T., Nagler, J., Tucker, J.A. and Bonneau, R.(2015), Tweeting from left to right: is online political communication more than an echo chamber?, *Psychological Science*, 26(10), 1531–1542.

© The Author(s), under exclusive license to Springer Nature Switzerland AG 2022
N. Ind, O. Iglesias, *In Good Conscience*, https://doi.org/10.1007/978-3-031-09338-8_3

systems but in being able to imagine things from the point of view of others; of being conscious and attuned to the things that matter in the world.[3] Some leaders and managers have managed this. They have embraced openness, taken the time to reflect, encouraged critical discussion and enabled their organizations to adapt and become conscientious.

As an illustration of this in practice, Wiebe Draijer, CEO of the Dutch co-operative bank, Rabobank, encourages employees to address the tensions in managing risk while promoting change in line with the bank's mission of 'Growing a better world together' by promoting critical thinking. This involves such mechanisms as an annual co-operative week of conversations whereby individuals can talk about and reflect on the dilemmas they face in doing the right thing while meeting client demands and an ethics committee that meets six times a year, chaired by Dreijer, to provide input on difficult ethical issues, submitted by staff—rather than deal in simple solutions the committee tries to critically analyse the underlying problem and to judge it against Rabobank's moral compass. As two members of the bank's ethics office note this is a complex process, which tends to involve a 'right-versus-right issue, meaning that the positively formulated interests of all stakeholders are considered as well as the organisation's norms and values. This leads to a choice between a range of alternatives. There are sound arguments for each of these alternatives. The eventual choice almost invariably leads to moral cost, since some arguments will be given a lower priority than others. In other words, making choices is not without consequence.'[4]

Second, conscience fails through inaction. Businesses too easily make fuzzy promises about a future state without really considering the implications that will enable such promises to be kept. Take the various commitments that have been made to tackle climate change or racial inequality and the gap between intention and action. As the activist, Greta Thunberg made clear in the run up to COP26, words are not sufficient: 'Build back better. Blah, blah, blah. Green economy. Blah blah blah. Net zero by 2050. Blah, blah, blah. This is all we hear from our so-called leaders. Words that sound great but so far have not led to action. Our hopes and ambitions drown in their empty promises.' In place of rhetoric, businesses need to demonstrate their commitment and engage with issues at a systemic level, build co-creative relationships with partners and suppliers and to act with others in alignment with their conscience.

---

[3] Parekh, S. (2008). Conscience, morality and judgment: An inquiry into the subjective basis of human rights. *Philosophy & Social Criticism, 34*(1–2), 177–195.
[4] Van Tonningen F.M.R and Louwers S.J.P. (2019) Rabobank Ethics Committee: about reflection platforms, moral cost and moral case law.

Conscience = Critical thought + acting together to effect change

Thus, our formula for the conscientious business is built on a willingness to think issues through in a critical way, from the perspective of all stakeholders (which requires both self-insight and awareness of others) and the will to work together to deliver transformative change'[5] The formula addresses the twin challenges of 'the comfort of opinion' and 'empty promises' and creates a basis from which conscience can guide decisions. There may be a temptation here to conflate conscience with sustainability or corporate social responsibility, but we argue that conscience sits above these and sets the framework within which environmental, social and governance decisions are taken. Sustainable actions can, and indeed are, taken without recourse to conscience, but this also can hollow them out. Much of the over-claiming and the ineffective actions around sustainability occur because they are driven by short-term pressures or opportunities rather than conscience. Yet, as Vincent Stanley of Patagonia notes about sustainability, 'when I look at real instances in which people have made changes, it really comes down to moral commitment'. When conscience is in play, it both drives sustainability strategies and creates commitment. And gives pause for reflection and discussion, when things go wrong. This creates a connection back to the conscience as the assumptions that drove a decision are re-evaluated and critical thought is used to plot a new course of action that is more robust (Fig. 3.1).

In this chapter, we'll explore the attributes of a business with a conscience that underpin our formula. First, let's look at an example of a company that really uses (and talks about) conscience as a guide to delivering sustainability: the luxury hospitality brand, Soneva.

Soneva: Integrating Conscience

The words 'luxury' and 'sustainability' do not sit comfortably together. One suggests indulgence, excess and waste, while the other indicates constraint and temperance. Yet, the Maldivian-based business, Soneva, has managed to marry the two by integrating conscience into the heart of its activities (one of the founders is the 'conscience' of the business and each resort has a

---

[5] This argument aligns with Kant, who believes that actions are determined by the adoption of a principle that is jointly determined together with others through interaction that governs their conduct. In her analysis of Kant, the philosopher Christine Korsgaard notes the moral motivation he ascribes to people and how Kant's conception of action allows us to deliberate and act together in a deeper way. Korsgaard C.M. (2009) Natural Motives and the Motive of Duty: Hume and Kant on our duties to others. *Contemporary Readings in Law and Social Justice.* 1(2), 9–36.

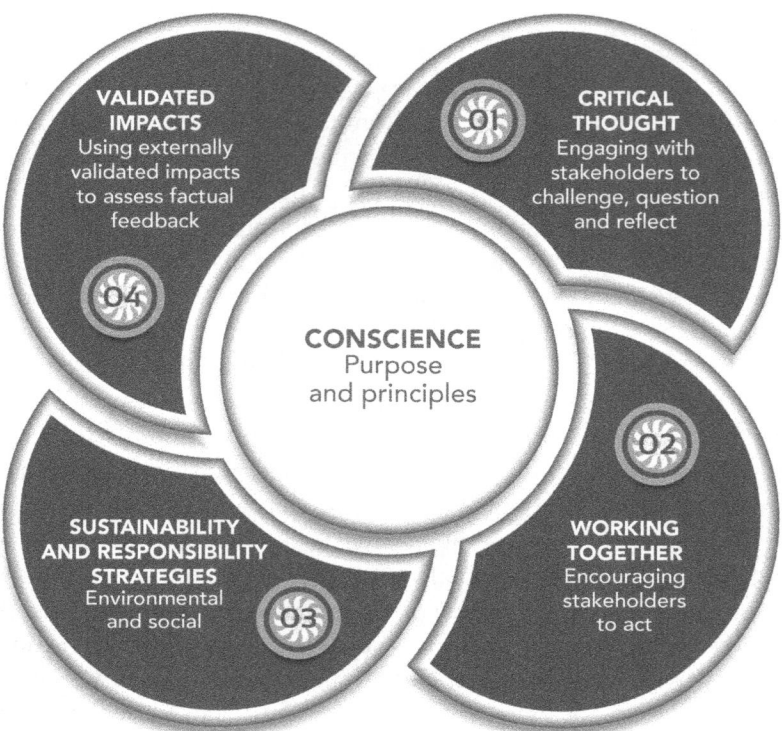

Fig. 3.1 The relationship between conscience and sustainability

conscience manager, who has responsibility for environmental and social initiatives) and by using it as a spur to think different and to innovate. This approach derives from the founders' beliefs, but also an awareness of the proximity of nature. The evidence of the impact of actions on the environment and on people is not abstract, but there to be seen in front of one's eyes. Sonu Shivdasani, who founded Soneva, together with his wife Eva Malmström in 1995, notes that the beauty of the islands was the primary attraction for tourists, yet early developers despoiled the environment, building groynes on the reefs, dredging harbours, throwing waste into the sea and cutting down trees. Shivdasani challenged this way of working. He recognized that the long-term viability of the Maldives could not be based on an extractive mindset that simply uses resources without consideration but rather had to be rooted in sustainability; in preserving the natural infrastructure and in minimizing the impact of tourism. The widely held belief in the industry was that such an approach was not economically viable, but he thought differently. Rather than seeing sustainability as a cost, he saw it as an opportunity.

Chief Financial Officer and Guardian of the Mission, Bruce Bromley, notes that the Mission is about growth and about adhering to the values of Soneva in a symbiotic way: 'in almost every single example I could give, the sustainable way of doing business creates more value for the business top line, bottom line and value than anything else'. As an illustration of this approach, Soneva generates more than $500,000 a year from the recycling of waste, through a Waste to Wealth initiative, which includes, using packaging materials such as Styrofoam in constructing buildings, making charcoal, composting some 20,000 kg of organic matter each month that is used to grow vegetables and herbs for the restaurants, and upcycling glass in its art and glass studio, which produces functional glasswear and glass art for sale. Similarly, Soneva now recycles almost all of the water it uses and is working with the Maldivian government to build a waste management system for all the islands. With around 90% of Soneva's waste recycled, you could argue, job done, but the company continually searches for new ways to solve problems. For example, while the reuse of Styrofoam is creditable, Soneva has been working with its food suppliers, who use it to transport food, to find alternative materials. Remon Alphenaar, Guardian of the Experience, notes that Soneva is not such a big company that it can dictate to its suppliers, but it has influence and companies can also see the potential of new revenue streams if they innovate to produce more sustainable packaging that is then endorsed by Soneva.

Soneva's Slow Life

While doing the right thing delivers long-term value for the business, another issue is whether it matters to customers. Do they care about sustainability? Soneva observes that the importance of sustainability varies depending on where guests come from, but for most it is a secondary factor in their choice of resort. The primary motivation is connected to Soneva's core purpose, which is 'to create imaginative and engaging slow life'. This idea of slow life is designed in opposition to the values connected to the speed of everyday life. It links people to the natural world and incorporates sustainability, wellness and inspirational experiences. Carissa Nimah, Guardian of the Brand, says, 'magical, rare experiences are wrapped up in this Soneva package, which is sustainable while at the same time, healthy and ethical and purpose-driven'. In practice this means a focus on the guest experience, while incorporating sustainability into it, so that it becomes an integral part of the Soneva offer. Thus, guests participate in the work of the eco centre, take part in workshops with marine biologists and entomologists and learn to blow recycled glass. Indeed, it is this interaction with employees (known as hosts) that Shivdasani sees as the most important element in delivering on the purpose. His argument is that luxury is not defined by the size of the villas, spa services or the food, but by exceptional service delivered by people who believe in the purpose. The purpose and the values are a central feature in recruitment and personal development and a means of engaging with local people—around half of the hosts come from the atoll where Soneva is based.

Putting Conscience at the Core

Soneva's conscience derives from the founders and emphasizes the vital role that leaders play, but it also inspires and guides the choices of the guardians and hosts in their day-to-day work. There is no distinction here between being responsible and being profitable, not only in terms of finding innovative solutions to challenges connected to society and the environment but also in tackling the impacts of suppliers and consumers. The last are particularly important, because the scope 3 carbon generated by consumers contributes most to emissions. There is no way to avoid the impacts that come from people travelling to the Maldives and consuming while they are there—even if Soneva tries to limit the negatives of consumption through its initiatives on reuse and recycling. To offset the emissions, Soneva charges a mandatory 2% carbon levy to its guests, which the Soneva Foundation (the charitable arm of the business) uses on such projects as green energy in India, planting trees in Thailand and supplying energy-efficient cook stoves to families in Myanmar.

The range of initiatives employed by Soneva and their seemingly restless quest to innovate in a sustainable way demonstrates how a business can use its conscience to make a transformative impact on the world while delivering profitable growth. Soneva demonstrates that luxury and sustainability can be integrated in the pursuit of social equity, environmental responsibility and long-term profitability.

The Attributes of a Business with a Conscience

In our studies of conscientious organizations, we have identified a set of consistent attributes that demonstrate the existence of a moral compass that guides people (managers, employees and partners) and the choices that they make.[6] Such businesses are driven by a desire to do the right thing and in so doing transform an industry and the attitudes and behaviours towards the environment and/or society. They think in a critical way and act on their beliefs, not at the expense of long-term profitability, but in support of it. We also see that at certain stages in their development, businesses will feel the need to articulate these moral beliefs that give direction to strategic decision-making and that inspire concrete behaviours. Businesses do have different ways of expressing these including mission, vision, DNA and values. However, we argue that the most appropriate way to bring a conscience to life is through the use of 'purpose' and 'principles'. We will define and discuss these in the next chapter, but what should be noted are three things: (a) purpose is widely used and encompasses a business and societal orientation—it states the case for why an organization exists; (b) principles serve as the foundation for a belief system and as such have to be precise and contextualized; (c) purpose and principles are performative in the sense that together they drive appropriate action and lead to new organizational realities.

This raises the question of where conscience comes from. Often it emanates from the beliefs of a leader or a founder, which is born out of their life view and moral sense of right and wrong. In reviewing such conscientious businesses as Patagonia, Tony's Chocolonely, John Lewis Partnership and Unilever, we see again and again how the conscience of an individual defines a direction, and then is sometimes adapted to changing circumstances, before becoming embedded in organizational practices. In these examples, we also see that such leaders question and then act against prevailing norms, from Yvon Chouinard at Patagonia making environmentalism central to the company's purpose to Wiebe Dreijer's redefinition of co-operative banking to Paul Polman's commitment to combine sustainability and profitability at Unilever. All of these leaders had naysayers, who argued against their ideas, but all of them kept true to their beliefs, and as we saw with Soneva found innovative ways to redefine their businesses.

An implication of this orientation is that a business with a conscience has a strong internal drive combined with the ability to empathize with stakeholders and to bring them into the organization's ecosystem and encourage their participation in the co-creation of value. A business with a conscience cannot act alone; it is always dependent on the actions of others. Patagonia cannot make claims about the materials in its garments nor Dutch chocolate brand,

---

[6] Iglesias, O., & Ind, N. (2020). Towards a theory of conscientious corporate brand co-creation: the next key challenge in brand management. *Journal of Brand Management*, *27*(6), 710–720; Ind, N., & Horlings, S. (Eds.). (2016). *Brands with a conscience: How to build a successful and responsible brand*. Kogan Page Publishers.

Tony's Chocolonely, about the cocoa beans and ingredients in its chocolate bars without trusted partners who align with the business and its beliefs and can produce to the necessary standards. Similarly, Unilever cannot reduce its environmental impacts without the involvement of its consumers and changes in consumption habits. This means conscientious businesses must look outwards, as well as inwards to their conscience, as they seek to make a positive transformative impact.

Adherence to one's conscience can, of course, be dangerous if it is misdirected. It also requires judgement. We laud the actions of Paul Polman, Yvon Chouinard and other leaders for their courage and commitment, but we would hardly celebrate the actions of leaders who justify corrupt actions because of their beliefs. Choices need to be leavened by virtue and by the other attributes of conscience: being **fair**, **open** and **responsible**. We can see conscience at work in the way that Tony's Chocolonely will not introduce flavours, if it cannot guarantee that the ingredients are fairly and responsibly sourced or the way that Spanish fashion brand Ecoalf acts against irresponsible consumption and encourages responsible consumption through product care and repair communications. Then, by contrast, look at the way some major companies signed up to an open letter to the *Wall Street* Journal urging the US to remain in the Paris Agreement on climate change, while at the same time supporting a lobby group that was pushing for withdrawal[7] or the way Jes Staley, former CEO of Barclays Bank went in pursuit of the identity of an anonymous whistleblower, in defiance of the Financial Conduct Authority's belief that whistleblowing plays a vital role in exposing misconduct.[8] These instances demonstrate what Kant is keen to call our attention to, in the way that individuals expect others to follow moral rules while making exceptions for themselves.[9] Indeed, Staley exhorted staff when he joined the bank in 2015 that 'there can be no retreat from becoming a values-driven organization which conducts itself with integrity at all times'.[10]

---

[7] Lyon, T. P., Delmas, M. A., Maxwell, J. W., Tima Bansal, P., Chiroleu-Assouline, M., Crifo, P., et al. (2018). CSR needs CPR: Corporate sustainability and politics. *California Management Review*, 60(4), 5–24. https://doi.org/10.1177/0008125618778854.

[8] Binham C and Arnold A. (2018) Barclays chief Staley fined £640,000 over whistleblowing scandal. *Financial Times*. May 11 2018.

[9] Wood. A. W. (2005) Kant. Blackwell Publishing.

[10] Masters B (2021) Staley's departure from Barclays reminds CEOs not to believe their own hype. *Financial Times*. November 5th, 2021.

Fair

These illustrations of conscience in action demonstrate the importance of having a human-centric view that respects the needs of internal and external stakeholders. Businesses with a conscience also understand the mutuality of employees, customers, suppliers and investors. The interdependence of these audiences ought to be self-evident, but as regular scandals and financial crises demonstrate they can easily go out of kilter. Former Governor of the Banks of Canada and England, Mark Carney notes, for example, that the cause of the 2008 financial crisis can be attributed to finance losing track of its core values of 'fairness, integrity, prudence and responsibility'.[11] Fairness matters because it creates the social capital that enables organizations to function effectively: fairly treated employees think about the wellbeing of partners, suppliers and customers; in turn customers and investors trust an organization to deliver on what it claims. Fair processes matter inside organizations because it motivates people to work together. By involving employees in fair and transparent processes and being clear about expectations, a feeling of ownership and trust emerges. The opposite is also true. Unfairness diminishes trust and upsets people: 'Fair process responds to a basic human need. All of us, whatever our role in a company, want to be valued as human beings and not as "personnel" or "human assets". ... People are sensitive to the signals conveyed through a company's decisions-making processes. Such processes can reveal a company's willingness to trust people and seek their ideas—or they can signal the opposite.'[12]

Clearly, fairness requires organizations to empathize with their stakeholders and their emotional needs and wants and to see beyond transactions to a relationship rooted in shared values. For example, Tony's Chocolonely, whose purpose is explicitly about fairness in terms of its quest to end the widespread use of slavery in the chocolate trade (estimated by the brand as 2.3 million children and slaves in Ghana and Ivory Coast), features on every pack the slogan, 'crazy about chocolate, serious about people'. For Chief Chocolate Officer, Henk Jan Beltman, the 'serious about people' piece means paying fair wages to farmers and workers, involving activist consumers in campaigning for change and co-creating the brand together with partners. Similarly, Nand Kishore (NK) Chaudhary, who founded the social impact company, Jaipur

---

[11] Carney M (2020) Value(s): building a better world for all. Harper Collins, p. 182.

[12] Kim, W. C., & Mauborgne, R. (2003). Fair process: Managing in the knowledge economy. *Harvard business review, 81*(1), 127–136.

Rugs, was motivated by the opportunity to provide security and fulfilment for artisans (especially women, who constitute 80% of the company's 40,000 weavers). Traditionally, the weavers were seen as untouchables and were often exploited by intermediaries. Chaudhary says, there was a lack of transparency in the supply chain and the artisans were treated unfairly. His solution was to introduce fair payments by enhancing the designs so that higher prices could be charged and by cutting out the intermediaries. He also encouraged the weavers to open up the villages where they worked and to connect directly with customers. This also changed the buyer/seller relationship and helped to build the brand by bringing the Jaipur story to life. When he talks about his philosophy, Chaudhary uses a word rarely used by business people: love. It is this love of human beings, of empathy with them and their desires, hopes and needs that guide the company and the way it supports people in terms of education, health care and social and economic development. Like other businesses with a conscience, Jaipur Rugs believes that profit and purpose can be combined. Treating people fairly is not only the right thing to do, it is also value creating.

An integral part of Chaudhary's vision of love as transformative is the sense of inclusion and his willingness to challenge India's caste system by embracing the untouchable weavers. Untouchability might seem a very Indian construct, but, when Martin Luther King Jr and his wife visited India in 1959, he was introduced as a 'fellow untouchable'. At first he was affronted by the connection, but then he came to realize 'Yes, I am an untouchable, and every negro in the United States of America is an untouchable'.[13] King saw the systemic unfairness of racial bias. In the contemporary environment, ensuring people are treated fairly means that no one should be excluded from work, education or health because of caste, gender, disability, sexual orientation or race. Conscientious organizations understand this because inclusion stimulates greater diversity of ideas and helps strengthen consumer-brand relationships. For example, over 60% of people believe that paying attention to diversity and inclusion is an important reflection of their own values and more than 70% say they are more likely to recommend or purchase a brand that takes a stand in support of diversity and inclusion.[14]

---

[13] Wilkerson I. (2020) America's 'untouchables': the silent power of the caste system. The Guardian 28 July 2020.
[14] Ind N and Payton K. (2021) *op cit.*

Open

In our research the importance of openness comes up consistently. Whether it is consumers, managers or partners, there is a belief that a business with a conscience should be open, transparent and honest about its intentions. There are factors, such as fear of proprietary knowledge leaking, competitive disadvantage and security concerns, that inhibit this orientation and there is also a recognition that secrecy is a strong corporate trait, not least when it comes to activities connected to political lobbying and corporate taxation. However, there are three factors pushing companies to be open. *First*, companies are not islands; they are parts of ecosystems that require knowledge to be shared and products and services to be co-created. For example, the German software company SAP has some 440,000 customers and 21,000 commercial partners. It could simply see these customers and partners as the means to deliver products and services, but this would deny SAP the opportunity to learn from, and innovate together with, a highly diverse set of organizations. Recognizing this opportunity, SAP has evolved its purpose from a company-centric, transactional view of to 'help the world run better' to a collaborative, co-creative one of to 'help the world run better and to improve people's lives'. This expanded purpose recognizes the way value is realized together with customers and partners both through ongoing symbiosis and through its global network of co-innovation labs.

Second, the number of contact points between a business and its stakeholders has multiplied. Whereas once external communications was limited to a cadre of corporate spokespeople and marketers, now diverse employees interact with stakeholders on a daily basis on social media. This makes control of communications much more complex, but also offers opportunities to enrich meaning through networks of exchange that bring consumers together in fan-based and company-sponsored communities. The upside of this is that the business can become closer to consumers and learn together with them about the role it plays in their lives and the specifics of product and service performance. The downside of this is that the multi-voiced expression can lead to meaning becoming obtuse as people receive different and perhaps contradictory messages.[15] To realize the opportunities of greater openness, businesses need to listen to, and work with, their internal and external stakeholders, and to have the confidence to share and the humility to learn. Notably some companies, like Patagonia and Ecoalf, are attentive to the feedback they receive

---

[15] Schmeltz, L., & Kjeldsen, A. K. (2019). Co-creating polyphony or cacophony? A case study of a public organization's brand co-creation process and the challenge of orchestrating multiple internal voices. *Journal of Brand Management, 26*(3), 304–316.

and admit their fallibility and then demonstrate a desire to improve their products and processes. Such companies recognize the move to openness is a journey that shapes and modifies them.[16]

Third, there is a growing consumer expectation that businesses not only deliver functional and emotional benefits, but that they also contribute to peoples' sense of identity. This requires companies to be explicit about their beliefs. Such transparency helps to induce social action and to engender the trust that is a requirement in stakeholder relationships. If we feel we cannot trust what a company tells us and that it seems to be hiding inconvenient truths or obfuscating, we are less likely to invest in it, work for it, partner with it or buy its products. On the other hand, transparency makes us feel closer to a business, to trust its claims and to reward it with our loyalty. Businesses may feel that they can avoid being transparent. For example, corporate political activity is often cloaked behind a veil designed to hide a business's real agenda, but this has side-effects in the diminution of trust when actions are exposed.

Asket and Transparency

A company that has committed to transparency is the Swedish fashion brand, Asket. Started in 2015 by August Bard Bringéus and Jakob Dworsky, Asket (which means ascetic in Swedish) started out with a clear purpose, of enabling customers to live with less, by producing a limited range of classic, high-quality fashion items that would be long-lasting. At the outset, the company also defined a set of core values: simplicity, honesty and boldness. Simplicity was a reflection of the design ethos, boldness was about being outspoken and honesty came to be expressed as transparency. Bringéus notes, 'we found that being transparent in terms of pricing; what you're actually paying for—breaking down the costs as well as showcasing the factories and storytelling about the factories and the people behind them, was actually a digital manifestation of quality that helped to create trust for people to actually transact with us'.

For Asket, transparency became central to the business purpose, a differentiator from competitors and a reassurance of quality. Bringéus argues that it also pushed the company into being values driven. However, the desire to be transparent came with challenges. The materials used in fashion garments are hard to pin down and the labelling used often hides where items are sourced. A material that claims to be made in Italy, for example, might only be washed there. Asket's first quest was to trace back all the materials in its classic Oxford

---

[16] Albu, O. B., & Flyverbom, M. (2019). Organizational transparency: Conceptualizations, conditions, and consequences. *Business & Society, 58*(2), 268–297.

shirt, including the thread, the buttons and the cotton through the supply chain, but it wasn't until 2018 that the company managed this. However, once the principle of traceability had been established, Asket knew it could do the same with other products—'it enabled us to jump start into being more activist and even more value-driven'. At the end of 2021, Asket could trace 90% of its materials and is aiming for 100%. This provides the company with the confidence to be more explicit in its communications about its commitment to traceability and also to educate customers with information about their purchase. This is realized both through the stories the company tells through text and films about the provenance of its products on its website and also through the impact receipt that comes with a purchase (Fig. 3.2).

The Impact Receipt, which was launched in 2020 derives from the lifecycle analysis, conducted together with RiSE (Research Institute of Sweden), of the company's range of products, and shows the water, energy and CO_2e emitted at the different stages of the production process. Based on customer research, the receipt also specifies the number of times the product can be expected to be worn. On the website, the costs of each item are broken down and Asket's margin specified.

Asket uses considerable resources to validate its supply chain and the founders visit all their key suppliers once a year. They see this as part of the process of ensuring that customers can trust the brand and the company's conscientious commitment to challenging the norms of the fashion industry. In place of fast fashion is Asket's idea of enabling people to live with less; of encouraging emotional gratification through storytelling over the material satisfaction of consumption. Bringéus says, 'So even if you don't care about social conditions or environmental impact, so long as you're interested in quality goods you will appreciate that storytelling and knowing where your goods come from. And that's kind of the key driver to helping people live with less also. Once you know the story of your garments, you will appreciate them more.'

Responsible

Fair and responsible are sometimes treated as conjoined concepts, but responsible is clearly different from fair. If a manager were to be focused solely on fairness, she would have to create processes and reward systems that treated people the same. However, fairness cannot be absolute. Even if everyone in an organization had the same extrinsic reward for their work, their intrinsic reward would be different. People approach their working lives with different expectations and to realize different outcomes. Therefore, what managers should aim at is a relative fairness that treats people with respect and rewards

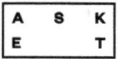

The Impact Receipt

ORDER: 001

THE T-SHIRT

RAW MATERIALS

Impact (CO_2)	0,29 kg
Water	33,27 m^3
Energy	12,41 MJ

MILLING

Impact (CO_2)	1,12 kg
Water	0,50 m^3
Energy	20,00 MJ

MANUFACTURING

Impact (CO_2)	0,24 kg
Water	1,30 m^3
Energy	5,40 MJ

TRIMS

Impact (CO_2)	0,13 kg
Water	0,03 m^3
Energy	5,14 MJ

TRANSPORT

Impact (CO_2)	0,11 kg
Water	0,00 m^3
Energy	1,20 MJ

TRUE COST

Impact (CO_2)	1,89 kg
Water	35,10 m^3
Energy	44,1 MJ

----

180 WEARS
MIN. EXPECTED LIFETIME

0,19 EUR	**0,01KG**
COST PER WEAR	CO2 PER USE
0,20 m^3	**0,25 MJ**
WATER PER WEAR	ENERGY PER USE

> KNOW YOUR IMPACT, BUY LESS,
> KEEP IT LONGER

I'VE READ AND UNDERSTOOD THE
IMPACT OF MY CHOICE:

ASKET.COM

Fig. 3.2 Asket's impact receipt

them in a coherent way for their effort. In most cases though, a desire for fairness needs to be tempered by a sense of responsibility. Responsibility requires an organization to balance the expectations and needs of different stakeholders and to align actions with principles and values. For example, with COVID-19 the issue of fairness emerged as people began to consider the contribution of healthcare workers in tackling the pandemic. After all, didn't each health care worker form part of a system of delivering vital care to the sick and the dying? And shouldn't their heroic and applauded efforts be rewarded? In England and Wales, there was a groundswell of support for this, but in the end the increase in extrinsic rewards was not so significant. After initially offering National Health Service workers a 1% salary increase, the government increased the offer to 3% (well below the rate of inflation). The government claimed this was fair, which doesn't seem a very plausible argument, but it could be an argument for responsibility. The government has to think responsibly about the consequences of the costs of funding salary increases for 1.3 million staff and the implications that has for tax paying citizens and the long-term funding of the NHS, where around 50% goes in salaries. So, being fair pushes in one direction and responsibility pulls in another. This creates a moral dilemma for decision-makers that ought to be solved through a recourse to conscience, by thinking critically and acting together to effect change. Often though, the comfort of opinion seems to win, as managers follow well-established tropes rather than reconsidering whether they have the courage to be conscientious.

As we described in Chap. 2, a trope that was unquestioned for a long time was shareholder primacy. In this view, the only responsibility is to meet the needs of shareholders. Yet such a narrow view of responsibility can distort behaviour. This can be seen very explicitly in the actions of Boeing in the wake of the launch of its 737 Max plane and two crashes within 5 months of launch and the deaths of 346 people and the way it sought to blame pilots rather than accepting its own culpability. As the drip, drip of truth emerged, it became clear that the source of the problem was systemic and the result of a post-merger shift from an engineering led culture to one that was more shareholder focused and 'celebrated managers for cost-cutting, sought to co-opt regulators with lobbying and political pressure, and pressured suppliers with Walmart-style tactics'. In an email handed over to congressional investigators, a Boeing employee had written about the Max: 'This airplane is designed by clowns, who in turn are supervised by monkeys'.[17]

---

[17] Robison P (2021) *Flying Blind: the 737 Max Tragedy and the Fall of Boeing.* London: Penguin Business.

Boeing's narrow view of responsibility can be countered by the stakeholder view, which recognizes that companies not only exist to deliver profits but also 'to improve our lives, expand our horizons, and solve society's problems large and small'.[18] In the past this led to the development of corporate social responsibility (CSR) programmes that aimed at delivering benefits not directly linked to profitability. CSR has certainly helped companies to develop a more conscientious approach[19] while also generating such positive outcomes as higher levels of customer loyalty, stronger brand equity and higher levels of employee commitment.[20] However, too often CSR has been a palliative: a reaction to external pressure to behave in a more responsible manner, an attempt to burnish reputation or as a mechanism to manage and reduce potential risks.[21] This has led to concerns about the corporate motivations and ethics behind CSR and a sense that CSR practices are insincere, manipulative and disconnected from strategic goals.[22] In short, all too often CSR is not properly linked to the organizational conscience or the business strategy. As Frank Cooper III, Executive Board member at BlackRock and Chief Marketing Officer, says in an interview with consultant and author, Andy Last, 'What I've seen in the past five years is an evolution from CSR to putting the question of how a business contributes to society in a positive way into the operation of the business. In the past, businesses could proceed under this idea of benevolence on the side, but not making it part of the corporation. But what we've seen in the past several years—and accelerated in the last two years—is a greater pressure against businesses directly and a greater awareness among the general public about the role of corporations in society.'[23]

---

[18] Carney M. (2020) *op cit.*, p. 315.

[19] Golob, U., and K. Podnar. 2019. Researching CSR and brands in the here and now: an integrative perspective. *Journal of Brand Management* 26: 1–8.

[20] Lee, E.M., S.Y. Park, M.I. Rapert, and C.L. Newman. 2012. Does perceived consumer fit matter in corporate social responsibility issues? *Journal of Business Research* 65 (11): 1558–1564; Hur, W.M., H. Kim, and J. Woo. 2014. How CSR leads to corporate brand equity: Mediating mechanisms of corporate brand credibility and reputation. *Journal of Business Ethics* 125 (1): 75–86; Skudiene, V., and V. Auruskeviciene. 2012. The contribution of corporate social responsibility to internal employee motivation. *Baltic Journal of Management* 7 (1): 49–67.

[21] Walsh, G., and S.E. Beatty. 2007. Customer-based corporate reputation of a service firm: Scale development and validation. *Journal of the Academy of Marketing Science* 35 (1): 127–143.

[22] Joyner, B.E., and D. Payne. 2002. Evolution and implementation: A study of values, business ethics and corporate social responsibility. *Journal of Business Ethics* 41 (4): 297–311; Pope, S., and A. Wæraas. 2016. CSR-washing is rare: A conceptual framework, literature review, and critique. *Journal of Business Ethics* 137 (1): 173–193; Maon, F., V. Swaen, and A. Lindgreen. 2017. One vision, different paths: An investigation of corporate social responsibility initiatives in Europe. *Journal of Business Ethics* 143 (2): 405–422.

[23] Last, A. (2022). *Business on a Mission: How to Build a Sustainable Brand.* London: Routledge. Introduction to 2nd edition.

While many companies still refer to CSR, we also see in our research that there is tendency as Frank Cooper says, to see it as 'benevolence on the side', that enables companies to absolve themselves for sins already committed. However, it would be better to avoid the sin in the first place by embedding positive and transformative actions into the core of the business. There is nothing wrong with CSR *per se*, but in practice it is not linked to conscience and often lacks organizational commitment. It is only when corporate responsibility adopts a systemic view that it begins to move from relieving negative impacts to dealing with the underlying conditions. The implication of this is that responsibility infers a long-term perspective, because it suggests the value in building multi-stakeholder relationships over time and foregoing, if necessary, short-term gains that might be expedient, but are not sustainable. Such responsibility weighs heavy because it recognizes the considerable power of companies to affect lives, the enormous capabilities of business to deliver transformative change, the potential negative impacts of misdirected actions and the challenge of meeting the sometimes competing demands of ethics and profits.

Facing up to Conflicts Between Ethics and Profits: Against Wishful Thinking in Business

Brian Berkey

Most of the difficult ethical questions that we face in our lives arise because we are confronted with unavoidable conflicts between competing values or principles. Often, though not always, these conflicts involve, on the one hand, an agent's self-interest, broadly understood (to include, e.g., the interests of her loved ones), and on the other, the interests, rights or claims of others, or, more generally, impartial values or principles. For example, a parent might have to decide whether to take advantage of a colleague's connection at a prestigious school in order to provide her son with a significant advantage in the admissions process, or instead to allow him to compete for admission on equal terms with all of the other applicants. She may, quite reasonably, take herself to have moral reasons, deriving from her relationship to her child, to do what she can to provide him with the best education possible. But she may also take herself to have moral reasons to ensure fairness in the admissions process and equal opportunity in education for all children more broadly. The choice that the parent has to make in this case is ethically difficult because whichever choice she makes, she will be failing to act in accordance with at least one of the values or principles that it seems plausible to appeal to in deciding what she ought to do. There is no option that will both maximize her son's prospects for the best possible education and ensure maximal fairness and equal opportunity in the admissions process.

(*continued*)

(continued)

In discussions of most of the important ethical issues that individuals confront in their lives, it is widely accepted, and indeed typically taken as a starting point for debate about the nature and scope of our moral obligations that we regularly face conflicts of this kind. We have to choose, for example, whether to spend some of our disposable income on desired luxury items for ourselves or to instead donate the money to a charity that provides life-saving aid to people in great need. Again, there is no option that will both satisfy our desires for the luxuries and ensure that fewer people die from preventable causes. There are moral principles that seem quite compelling that suggest that it would be wrong to buy the luxury items when lives could be saved instead. At the same time, it might seem overly demanding to hold that it is never morally acceptable for individuals to choose to indulge in luxury purchases so long as there are potentially life-saving uses for the money that they would be spending.

It is one of the central tasks of moral philosophy, and of the ethical thought and reflection that we all engage in when we face morally important choices in our lives, to determine, as best we can, how these conflicts ought to be resolved. Serious moral reflection requires facing head-on the conflicts that can, and often do, arise between competing values and principles, and attempting to arrive at a coherent and well-justified view about how we can live an ethical life in a world in which these conflicts are pervasive.

If someone were to suggest that such reflection is unnecessary, because in fact there are no, or few, deep conflicts between competing values of the kind that I have described, we would likely think that they have either an extremely shallow understanding of morality or an excessively rosy picture of what the world is like (or, perhaps most plausibly, some combination of the two). And in fact, when it comes to the morally important choices that we face in most dimensions of our lives, virtually no one denies that there are often difficult conflicts of competing values or principles that arise.

In discussions of decision-making in business, however, there is a much stronger tendency, at least in certain circles, to deny that the world presents decision-makers with unavoidable conflicts between conflicting values or principles. Consider, for example, how many of my students are initially inclined to respond to Milton Friedman's well-known view about the responsibilities of corporate managers. Friedman claims that managers of firms act wrongly whenever they deploy company funds in ways that aim to satisfy purported 'social responsibilities' at the expense of any amount of legally obtainable profits. One of the first things that many students say when confronted with this claim is that socially responsible behaviour by firms and their managers will also increase profits, because, for example, such behaviour enhances firms' reputations and contributes to greater employee satisfaction and thus productivity. In other words, they deny that managers will tend to face difficult choices between profit-maximizing actions that seem ethically objectionable and ethical choices that involve foregoing opportunities to increase profits.

Importantly, when asked whether this claim suggests that Friedman is wrong, some students say that it does, while others say that it does not. This is not surprising, since the denial of the conflict between profits and broader ethical considerations makes it impossible to assess Friedman's view on the proper terms,

(continued)

that is, as a matter of principle. On the one hand, some students say that the claim that there is no conflict shows that Friedman is wrong, since it shows that managers clearly should choose socially responsible policies for their firms—after all, doing so will, it is claimed, maximize profits anyway. On the other, some say that it shows that Friedman is right, since managers should choose policies that will maximize profits—after all, doing so will, it is claimed, involve making socially responsible choices anyway.

The claim that there are no deep conflicts between ethics and profits is an extremely convenient one for those in the business world (and those, like my students, who intend to work in that world) to accept. Accepting it allows them to believe that they do not need to engage in serious ethical reflection about their business decisions and take seriously the possibility that they may be morally obligated to forego at least some profitable opportunities. The belief that there are no deep conflicts, however, surely constitutes a kind of wishful thinking that is unsupported by the available evidence about what the world is like. It would be extraordinary, indeed unbelievable, if the kinds of conflicts between competing values and principles that virtually all of us acknowledge arise regularly in our lives outside of business, somehow virtually never arose in business contexts. Surely the world is not nearly that conveniently structured for those involved in business decision-making.

It is not only business students and those who work in the business world, however, who suggest that there are no deep conflicts between ethics and profits. Prominent scholars whose work has been influential within managerial circles have also, in effect, suggested that business decision-makers need not think about the choices that they face in terms of potential conflicts between competing values, and in particular between ethics and profits. It is not surprising that many in the business world (along with many in business academia) have responded positively to work of this kind, while largely ignoring the work of those in business ethics who accept that there are conflicts and develop views about how business decision-makers ought to respond to them. But denying the possibility of deep conflicts between ethics and profits is dangerous and will tend to lead those who do so to fail to properly grapple with some of the most important issues that are relevant to the business decisions that they may face.

To see why this is the case, consider, for example, Michael Porter and Mark Kramer's influential 'creating shared value' approach to managerial decision-making.[24] Porter and Kramer define shared value as 'policies and operating practices that enhance the competitiveness of a company while simultaneously advancing the economic and social conditions in the communities in which it operates' (p. 66). They emphasize that their approach treats creating shared value as 'integral to profit maximization' (p. 76) and maintain that '[e]very firm should look at decisions and opportunities through the lens of shared value' (p. 65).

(continued)

---

[24] Porter, M. E., & Kramer, M. R. (2011). Creating shared value: How to reinvent capitalism—and unleash a wave of innovation and growth. *Harvard Business Review 89*(1–2), 62–77.

(continued)

Porter and Kramer's view embodies the kind of wishful thinking that I have described, and therefore fails to offer the kind of guidance to business decision-makers that a serious approach requires. To see this, note, first, that to the extent that 'creating shared value' is intended to provide a general framework for managerial decision-making, it provides no guidance regarding what ought to be done in situations in which a firm's best means of enhancing its own competitiveness would not be, on net, beneficial for the communities in which it operates. It is, of course, true that managers are sometimes in a position to make business decisions that are beneficial for both their firms and the communities in which they operate, and there are strong reasons for them to take advantage of these opportunities where they exist. However, Porter and Kramer present the 'shared value' approach in a manner that suggests that, if managers simply think through the opportunities available in *any* situation hard enough, they will always arrive at an option that is beneficial for all relevant parties. But this is just to deny that deep conflicts between the interests of distinct parties can arise in business contexts. This kind of optimism about the pervasiveness of options that are beneficial for all concerned, and especially optimism about the profit *maximizing* options always being beneficial for all concerned, however, is not merely implausible, but dangerous, because it denies the possibility of conflict. For example, the view refers only to business firms and the communities in which they operate as the parties among whom the value created by business activity ought to be shared. However, some of the most ethically important implications of business activity are not limited to the communities in which firms operate. The climate crisis, for example, is both global and intergenerational, impacting people all across the world, as well as those who will not exist until centuries in the future. Any approach to managerial decision-making that does not explicitly build in a requirement to take account of the global and intergenerational effects of business activity is virtually certain to permit business decisions that will be deeply damaging to vulnerable communities around the world, as well as to future generations.

In order to be in a position to reflect in an appropriately serious way about the ethical issues that they will inevitably face, managers need to become familiar with at least the basic methods of reasoning and argument in moral philosophy. They should, for example, be able to identify plausible moral principles, think through their implications for particular cases and recognize when their initial intuitive reactions regarding what ought to be done in a particular case conflict with a principle that they are otherwise inclined to accept. They should also be able to identify when their intuition conflicts with their belief about another case that seems analogous in morally relevant respects. These kinds of conflicts in our moral thinking tend to arise when (though not only when) there are significant conflicts between our own interests and the morally important interests of others that we would like to resolve in our own favour. Reflecting on whether doing so is consistent with principles that we are willing to accept on reflection (which might require acting against our own interests in other cases), and consistent with our beliefs about other cases that share similar morally important features, is necessary in order to maintain and act on a consistent, and hopefully well-justified view about how one's conduct ought to be guided, both in business and more generally.

(*continued*)

(continued)

Business decision-makers, then, must recognize that conflicts between ethics and profits can and will arise and must be prepared to think critically and systematically about which values ought to be prioritized. The kind of wishful thinking that I have described, which presents the world as inevitably providing business decision-makers with opportunities that are both highly (or even maximally) profitable for themselves and their firms, and also meet the highest of ethical standards (in terms, e.g., of impacts on important social and environmental concerns), must be avoided. The world is simply not that convenient, and addressing the urgent ethical issues that we must, as a global community, confront, many of which are extensively bound up with the activities of business and the choices that business decision-makers face, requires that we not pretend that it is.

Brian Berkey is an Assistant Professor in the Legal Studies and Business Ethics Department at the Wharton School of the University of Pennsylvania.

Becoming a Business with a Conscience

We started this chapter with a quote from John F. Kennedy and we close it with a quote from his brother Robert F. Kennedy from a 1968 speech at the University of Kansas, when he was standing to be the Democratic nominee for the US Presidency and observed that while the Gross National Product of the US was $800 billion a year it also was an inadequate measure:

Yet the gross national product does not allow for the health of our children, the quality of their education or the joy of their play. It does not include the beauty of our poetry or the strength of our marriages, the intelligence of our public debate or the integrity of our public officials. It measures neither our wit nor our courage, neither our wisdom nor our learning, neither our compassion nor our devotion to our country, it measures everything in short, except that which makes life worthwhile.[25]

There have been more recent and deep critiques of the way we measure—and hence value—what's important in our societies,[26] but Kennedy's brief formulation is eloquent and compelling and serves to remind us about the importance of valuing the things that matter to us as human beings. Yet, when

---

[25] https://www.jfklibrary.org/learn/about-jfk/the-kennedy-family/robert-f-kennedy/robert-f-kennedy-speeches/remarks-at-the-university-of-kansas-march-18-1968.
[26] Mazzucato, M. (2018). *The value of everything: Making and taking in the global economy*. Hachette UK; Carney M (2020) *op cit.*

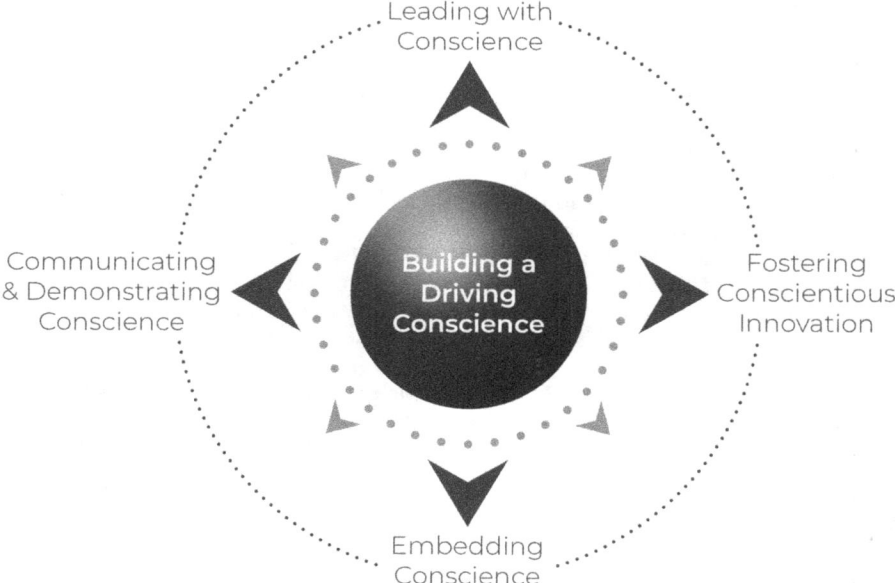

Fig. 3.3 Model of business with a conscience

we sit at work and are confronted by targets to achieve and roles to play, we can become blindsided and ignore the broader impacts of our actions and miss the opportunity to contribute to the wellbeing of others. It is at this point that we need to draw on our individual conscience and that of the organization, and act. The question this poses is, How can a business develop a collective conscience that guides its actions? This is the subject of the inter-connected elements in the model below and the forthcoming chapters of the book. Having defined what a business with a conscience is, we need to establish how to become one—not as a finished state, but as an ongoing journey (Fig. 3.3).

Building a driving conscience. This concerns the belief system that drives the organization forward and guides the choices that people make. As individuals we do not normally write down what our conscience is. But for a business of any scale there comes a point where conscience needs to be elucidated and shared, ideally in the form of a purpose (what the company seeks to achieve in the world) and principles (the fundamental tenets that guide actions). As noted in the Introduction this is not conscience itself, which is irreducible, but is a proximation of it. Of course, what gives the conscience relevance and meaning is not the words in themselves that are used to describe it, but their performative value. In other words, how does a business with a conscience act. This is why we refer to 'Building a Driving Conscience'. This phrasing is designed to convey the way conscience develops over time through the practice of thinking and acting. As the philosopher Maurice Merleau-Ponty suggests, we often believe that we think our way into action, but we also act our way into thought.[27] Thus, it is important to use conscience to help us judge situations and make choices, and also to use it to reflect on the choices we have made. However, this critical reflection can only occur if conscience is embedded in the business such that the words that describe the purpose and principles are understood by stakeholders and integrated into the processes and culture.

Embedding conscience. Embedding is a vital element in the Business with a Conscience model, because it is the only way to ensure that conscience becomes core to decision-making. Embedding contains two aspects. First, is the need to curate conscience. This means looking inwards to understand organizational capabilities and outwards to understand the needs of stakeholders, society and the environment. Bringing the inside and the outside together enables the business to determine which issue or issues it will focus on. This doesn't suggest that a company should ignore its broader responsibilities as a good corporate citizen, but it does indicate it should reflect critically on where it can have the most impact. Second, is the process of embedding itself, which is concerned with how to ensure that what has been curated becomes meaningful for an organization's stakeholders.

Fostering conscientious innovation. Conscience should also drive the approach to innovation by encouraging managers to think of innovation in a holistic way. This suggests developing innovation processes that are driven not only by consumer desires for the next new thing but also tapping into their desires to do the right thing. Amongst other things, this might involve slowing the lifecycle of products or creating new business models that change patterns of behaviour, while delivering environmental and social benefits. We know from research that innovative brands are more attractive to consumers, but this is not simply because of product or service innovation but also because such brands also innovate in the arena of social responsibility.[28] Our argument here is that socially responsible and commercially focused innovation goes hand in hand.

---

[27] Merleau-Ponty, M. (1945) (2002). *Phenomenology of Perception* (Phénoménologie de la perception, Gallimard, Paris). Translated by C. Smith. London: Routledge.

[28] Kurtmollaiev, S. Lervik-Olsen L. and Andreassen T.W., (2022) 'Honey or Condensed Milk? Improving Relative Brand Attractiveness through Commercial and Social Innovations' in The Routledge Companion to Corporate Branding. Edited by Oriol I., Ind N. and Schultz M. London: Routledge: 211–227.

Communicating and demonstrating conscience. The central problem with communication is the prevalence of over-claiming. As businesses have become aware of the sustainability expectations of stakeholders, so they have begun to harvest its appeal in communicating their initiatives. This has led to the misuse of the word sustainability and the practice of greenwashing and wokewashing. This is why, when it comes to communicating conscience and making promises, companies need to ensure as best they can that they can demonstrate the substance behind their claims. This means validating what goes on in supply chains and ensuring a strong factual basis in communication activities. To communicate conscience in a credible way requires deep insight into stakeholder beliefs and behaviour such that the company knows how to present environmental and social attributes and how to tap into stakeholders' needs and nudge them to make good choices.[29]

Leading with conscience. Some of the leaders that we feature in the book have built businesses that are driven by their own conscience, yet we should also note that a corporate conscience requires that sense of conscience to be shared with others if it is to have meaning. This indicates that while leading with conscience is about inspiring others it is also about humility, vulnerability and providing organizational members with the opportunity to express themselves and to sometimes challenge managerial assumptions. Thus, leading with conscience is complex and demanding and no individual can possess all the necessary attributes, which argues that it requires a collective approach to bringing conscience to life and making it an active element in decision-making.

Conclusion

This chapter has focused on describing what a business with a conscience is like. It is built on a simple formula of **Conscience = critical thought + acting together to effect change**. The formula indicates that a business with a conscience must look inwards and outwards and act without succumbing to expediency. This is not always easy, but the examples of Soneva and Asket show that if a business is willing to challenge accepted norms and act with integrity, it can establish new business models and find different ways of working. In the 'How to' model, we show the key areas a business must address if it is to define, and then live, according to its conscience. In the chapters to follow we will show how this model works in practice.

---

[29] Schubert, C. (2017). Green nudges: Do they work? Are they ethical? *Ecological Economics, 132,* 329–342.

4

Building a Driving Conscience

In Chap. 2 we set out what conscience is and why it is relevant, while Chap. 3 explained what a business with a conscience is and introduced a management model for shaping such an enterprise. In this chapter we will focus on the centrepiece of this management model, the corporate conscience, and how to articulate it through a transformative purpose and a set of principles to guide a company's stakeholders. Here it is worth reminding that, as we saw in Chap. 3, conscience is about critical thought and acting together to effect change. To give voice to this conscience, companies have to think critically about their raison d'être and the principles that guide collective action. However, this is not a linear process and neither is it unidirectional. Instead, actions also spur further thinking, which can lead to the evolution or redefinition of the corporate purpose.

The Corporate Purpose

A business with a conscience defines, fosters and puts corporate purpose into action. Purpose sets out why a company exists and the positive transformative impact it seeks to make in the world beyond creating profits for its owners or investors. Here, one should note that conscientious companies are not non-profit entities. That is because a company with a conscience legitimately seeks to build a profitable business. Yet at the same time, such a company also wants to create value in a balanced way for its various stakeholders. Thus, defining a corporate purpose is relevant for two key reasons. First, a purpose recognizes that an enterprise cannot be run by only considering the interests of its

© The Author(s), under exclusive license to Springer Nature Switzerland AG 2022
N. Ind, O. Iglesias, *In Good Conscience*, https://doi.org/10.1007/978-3-031-09338-8_4

shareholders. Instead, it forces an organization to embrace a wider stakeholder perspective and to acknowledge that it should also consider how its activity impacts society and the environment. Second, a corporate purpose encourages the organization to strengthen its capabilities in order to generate value beyond profits. From such a perspective, an enterprise is a vehicle for innovation and the collective creation of shared value.[1] Both arguments underscore that a business with a conscience must not only 'avoid doing harm' but also aim 'to do good'.[2]

The relevance of corporate purpose and its potential to foster a transition from shareholder primacy to a stakeholder perspective has given rise to changes in corporate law at the international level. For instance, two new forms of corporation have emerged in the US, the 'benefit corporation' in Maryland in 2010 and the 'social purpose corporation' in California in 2012. Similar changes have recently occurred in Europe, such as the adoption of the 'Società benefit' in Italy in 2017 and the 'Société à mission' in France in 2019. The generic term 'profit-with-purpose corporation' (PPC) encompasses all these different corporate forms that have emerged. Three legal innovations are at the core of the PPC governance model.[3] First, PPCs legally require the formulation of a corporate purpose that must go beyond profit maximization. Second, directors and managers need to accept the corporate purpose as an intrinsic part of their mandate. On one side, this implies that they need to ensure that the company strategy facilitates an appropriate progress towards fulfilling the purpose. On the other, this implies that they will be assessed in relation to the achievement of the purpose. Third, PPCs need to create accountability mechanisms aimed at ensuring that purpose is embedded into strategy-making and organizational behaviour. These three changes aim to decouple the focus on purpose from the 'contingent engagement of one particular leader or the consent of changing stakeholders'.[4] Patagonia and Danone are among the first corporations to have become PPCs.

Patagonia, the American outdoor sports clothing and accessory company, is an excellent example of a business with a conscience with a very strong

[1] Segrestin, B., Hatchuel, A., and Levillain, K. (2021) When the law distinguishes between the enterprise and the corporation: the case of the new French law on corporate purpose. *Journal of Business Ethics*, 171(1), 1–13.

[2] Scherer, A. G. and Voegtlin, C. (2020) Corporate governance for responsible innovation: Approaches to corporate governance and their implications for sustainable development. *Academy of Management Perspectives*. 34(2), 182–208.

[3] Levillain, K. and Segrestin, B. (2019) From primacy to purpose commitment: How emerging profit-with-purpose corporations open new corporate governance avenues. *European Management Journal*. 37 (5),637–647.

[4] Levillain and Segrestin (2019) ibid., p. 642.

purpose. This firm was originally founded by Yvon Chouinard in 1965 as the Chouinard Equipment Company. Chouinard was a climber and self-taught blacksmith whose company made pitons—spikes hammered into a rock crack or seam. However, one day he had an epiphany climbing a rock formation called El Capitan in Yosemite National Park, when he discovered the damage that the pitons did to the rock face. He felt this was wrong. He found an alternative in the form of aluminium chocks, which did not need to be hammered in, and started a campaign for what he called clean climbing. The close connection to nature and belief in the importance of preserving the natural environment led to the formation of a new company in 1973 focused on outdoor clothing, called Patagonia, after an inspirational trip he had taken there with friends to climb and ski. Later when Patagonia defined its corporate purpose that belief in the importance of the environment was core: 'To build the best product without causing unnecessary harm to the environment, as well as a business that inspires and implements solutions to combat the environmental crisis'. The purpose enshrined the company's business philosophy and served as a moral compass guiding all the enterprise's strategic decisions, even when doing the right thing has meant bearing major costs, such as when the company replaced conventional cotton with 100% organic cotton. Back in the early 1990s, this was a bold high-risk decision but was in alignment with the company's purpose. At the time cotton products made up 20% of Patagonia's business volume and $20 million in turnover a year. Furthermore, there were virtually no suppliers of organic cotton worldwide. The decision to switch to organic cotton meant that the company had to find and foster a wholly new supplier network at a time when organic made up under 1% of the world's cotton output.

In 2018, Patagonia decided to alter its original purpose to something more direct and forceful: 'We're In Business To Save Our Home Planet'. This seeks to convey both a more direct message and a sense of urgency. That is because global warming calls for urgent change and the need to act now. As Chouinard says:

> This is Pearl Harbor. The whole country, and whole world, has to mobilize to do this. [...] That's what has to happen now. So I didn't think we were taking climate change seriously enough. We were supporting too many causes that were working on symptoms and not actual causes and solutions.[5]

---

[5] https://www.fastcompany.com/90280950/exclusive-patagonia-is-in-business-to-save-our-home-planet.

As Vincent Stanley, Director of Patagonia Philosophy adds, the addition of the unnecessary but distinctive word 'home' is also 'a reminder that the planet is not an abstraction, but it's something intimate'. The redefinition of Patagonia's purpose gives us some clues as to how a corporate purpose should be built. First, a corporate purpose should reflect what makes a company unique and how it can positively impact the world. Primarily this involves a company looking inwards and reflecting on itself. When defining a corporate purpose any organization needs to look back, conduct a form of organizational archaeology and understand its distinctive heritage. The new Patagonia purpose connects with the company's past and reinforces its foundational philosophy. However, at the same time, when defining a purpose, a company should also open-up and look outwards and reflect on its potential role. What are the key expectations of stakeholders? How can our identity be relevant to the outside world? The new Patagonia purpose is more concise and direct because, when looking at the outside world, the company felt that every year the climate change challenge was becoming more urgent. This led Patagonia to the conclusion that their identity was more relevant than ever and that they had to make explicit an even stronger commitment. Thus, the new purpose strengthens the company's conscience, driving it forward and spurring Patagonia to take more committed positions and to engage in political activism. For example, during the 2020 American elections, Patagonia campaigned in favour of candidates advocating a circular economy, renewable energy and sticking to the Paris Climate Accord. In addition, the company closed its headquarters, stores and logistics centres on polling day to boost voter turnout among both its staff and customers.

Patagonia is a pioneering business with a conscience. Over the last decade, many other companies have tried to become more conscientious by formulating a corporate purpose; though few have seen it through with the same commitment as Patagonia, who have not only thought about conscience at the corporate level but have also driven it down to the level of individual conscience. This has also been realized by Unilever, who as a multi-brand company, work at three levels: corporate, brand and individual.

Unilever and the Three Levels of Purpose

In 2009 Unilever found itself in a tight spot. In less than a decade it had gone from being the world's largest consumer products company to trailing third behind Nestlé and Procter & Gamble. In fact, the share price in 2009 was the same as it had been ten years earlier in 1999. With the aim of reviving the company, Paul Polman was recruited as the new CEO—the first in Unilever's history to come from outside the company's ranks. Three years before joining Unilever, Polman had served as Nestlé's CFO and had run its business in the US.

Polman launched a growth strategy known as the Unilever Sustainable Living Plan (USLP), which was built around a new corporate purpose that was 'to make sustainable living commonplace'. The idea was to de-couple the company's growth from its environmental footprint and make Unilever a leader in sustainability. The guiding principle also sought to strike a balance between the company's diverse stakeholders and to ensure a positive social impact. In an interview, Paul Polman stated:

> I don't think our fiduciary duty is to put shareholders first. I say the opposite. What we firmly believe is that if we focus our company on improving the lives of the world's citizens and come up with genuine sustainable solutions, we are more in synch with consumers and society and ultimately this will result in good shareholder returns.[6]

The new strategy thus set ambitious goals for incorporating sustainability into Unilever's core business. Moreover, the timescale for achieving some of them was very short. These goals included such things as cutting out plastic in the firm's products and slashing waste and CO_2 emissions. Another step taken was to restrict the quarterly reports issued to shareholders. The aim here was to help foster a longer-term vision of the business. To the same end, Polman also forged highly pro-active agreements with new investors that were in tune with his long-term vision of creating value for all the company's stakeholders.

The work on 'corporate purpose' begun by Polman mainly focused on the corporate level and enabled Unilever to evolve into a company with a conscience. However, it took a little time before the company fully grasped what gaining a corporate conscience really entailed. The process involved defining and implementing a purpose for the company's product brands, which while expressing their own unique role had to be inspired by, and aligned with, the corporate purpose. This second level of purpose was vital for putting conscience at the heart of the organization's value proposition. It was one of the key strategic bets made by Polman's successor, Alan Jope.

---

[6] https://news.mongabay.com/2020/10/putting-sustainability-at-the-center-of-business-strategy-an-interview-with-paul-polman/.

For example, Dove exemplifies a product brand that has built its entire value proposition around its purpose. In fact, it was the first Unilever brand to work in this way. Dove's purpose is stated thus:

> We believe beauty should be a source of confidence, and not anxiety. That's why we are here to help women everywhere develop a positive relationship with the way they look, helping them raise their self-esteem and realise their full potential.

This purpose is relevant because only 4% of women around the world consider themselves beautiful[7]—this lack of self-esteem tends to generate anxiety at very early ages. Additionally, 6 out of 10 girls are so concerned with their appearance that it affects their daily life. *The Dove Campaign for Real Beauty*, which launched in 2004, aligns with the brand's purpose and uses 'real women' (rather than professional models) in its advertising. As part of its stance, the brand undertook never to 'PhotoShop' pictures to falsify natural beauty. Dove's purpose and value proposition were clearly in tune with consumer attitudes and global sales leapt from $2.5 to $4 billion in the campaign's first ten years, making it Unilever's best-selling brand globally. In 2019 Dove launched another major initiative, the #ShowUs project. It was drawn up in collaboration with Getty Images and the Girlgaze network of creators. Its goal was to build up a photo archive that broke with traditional stereotypes of beauty. Currently, the archive collection has over 11,000 pictures of individuals who identify as women or as trans-sexual. The pictures are available to communication agencies and advertising companies for use in their campaigns. All the photos depict people as they are and have not been retouched in any way. The brand's quest for social impact is complemented by its firm commitment to environmental sustainability. In fact, Dove has launched a 100% recyclable plastic bottle as part of the company's goal to cut plastic consumption by 20,500 tonnes a year.

While working on purpose at the corporate and product brand levels, Unilever has also been working hard on purpose at the individual level. The seed for this third level of focus on purpose emerged from the Unilever Leadership Development Programme (ULDP), which Polman pioneered. This was a one-week programme in which Unilever's top 100 executives and the CEO himself took part. The programme explored what kinds of managers the company would need over the next decade and included activities designed to help Unilever's top managers find their own individual purpose. Thus, executives reflected on who they were and what they wanted from their lives,

---

[7] https://www.dove.com/us/en/stories/about-dove/our-vision.html.

as well as on how their work could help them in this quest for meaning. The initial exercise proved so inspiring and made such an impact on senior management that the programme was later extended to all Unilever staff. The upshot is that the company offers individual-purpose training to all employees, of whom 60,000-plus have taken the programme.[8] In this discover-your-purpose training, individual employees explore their own passions and causes to define the things that they really care about and to put them at the centre of their career development. Getting each employee to reflect on his or her purpose helps Unilever come up with personalized training plans that are tailored to advancing individual careers. Finally, one should note that the corporate purpose helps Unilever attract and recruit talented individuals whose own purposes and values are in keeping with the firm's. In this regard, no less than three-quarters of new recruits say that they joined Unilever because of its business purpose and philosophy.[9]

To sum up, businesses with a conscience have a transformative corporate purpose that clearly defines why they exist and how they seek to make the world a better place. Both goals go beyond making profits but do not renounce them. In addition, these firms place conscience at the heart of their value proposition by defining a purpose for each of their product and/or service brands, which in turn are inspired by and aligned with the overarching corporate purpose. Finally, companies with a conscience encourage their staff members to reflect on and build their own individual purposes. This approach furthers professional and personal development, giving employees meaning. It also fosters in-house talent that is at one with the company's purpose and principles.

The Corporate Principles

So far, we have seen purpose's central role in articulating corporate conscience. However, for corporate conscience to work well, it needs also to operate through a set of corporate principles that operationalizes how the organization will achieve its purpose and encourage specific behaviours.

Unfortunately, most companies still work only with corporate values rather than also using principles to put the former into action. Corporate values are often expressed through one-word labels such as 'innovation', 'quality' and

---

[8] Polman, P. and Winston, A. (2021) *Net Positive. How courageous companies thrive by giving more than they take*. Harvard Business Review Press, p. 86.
[9] Polman, P. and Winston, A. (2021) ibid., p. 87.

'honesty'. The problem is that such an approach is highly ambiguous and can be interpreted in any number of ways. For example, what does 'innovation' mean? Does innovation embrace incremental change? Is it continuous improvement? Does it imply radical change? The word itself gives no inkling of the answer and thus the concept remains nebulous. Such ambiguity and lack of precision renders corporate values highly subjective. That is why company employees tend to have individual interpretations of what such value words as 'innovation', 'quality' and 'honesty' might mean. The danger with this is that a host of varying interpretations can spawn highly heterogeneous corporate cultures and communication. Instead of defining the uniqueness of an organization, much of the value language could apply to any business. Finally, corporate value words are often static. However, conscience is performative. Therefore, it makes sense to define conscience in a way that guides people in their decision-making, deeds and behaviours. In other words, corporate principles must be clearly action-oriented. So, when we try to articulate corporate conscience, it is always much better to do so through a set of corporate principles.

As we saw earlier, the statement 'Patagonia exists as a company to save our home planet' enshrines the corporate purpose. To support this, Patagonia also has a set of corporate principles that operationalize how the company will do business in ways that reflect its purpose and inspire the right behaviours.

Patagonia's first corporate principle is:

> Build the best product. Our criteria for the best product rests on function, repairability, and, foremost, durability. Among the most direct ways we can limit ecological impacts is with goods that last for generations or can be recycled so the materials in them remain in use. Making the best product matters for saving the planet.

This principle is specific in defining the criteria for a good product, which guides employees and partners and lessens the risk of the corporate purpose being misinterpreted. Furthermore, stating the enterprise's philosophy on what a good product is helps Patagonia frame a corporate conscience that is all its own. The principle also inspires highly specific actions and behaviours. These include such things as making recycling a strategic priority and ensuring that the company can repair customers' products when they have become badly worn.

Another of Patagonia's corporate principles is that the business is:

Not bound by convention. Our success—and much of the fun—lies in developing new ways to do things.

This highlights the value the company sets on 'thinking outside the box', breaking with traditional industry norms and taking risks when needed, to achieve its purpose. This corporate principle led Patagonia to successfully develop and scale bold, unconventional initiatives such as its worn wear programme. In the first place, Patagonia's programme gives its customers the option of returning their worn products to the company, either by handing them over at a shop or by posting them. The company's goal here is to resell these products to other users. So, when anyone goes to Patagonia's website, they can buy any product in Patagonia's catalogue in the form of either a new product or a used one. Customers handing in worn Patagonia garments are rewarded with credits that they can offset against future purchases. This circular commitment has three main advantages. The first is that buying used products extends their useful life by almost two years, cutting the company's carbon footprint by around 82% through both savings on water and materials.[10] The second is that Patagonia offers to mend those products that can still be saved. The company has one of the largest clothing repair centres in the US, which since 2005 has repaired over 415,000 items. Also, together with its ally iFixit, Patagonia has produced many online tutorials that enable users to mend their products by themselves at home. Third, the company tries to recycle all those products that cannot be resold or repaired. In 2019 they announced the ReCrafted initiative which launched a new collection of clothing and accessories produced with recycled materials. The scheme covered badly damaged products that were not worth repairing or reselling, but could still be 're-crafted'. These modified or repurposed items were then returned to the company's customers.

Patagonia, like Unilever, looks inwards to understand its capabilities and outwards to the positive impact it can have on the world. What gives both Patagonia and Unilever clarity is an awareness of a corporate conscience that is given voice through a multi-layered approach to purpose and to a set of corporate principles that operationalize the purpose. Here we should note that corporate principles are not rigid rules. Instead, they are guidelines which should empower each employee to critically assess what the right thing to do is. Additionally, corporate principles should also inspire and promote certain specific behaviours capable of activating the corporate purpose.

---

[10] https://wornwear.patagonia.com/.

The Benefits of a Driving Conscience

So far, we have seen how corporate conscience can be articulated through corporate purpose and principles. We'll now delve into how this conscience benefits companies.

First, corporate conscience provides a moral compass that helps staff make better strategic decisions. According to Hannah Arendt, morality is our ability to define what is right or wrong, regardless of what the Law says. Thus, morality bears on our self-awareness and ability to relate to ourselves. From this standpoint, morality depends on our conscience, our ability to live with ourselves and with the implications of our decisions. In fact, Arendt stresses that what human beings fear most is the nagging voice of conscience. Therefore, conscience limits and determines what someone is willing to do given that she will have to live with the consequences of her decisions. At the end of the day, our conscience decisively influences our judgements and the decisions we make. In fact, 'the fundamental task of conscience is to determine what I can and cannot do and still remain in harmony with myself'.[11]

In essence, corporate conscience helps employees examine options and aid better decision-making. This is precisely how Patagonia draws on its purpose and principles. An example is furnished by the labels that Patagonia's design team came up for some of the company's products during the 2020 American presidential elections. Specifically, Patagonia's designers fashioned new labels, which were sown into the company's 'Road to Regenerative' line of shorts. The label bore the phrase 'VOTE THE ASSHOLES OUT'. When consumers discovered these tags, they shared photos of them on social media and they went viral. The aim of the labels was to make consumers aware of the need to abstain from voting for those politicians either denying climate change or unwilling to lift a finger to stop it. The design team felt it was the right call at the time given that the company's corporate purpose is 'to save the world'. It was also in keeping with the idea of acting in unconventional ways when called for. Thus, Patagonia's corporate conscience made it easier for the team of designers to come up with what was a highly provocative and controversial slogan given the context of the 2020 US Presidential Election.

Second, corporate conscience confers agility. Those companies with a sound conscience that is shared by employees not only make swifter, better decisions but they also put them into action faster. In times of crisis or uncertainty, conscience makes clear what the right thing to do is. Additionally, when a corporate conscience is linked with the company's capabilities, it

---

[11] Parekh, S. (2008) op cit.

makes the implementation of strategic decisions much quicker. A good example of this is how SAP acted when the COVID-19 pandemic hit and it used its purpose of 'To help the world run better and improve people's lives' to drive a variety of initiatives. The company activates its purpose by linking it with its distinctive capabilities, its products and through collaboration agreements with sundry partners, including non-profit organizations and NGOs. During the first peak of the pandemic and driven by corporate purpose, SAP staff harnessed the company's special software capabilities to deal with the major challenges and emergencies posed by the pandemic.

For example, SAP was able to produce an app for Germany's Ministry of Foreign Affairs (*Auswärtiges Amt*) in under two days. This made it possible to co-ordinate the repatriation of 120,000 citizens who had been stranded in other countries due to lock-downs and transport restrictions arising from efforts to contain the disease. During the first month of the pandemic, the German government had already decided to launch a €50-billion emergency fund to help the economy. Management of these funds was in the hands of the Federal Government, regional governments (*Länder*) and municipalities. Driven by the company's purpose, SAP employees developed a mobile application for Hamburg and for its development bank, IFB Hamburg (*Die Hamburgische Investitions und Förderbank*), in just a few days. This initiative allowed rapid disbursement of funds to small businesses and medium-sized companies, as well as to the self-employed (all of whom were hard-hit by the pandemic). Some 40,000 users signed up within hours of the App going live, and over 16,000 requests were handled. The App let users automatically apply for emergency aid online, without needing to print and fill out PDF forms. Thanks to the App, IFB Hamburg was able to approve the first aid package in under 24 hours from the moment applications were sent, thus providing almost immediate financial support to those most in need.

Third, corporate conscience inspires and motivates diverse stakeholders. As already seen in Unilever's case, a business with a conscience tries to connect its corporate goals with the purposes of each and every one of their employees. To make this possible, companies also make it easier for employees to discover what their own personal and professional goals are and the individual purpose which gives them meaning. A study by McKinsey[12] in 2020 showed that those who realize their own goals at work are more productive than those who do not. Furthermore, such employees are also more resilient, healthier and tend to stay in the company for longer. Thus, being able to develop individual

---

[12] https://www.mckinsey.com/business-functions/people-and-organizational-performance/our-insights/purpose-not-platitudes-a-personal-challenge-for-top-executive.

purpose at work brings clear benefits to both employees and employers, particularly, when corporate purpose is aligned with the purpose of the firm's employees. This requires the corporate purpose to be activated such that strategic decisions and leaders' behaviour are in keeping with the purpose. In this case, alignment of corporate and individual purposes yields high levels of staff commitment and loyalty, with employees recommending the company to others.

The good news is that a growing number of employees and candidates are asking companies to pin down their business purpose so that they can see whether these align with their own goals. Here, one should note that in a recent interview with Nestlé Spain's CEO during a Round Table, he stressed that there had been a major change in recruitment dynamics over the last few years. Hitherto, when evaluating a job candidate, the CEO used the last interview to ask what the applicant felt he (or she) could bring to the company. Nestlé Spain's CEO noted that today the boot was on the other foot, with candidates asking him how his company could make the world a better place instead of only thinking of how to rack up profits. This change in 'the conversation' shows how employees make their careers part of their quest for leading a meaningful life. From this standpoint, corporate conscience is clearly a source of inspiration and motivation for a firm's staff.

From an external perspective, corporate conscience can inspire a company's diverse stakeholders, drive them to change and make long-term strategic commitments. As a Unilever senior manager, we interviewed in one of our research projects, put it:

> What we want to do as part of our strategy, of our purpose, is to build a movement. So, leading by example, we try to convince others that this is the right way to do business and we try to prove it through our results. This is the way we try to inspire our suppliers and partners to transform themselves and join us in this way of understanding business.

As we'll see in the forthcoming chapters, one of the hallmarks of businesses with a conscience is that they are committed to nudging their stakeholders to embrace conscientious ways of thinking and acting.

So far, we have discussed how corporate conscience should be articulated through corporate purpose and principles and what benefits can be gained from it. However, we should also ask, what is the best process for building corporate purpose and principles so that corporate conscience can yield the foregoing benefits? Our research suggests that this process should first exploit the company's history and heritage because this is what makes that firm unique. Second, the process needs to be rooted in participation and co-creation because a corporate conscience needs to be relevant to the outside world.

Driving Conscience

Uncovering the Corporate Heritage

In an article that we published in 2020 in *Business Horizons*, we argued that managers usually dwell on what the future holds as they strive to anticipate future customers' needs, trying to foretell what the firm's competitors will do, and launching new products and services to gain market share. This forward-looking approach is understandable. Yet an excessive focus on the future can lead managers to forget the organization's past and fail to appreciate the value of its history. This was precisely the case with Unilever, a company whose remarkable history lay forgotten for several decades until Paul Polman joined the company. He rediscovered the firm's past and leveraged it in drawing up the company's plan for the future.

Unilever is a company with a rich history and had strong corporate principles right from the outset. In fact, when William and James Lever founded the Lever Brothers company in 1885 (which became Unilever in 1929), their idea was to make cheap soap for poorer consumers who could not afford the soaps then on the market. From its foundation Unilever was a company with a conscience. Another example of Unilever's corporate conscience can be found in Port Sunlight, the industrial town that the Lever brothers began to build in 1888. The town was sited in Merseyside in North-Western England and featured high-quality housing with running water and bathrooms. Port Sunlight also had a school, a library, a hospital, a swimming pool, an art gallery and a church. In addition, William Lever made plans to foster the wellbeing of his workers, focusing on the education of families, running entertainment activities and promoting music, art and literature. Lever Brothers' workers also enjoyed better wages and social benefits than were typical at the time.

When Polman became Unilever's new CEO in 2009, and charted a new strategy for a brighter future, he delved into the company's past and drew inspiration from it. Given that Unilever already had a strong corporate conscience, the new CEO was able to leverage it to come up with a new purpose—namely to make sustainable living commonplace. Forging links between the company's heritage conscience and its new one became the cornerstone of Polman's strategic project. Not surprisingly, employees, customers and other stakeholders see a corporate conscience as more genuine when it builds upon a company's history. Our research also shows that digging into a company's past brings out a firm's unique character and the link between past and present bolsters the future strategy's authenticity and legitimacy. This explains why Unilever's conscience gained in terms of both perceived authenticity and legitimacy from Polman's approach. Additionally, the moral authenticity that comes from connecting a company's roots with conscience and strategy boosts managers' credibility, power and influence.

Similarly, the Dutch co-operative bank, Rabobank, founded over a century ago by a group of farmers who joined forces to gain better access to funding and share financial risks shows how the past can drive strategy. Inspired by the ideas of Dr Heinrich Raiffeissen, Rabobank was initially a Credit Union based on the idea of: 'What can't be solved alone, can be achieved together'. The founding identity of the bank acted as a 'corporate conscience' and was articulated through a set of principles based on reciprocity and the collective advancement of its members. Furthermore, these founding principles led to a culture of taking the long-term view, which was deeply rooted in a sense of social responsibility and a duty of care to both the co-op's members and the communities it operated in.

Over the next 125 years Rabobank grew to become one of the top three banks in the Netherlands and the world's largest specialist in banking services for the food and agriculture sectors. In 2021, Rabobank was present in 37 countries and had a workforce of over 40,000 staff. Rabobank has 10 million clients, of whom 2 million are a member and/or co-owner. These members are represented by local Member Councils which supervise the activity of the local Rabobank branches, while a global Member Council oversees the performance of the company's Management Team. The final goal of these Member Councils is to ensure that Rabobank and its management teams, both global and local, effectively serve the needs of clients and their communities.

For many decades these strong corporate principles helped Rabobank become the most reputable bank in its market. However, in late 2012 it was discovered that some Rabobank traders working in London had been involved in meddling with benchmark interest rates, specifically in the London Interbank Offered Rate (LIBOR). This, and similar behaviour by other traders and banks, sparked the so-called LIBOR Scandal. The bank took swift remedial measures to deal with the ensuing crisis. Nevertheless, Rabobank's members asked management to draw up a far-reaching plan to restore trust in the company. The scandal made it clear that Rabobank was not different from other banks, contrary to what its members believed. Furthermore, the bank's uniqueness was also diluted by a growing spate of regulations stemming from the Global Financial Crisis and its fallout. Just like any other bank, Rabobank was required to raise its capital reserves and its cost/income ratio, to centralize its decisions and operations and to speed up its digital transformation.

This context led to the appointment in 2014 of a new CEO, Wiebe Draijer, a former McKinsey partner and an executive that was highly respected for his commitment to social causes, as well as for his political activism. The new CEO had to tackle two challenges. The first was to transform the bank to comply with the new regulatory framework. This meant greater intervention by senior management to implement more centralized control of the bank. The second challenge was to restore and bolster the co-operativist principles that had shaped the bank's strategic decisions from the outset and that had guided all its members and communities over the years. To make matters worse, Draijer had to do all this when the bank's reputation was at its lowest and members were sceptical of the bank's probity.

Centralizing control was a tall order because it ran counter to the bank's co-op ethos and structure and the freedom enjoyed by bank branches serving their local communities. In fact, the company had some 150 local banks in The Netherlands that were used to unbridled autonomy, each having its own banking licence, management team and Member Council, as well as its own budget to support local causes. It is little wonder that efforts to centralize Rabobank's business and exert greater control over the local banks were seen as a frontal attack on the co-operativist nature of the company. In any case, the CEO had no other choice but to follow the dictates of the regulators. In his first years in the post, Draijer merged the various local banks, creating a single legal entity with just one banking licence while reorganizing and ratio-nalizing the company at the same time. These changes sparked stiff opposition among Rabobank's staff and its customers. At the same time, the company was slated in the media for abandoning its co-operativist founding principles.

By 2017 it was clear that Draijer had wrought a decisive change in the way Rabobank did business—something reflected by most of the key economic and financial benchmarks. Nevertheless, the CEO was keenly aware that he had yet to rebuild a corporate conscience rooted in the bank's principles. At the same time, Draijer also realized that the rediscovery of the bank's founding ethos would have to be re-contextualized for the modern world. To achieve this, the CEO formed a new management team whose members were drawn from both inside and outside Rabobank. Outsiders filled some of the key posts such as the directors of Human Resources, Communication and Sustainability. The challenges were to: (1) rediscover the organization's co-operativist principles; (2) make them relevant to today's setting and (3) place those principles at the heart of the company's new strategy. Deep reflection on what strategy should be pursued led to a new plan focusing on enhancing Rabobank's co-operativist nature. Such a focus, it was felt, would foster collaboration with many other entities, speeding up the transitions needed in the food and energy sectors to build a more sustainable world. This rediscovery of corporate conscience was articulated in the form of a new purpose, 'Growing a better world together', as well as a set of renewed and revitalized corporate principles. Over the following years, revitalization of these tenets was the key theme at all Rabobank global events, in internal company communications, in training projects and in employee performance reviews and promotions. From 2018 external stakeholders also started to notice and Rabobank reclaimed its position as the bank with the strongest reputation in the sector.

General Council members reacted positively to this new strategy. Yet they were also critical because they believed much more was needed to make sure that Rabobank's managers and staff worked in ways that were fully in keeping with the corporate conscience. Following on from this, internal consultations were held in 2018, which led to a 12-point strategic plan being drawn up to put co-operativist principles back at the heart of the bank's corporate culture. This plan was adopted by the bank's Board of Directors and detailed the steps to be taken. The goal was to ensure that the new purpose and corporate principles: (1) guided key strategic decisions; (2) resolved dilemmas; (3) prioritized investments in innovation and (4) developed new products and services. For instance, in 2021 Rabobank started the Rabo Carbon Bank, which is committed to developing climate-smart initiatives focused on Carbon Farming, thus helping farmers to reduce emissions and remove carbon from the atmosphere. Such initiatives are monitored by satellites and certified. Furthermore, rituals (such as Co-op Awards and Co-op Employees Week) were used to make employees think in pro-active terms about the meaning of co-operativism and what they could do to strengthen it. A key part of this philosophy was the belief that the deepest changes cannot occur if one views business as a zero-sum game. Rabobank wanted to foster the idea that the best solutions are win-win ones for everyone and that the whole is greater than the sum of its parts.

At the same time, the brand and corporate communication team also launched a strategy and an action plan to ensure that the co-op mindset was reflected in all new communication campaigns. They showed positive-sum examples (i.e. 'win-win' outcomes). A lot of effort was also put into explaining what the Rabobank co-operativist philosophy entailed. This new strategy was further reinforced by renewing the firm's visual identity.

Instead of only seeking to maximize profits, Rabobank tries to strike a balance that serves all its stakeholders. In addition, the company draws on its purpose and co-operative principles to work with its employees, customers and partners to improve society and thus to make the world a better place. Rabobank strives to ensure that everyone involved enjoys a financially healthy life and can contribute to the energy transition, food transition and a more inclusive world. Thus, the corporate principles set out in 1898 are still very much alive today. In a nutshell, the bank uses its corporate conscience (articulated as the corporate purpose and principles) as a moral compass to help it make better, swifter decisions and to inspire its sundry stakeholders.

Embracing Stakeholder Co-creation

Another lesson to be learnt from Rabobank is that the CEO did not unilaterally define the new corporate conscience or the company's future strategy. Instead, he began a process of 'co-creation' in which many employees took part. As we have seen, this process not only led to a definition of corporate purpose and principles but also led to the drawing up of a 12-point strategic plan to boost corporate conscience and make sure that the bank's highest principles were observed as in days of yore.

Co-creation, which involves the process of engaging internal and external stakeholders in value creation processes, has gained relevance because of two main factors.[13] First, there has been a dawning recognition that customers are not simply passive recipients of what organizations chose to provide. Instead, they have relevant knowledge and ideas, which they want to share with companies and with others, in order to co-develop new products and services. In a similar vein, employees expect much more than the traditional top-down command and control approach to management, and instead want to express their views and share their concerns. Second, the rapid growth of social media and the emergence of online communities have shifted the power from organizations to stakeholder communities. This is a reality that companies and managers cannot ignore and that they should instead embrace. In essence, rather than trying to decipher what customers, employees or other stakeholders want, managers can foster communities and build participative networks to co-create strategy and innovations. Of course, this demands a leadership style that is more open, empathetic and participatory.

---

[13] Ind, N., Coates, N., Lerman, K. (2020) The gift of co-creation: what motivates customers to participate. *Journal of Brand Management*, 27(2), 181–194.

Building a corporate conscience and corporate strategy through co-creation not only tends to lead to better outcomes but also lends them greater legitimacy. Research we conducted in the health insurance sector showed that co-creation boosts trust in strategy and enhances perceptions of its rationale.[14] The same research also shows that staff and/or customer involvement in co-creation boosts loyalty to the company and commitment to the corporate strategy. Getting stakeholders involved in drawing up the strategy leads to greater engagement, making them much keener to carry out the plan.

Thus, co-creation is an invaluable tool for not only defining corporate conscience but also for linking this to corporate strategy. Co-creation can be used to enrich and activate corporate conscience and tie it in with the development and implementation of a firm's strategy. This is why Rabobank regularly uses co-creation. For example, in 2021 Rabobank promoted a structured dialogue with 5000 of its members in the Netherlands' 14 regions. The goal was to decide the bank's economic, ecological and social priorities in each region. This commitment was shared with the Dutch Government and led to the drafting of regional co-op investment plans. These plans foster collaboration between regional members and partners with a view to come up with co-investment initiatives benefiting all stakeholders while making profits for Rabobank.

The French multinational foods company Danone also fosters co-creation by linking its corporate conscience with corporate strategy. Danone was the first French-listed company to be legally recognized as an *Entreprise à Mission*. This designation means the company is obliged to strike a reasonable balance among its stakeholders and to have a purpose that fosters positive change in the social and environmental settings it operates in. Danone has drawn up a highly ambitious and innovative governance model, called 'One Person, One Voice'. Through it, some 100,000 company employees have taken part in drawing up the strategic priorities for 2030. This co-creative approach is intended to make the firm's staff feel that they own the plan and to make them play a key role in drafting both Danone's local and global future strategy. Furthermore, this strategic agenda aims to build a better future for the company, its employees and the communities in which Danone operates. Here, one should note that Danone regularly launches co-creation initiatives in which employees, key customers and other external stakeholders such as NGOs take part. Each of these initiatives has specific goals and performance

[14] Iglesias, O., Markovic, S., Bagherzadeh, M. et al. (2020). Co-creation: A Key Link Between Corporate Social Responsibility, Customer Trust, and Customer Loyalty. *Journal of Business Ethics* 163(1), 151–166. https://doi.org/10.1007/s10551-018-4015-y.

benchmarks in mind, which are pursued through the company's various social, environmental and governance strategies.

Conclusion

A business with a conscience needs a corporate purpose to give it direction and a set of corporate principles that guide action. Ideally, purpose also needs to be defined at product and individual levels. When a business has a solid conscience that drives it forward, it provides employees with a means to critically assess the right thing to do and to take better decisions. Additionally, such decisions can be taken with greater agility. Finally, a driving conscience inspires and motivates employees and stakeholders. However, it is important to remember that businesses with a conscience cannot be built from a classic, unambiguous, top-down, inside-out perspective. Instead, while nurturing a distinctive heritage, businesses must also weigh the perspectives of many interest groups and work with them to co-create a collective conscience that aligns with the corporate strategy. There are many benefits to a co-creative approach to building a brand with a conscience, but a vital one is that it strengthens the legitimacy of the strategy and boosts employees' commitment to it.

5

Embedding Conscience

We move now from how an organization defines its conscience in the form of a purpose and principles, to how it curates and embeds such a belief system into its actions. However, this makes it sound as if the process is a step-by-step progression from thought to action. Yet, the reality is somewhat different. Thoughts and actions intertwine as an organizational conscience emerges through discussion and reflection over time. Without discussion a conscience would be abstract, irrelevant to the opportunities, challenges and dilemmas an organization faces. As the philosopher, Mikhail Bakhtin notes, thought is born and shaped 'in the process of interaction and struggle with others' thought'.[1] This idea of emergence indicates that organizations have to be able to tolerate ambiguity and uncertainty as they move to deeper understanding.[2]

For most of the time conscience is not called upon. As people provide customer service, produce reports and write code, there is no need to consult conscience. It is only when there is a break in the pattern—when new choices need to be made—that conscience needs to be engaged and questions asked of oneself and the organization: what do my beliefs guide me to do? What

[1] Morris, P. ed. (2003) *The Bakhtin Reader: Selected Writings of Bakhtin, Medvedev, Voloshinov.* London: Arnold. p. 86.
[2] Weick, K. E. (2003) Organizational Design and the Gehry Experience. *Journal of Management Enquiry* 12(1), 93–97.

Electronic Supplementary Material The online version of this chapter (https://doi.org/10.1007/978-3-031-09338-8_5) contains supplementary material, which is available to authorized users. The videos can be accessed by scanning the related images with the SN More Media App.

does the corporate conscience as expressed in the purpose and principles suggest? To enable people to make conscientious choices, the purpose and principles need to be embedded and acted upon. Here it should be noted that the purpose and principles are not there to dictate patterns of behaviour but to enable the responsible use of freedom within a broad framework. They are there to enable agility not to constrain it.

In this chapter we will look at how companies select or curate what they consider to be important and then how they root conscience in the organization through new practices and by emphasizing stakeholder participation in a *power-with* approach.

Conscience as a Strategic Guide: La Casa de Carlota

La Casa de Carlota & Friends (LCDC) is one of thousands of design consultancies in Spain. Like many others in the field, it produces highly creative work and wins awards for its designs. The company has an inspirational, albeit generic sounding purpose—*to change the world with creativity*. Yet the company also has a key point of difference that is rooted in its conscience and deepens the meaning of the purpose: it uses disabled designers, because it believes in their creativity. This is not a token gesture but a key element in the company's success. As co-founder, Sergi Capell says, 'we emphasise capabilities not disabilities. And we provide the designers the opportunity for creativity; we let them break the rules.'

The idea for La Casa de Carlota came from a project run by co-founder, José Maria Batalla, called *Los peces no se mojan* ('Fish don't get wet'), that involved children with and without Down's Syndrome, making a documentary and an activity manual to explain to other children the nature of the disorder. Seeing, at first hand, the creativity of the disabled children, Batalla and Capell, wanted to incorporate this in an approach to design. Of course, they could have then created a design business that was run in the standard way with a team of professional designers—and perhaps done some free design projects for charities that work with disability. This would be the typical philanthropic approach. But the idea behind LCDC wasn't about philanthropy. Rather, drawing on the 'Fish don't get wet' project, they adopted a social issue—the challenge of finding meaningful and properly rewarded work for people suffering from autism and Down's Syndrome—and made it central to their business idea.

What the founders recognized was that the creativity of the autistic and Down's Syndrome individuals was raw and untainted by social conventions or design training. Give a brief to an established designer to create a logo and she would inevitably be influenced by awareness of graphic design tropes. Give the brief to an autistic designer and he would ask, what is a logo? Batalla and Capell saw that the unfettered and surprising responses from an autistic or Down's Syndrome designer delivered highly original ideas, but they also understood that working for commercial clients meant a need for structure and accountability. Consequently, they developed a consultancy with three connected but complementary groups: the designers with Down's Syndrome or autism; design students who could work together with the disabled designers; and professional designers and art directors who interpret the brief and help shape the ideas (Fig. 5.1).

La Casa de Carlota is a business with a conscience that is driven by the desire to do the right thing and be economically sustainable. This comprises giving a real opportunity to creative individuals to express themselves and to earn a salary, while responding to client briefs with a unique creativity. This is

Fig. 5.1 La Casa designs for Ecoalf T-shirts

not an occasional practice, but the way the company works day-in, day-out. It also guides the working practices of LCDC in that there is a belief in equality with empathy. All employees are treated equally by the company and are paid at rates typical for designers. There are no therapists to accompany people and no special facilities. Everyone brings their own unique capabilities to the team. The only special requirements are shorter working sessions with clear routines and a willingness to listen and be patient. For people with autism and Down's Syndrome who regularly encounter prejudices about their capabilities, the sense of being treated as an equal; of having *power with*, improves both self-esteem and cognitive abilities.[3]

Curating Conscience

La Casa de Carlota illustrates how a business can make a social cause the focus of its work and benefit from so doing. It also demonstrates how companies with impassioned leaders and a clear conscience can develop a virtuous and authentic business idea from the ground up. However, can this still be done as a company grows? And what about those companies that want to transition from shareholder primacy to a conscientious stakeholder approach. The first requirement is that the company sees value in adopting an approach rooted in conscience, but then it must determine how to transition, which involves defining and using its purpose and principles, as a guide to curate those issues, which are most relevant to society and which it has the competence to address, and to embed in the strategy, processes and culture.

To curate the issues that matter a company needs to look both inwards to critically assess its own motivations and capabilities and outwards to build insights into the needs of stakeholders and the planet. Given the growing requirements to deliver on environmental, social and governance measures, companies are under pressure to deliver on a whole range of issues, but most also understand the need to focus on those that create meanings that either reinforce or complement their core business activity.[4] When there is a good fit or congruence between what the business does and the issues it chooses to tackle, there is a stronger perception of authenticity among stakeholders.[5]

[3] For more on La Casa de Carlota see Magomedova N. and Bastida-Vialcanet R (2019). La Casa de Carlota: a studio where the diversity wins. *Entrepreneurship Education and Pedagogy* 2(4), 350–362 and https://www.theguardian.com/society/video/2017/dec/04/the-barcelona-design-studio-for-people-with-downs-syndrome-and-autism-video.

[4] Lawton, T.C., Doh, J.P. and Rajwani, T. (2014) *Aligning for Advantage: Competitive Strategies for the Political and Social Arenas,* Oxford, Oxford University Press.

[5] Napoli, J., Dickinson, S.J., Beverland, M.B. and Farrelly, F. (2014), "Measuring consumer-based Brand authenticity", *Journal of Business Research*, 67 (6), 1090–1098.

As an illustration of curation, take three companies mentioned so far—La Casa de Carlota, Tony's Chocolonely and Ecoalf—and the issues that they align with their core business activity. All these companies are B Corps, which requires them to be purpose-driven, have a stakeholder focus and be measured against non-commercial attributes. Companies that become B Corps cannot simply decide that is the structure they want. Rather they have to document their processes and are assessed on their performance in terms of environment, employment practices, community and governance. Whereas LCDC and Tony's Chocolonely are strong on employment and community (especially workforce development for LCDC and supply chain poverty alleviation, for Tony's), Ecoalf is strong on environment (especially resource conservation). These ratings reflect the orientation of their respective purposes, provide a focus area for new initiatives and help identify areas for improvement.

B Corps Impact Assessment Ratings

	Ecoalf	LCDC	Tony's Chocolonely
Overall	99.1	91.9	100.9
Governance	19.8	15.6	10.9
Employment	17.2	23.8	26.1
Community	18.3	32.7	45.2
Environment	45.5	5.6	18.7

Similarly, those companies that align their strategies with the UN SDGs generally do not try to focus on all 17 SDGs at once. Rather they curate those that are of particular relevance. Take SAP's approach to curation and strategic alignment. The various SDGs are evaluated against the purpose both in terms of business relevance and customer and consumer reach. Recall SAP's purpose of *To help the world run better and to improve people's lives,* which along with the company's core competency in business process management, provides a specific SDG focus. By enabling its partners and customers, SAP focuses on Decent Work and Economic Growth (8), Industry, Innovation and Infrastructure (9), Reduced Inequalities (10) and Responsible Consumption and Production (12). Taking the last (12) as an illustration, SAP grounds its work in partnership with non-governmental organizations such as the Ellen MacArthur Foundation, and industry coalitions such as the World Economic Forum's Global Plastic Action Partnership, where SAP provides the software tools and solutions to enable others to eliminate and reduce plastic waste in the oceans. Within SAP's own operations the focus is on Good Health and Wellbeing (3), Quality Education (4), Climate Action (13) and Partnerships for the goals (17).

These various examples, both large and small, illustrate the way conscientious businesses are selective in their approach. These companies recognize that while growing expectations of responsible corporate behaviour demand awareness of, and policies on, a range of practices, there is also a requirement to curate a conscience. Chip Bergh, CEO of Levi Strauss, says, 'You have to navigate all the different stakeholders and do the right thing. You also have to decide where you draw the line. Where do you weigh in? Because if you stand for everything, you stand for nothing. So we pick our spots about when we comment, and sometimes those are tough calls.'[6]

In making a choice as to where to focus, managers have to consider four questions:

1. *Does it align with our capabilities?* When curating conscience a company needs first to understand for which territory its capabilities are most appropriate. So, Patagonia's business area of outdoor sport clothing and its roots in climbing equipment makes it appropriate for the company to take a stance on environmentalism. This is an area where it has specific capabilities and the company can use its conscience and experience to be influential. By contrast, the infamous 2017 Pepsi-Cola advertisement, which suggested that Pepsi was a cure for social ills was clearly outside the scope of a soft drink and leaden footed in its execution to boot. Yet while for most companies, capabilities define the boundaries of what a company should engage with, there are also some businesses, such as Ben & Jerry's with its support for Refugee Rights and soap brand, Lush with Social Media safety, that have consistently immersed themselves in issues, that go beyond their core activities, but nonetheless resonate with their core audience. Such commitments enhance the symbolic capital and reputation of these brands and show how commercial success and commitment to diverse causes can be combined, when it is underpinned by sincerity.[7] However, it should be noted that the partisan nature of political discourse can make these stances risky.[8]

2. *What's the impact?* Increasingly companies engage in materiality analyses to identify their key stakeholders and to elicit their views on environmental,

---

[6] Bryant A (2020) If you stand for everything, you stand for nothing. So we pick our spots. Interview with Chip Bergh. 17 November 2020. https://www.excoleadership.com/articles/if-you-stand-for-everything-you-stand-for-nothing-so-we-pick-our-spots-%E2%80%8B/.

[7] Schmidt, H. J., Ind, N., Guzmán, F., & Kennedy, E. (2021). Sociopolitical activist brands. *Journal of Product & Brand Management*, 31(1), 40–55.

[8] Bhagwat, Y., Warren, N. L., Beck, J. T., & Watson IV, G. F. (2020). Corporate sociopolitical activism and firm value. *Journal of marketing*, 84(5), 1–21.

social and governance issues. This process helps managers to map and prioritize the impact of their initiatives on different stakeholders and also to define risks and opportunities for improvement. In the mapping process, companies are trying to evaluate, for each specific issue, both the significance for the business and the importance for society. Using a research-based approach is vital in the curation process, because even if it is 'a highly subjective process in which personal opinions, experiences and expectations are key elements',[9] it provides a basis for making judgements that can guide the company and enable it to evaluate progress. This is particularly important, in areas such as carbon offsets, which have been likened to the 'wild west', where there is a lack of structure. Rather than only relying on internal resources to validate impacts, there is value here in working with credible external partners to verify processes.

3. *Can we be consistent?* In selecting which issues to focus on, a company has to reflect self-critically on its motivations and the meaning of its purpose and principles. It should only opt to get involved with issues that it can properly engage with and put resources behind. There is little value in tokenistic gestures or short-term initiatives towards such issues as climate change or racial equality or immigration, if the systemic factors that underpin the issues are not addressed. This requires a longer-term perspective and a willingness to drive the issue into the core of the business. When a company makes this commitment, it gives it issue legitimacy among its internal and external stakeholders. Consumers, notably expect a brand to be faithful and true to itself as well as supporting consumers in being true to themselves.[10] When a business is an integral part of an individual identity, then employees and consumers too become invested in the stances that it takes.

4. *Why are we doing this?* The core argument of this book is the connection between doing the right thing and being profitable at the same time. Yet, sometimes companies just have to recognize their social role and focus on doing the right thing, no matter what. For example, consumers may possess little knowledge about the impact of buying fast fashion and the environmental consequences of discarding unworn or hardly worn clothes.

---

[9] Calabrese, A., Costa, R., Ghiron, N. L., & Menichini, T. (2017). Materiality analysis in sustainability reporting: a method for making it work in practice. *European Journal of Sustainable Development*, 6(3), p. 440.

[10] Morhart, F., Malär, L., Guèvremont, A., Girardin, F., & Grohmann, B. (2015). Brand authenticity: An integrative framework and measurement scale. *Journal of consumer psychology*, 25(2), 200–218.

And in business terms there may be little advantage in nudging them to change their behaviour, but from an impact point of view, there might be strong reasons to educate consumers and steer them towards making better choices. Similarly there may not always be strong business reasons to promote race and social justice, but there are clear societal reasons why this is important.[11]

Curating conscience cannot be treated lightly. It requires critical thinking and a questioning of assumptions, which brings with it internal conflicts that have to be navigated. In our research, we see that managers believe that taking a stance and integrating it into behaviours helps to differentiate the business, attract new employees, builds emotional and self-expressive benefits, boosts brand image and generates customer loyalty. Yet managers also have concerns about the challenge of aligning the organization's beliefs with the profile of the core target audience and the consequences of this when it goes wrong in terms of employee, customer and partner alienation.[12] A company should only engage if it has an authentic commitment; if its conscience is guiding it to do the right thing and it has the resources and will to implement the choices it makes.

How Oda Curates Conscience

Our mission is to create the world's most efficient retail system, of course it also has to be the most climate-friendly one.[13]

A company that has thought through the four questions listed above is the e-grocer, Oda, which operates in Norway, Finland and Germany. Unlike traditional grocery companies, an e-grocer has a different value chain with fewer links and a focus on technological efficiency. Director of Sustainability, Louise Fuchs, notes that the company had been building a set of competencies, since it started in 2013, that were focused on operational excellence but that also happened to deliver environmental and social benefits. Thus, the alignment of operative scope came about organically as the result of a focus on good systems

---

[11] Ind, N., & Payton, K. (2021). Do the Right Thing : How Business Can Respond to the Challenge of Racial Injustice. *California Management Review* https://cmr.berkeley.edu/2021/03/racial-injustice/. Accessed 14 July 2021.

[12] Schmidt H.J. et al., (2021) *op cit.*

[13] Oda Sustainability Report 2020. p. 10.

and the reduction of waste. As the company started to be more ambitious about growth (it became a Unicorn in 2021) and recognized the need to scale the right things in the right way, it became more concerned about knowing its environmental impacts. Fuchs put together a group of volunteers from different departments to develop an insight programme to understand more about its value chain and its customers and to uncover the areas it should focus on.

The group zeroed in on their use of plastic bags in the home delivery process. The set-up in the fulfilment centre, with its different temperature zones, meant that products were put in bags in the zones and consumers would get their groceries delivered in five or six different plastic bags. After vehicle transport and food production, the bags were the third largest emission driver in the value chain. At the same time, research showed that Norwegian consumers, while being high users of plastic bags, were also questioning their use. The sustainability group decided to test different options in terms of consumer acceptance and the viability in the fulfilment centre. The final solution was to move to a cardboard box, which reduced the environmental impact by 30%, made it easier for the operators to pack, cut down on damage to produce and was applauded by customers.

From these humble but significant beginnings, a larger grassroots movement emerged. Fuchs says, 'We have done a lot of sustainability work without having anyone leading sustainability work. It's just been kind of a part of our culture and DNA that, okay, so, we're redesigning grocery. And we're building a different future of grocery. Of course, it has to be sustainable.' Knowing that the culture of Oda and engaging with sustainability would require a scientific basis the group designed different work streams, which included as the first task to gather climate accounting data and align it with the UN SDGs and also animal welfare. Oda decided that it would map a climate receipt—Your Climate Footprint—that would show the impacts to consumers as they selected products. Regi Turid Pettersen, who works with sustainability strategy and materiality analysis at Oda observes,

> We know that they [Oda's customers] want to live sustainable lives, but they think it is really difficult, because there are a myriad of different certification schemes and also understanding the climate footprint for instance of different products. That's a really complex field for the average consumer to understand. And when you buy groceries, you do it on autopilot, so you might not have the time and capacity to be able to really understand the issues.

Working together with suppliers and with CICERO (the Center for International Climate Research), as a way to create an independent objective evaluation, Oda's aim was to inform customers about the consequences of their choices in an accessible way.

Driven on by grassroots passion which has developed over time, Oda's management has come to appreciate how sustainability and efficiency intertwine and the commitment to improving environmental and social performance has been reframed and incorporated into the business strategy. With a sense of urgency the company has brought forward its goals to reduce the climate footprint of its own operations by 50% to 2025—including a switch to 100% electric vehicle delivery. Oda is a vivid illustration of how a company can listen to, and curate, its conscience. This has enabled the company to deliver sustainable choices to customers whilst realizing benefits for the business. As Pettersen adds, 'There is some existential need, I think that you fulfill by working with sustainability, contributing to something larger than yourself—fulfilling that need for meaning and greater purpose, which in addition to being a prerequisite for attracting top talent and capital and customers in the future, it's just so much fun working with'. In the video (Fig. 5.2) you can see how Oda has worked to make sustainability an integral part of its business.

How to Embed Conscience

Moving from curating to embedding requires a business to integrate the social and environmental strategies that it has decided to focus on, into the core of the business strategy. As we saw with Oda, this can sometimes be driven from the bottom-up and in the case of British supermarket, Tesco, it sometimes emerges piecemeal as a commitment to taking action develops over time. Whatever the source, a significant barrier to overcome is the tendency to equate social and environmental initiatives with marketing or communication activity. This does not deny the value of communicating conscience, but

Fig. 5.2 Bringing sustainability to life at Oda (see Video 5.1)
[https://doi.org/10.1007/000-8kh]

being a business with a conscience relies on integrating initiatives into value creation processes. In the case of Oda, Louise Fuchs was previously Director of Sustainability and Communication, but decided the sustainability role lacked credibility internally and externally with 'Communication' appended. Similarly, Tesco's initial work on climate was largely done by communication experts, who got good media coverage for making announcements about Tesco's intentions, but lacked the technical knowledge to deliver on it. Kené Umeasiegbu, Campaigns Director at Tesco, notes that for all the coverage, 'not many of them [the announcements] had roots into the business, and what we were actually going to do'.

To move beyond a project-based approach, which is where both Oda and Tesco started, to embedding conscience, requires the organization to critically think about three different areas (Fig. 5.3). We'll describe these and then look at how Unilever has embedded conscience in its ecosystem and how John Lewis Partnership has adopted a participative approach to exploring its purpose and then embedding it into the business.

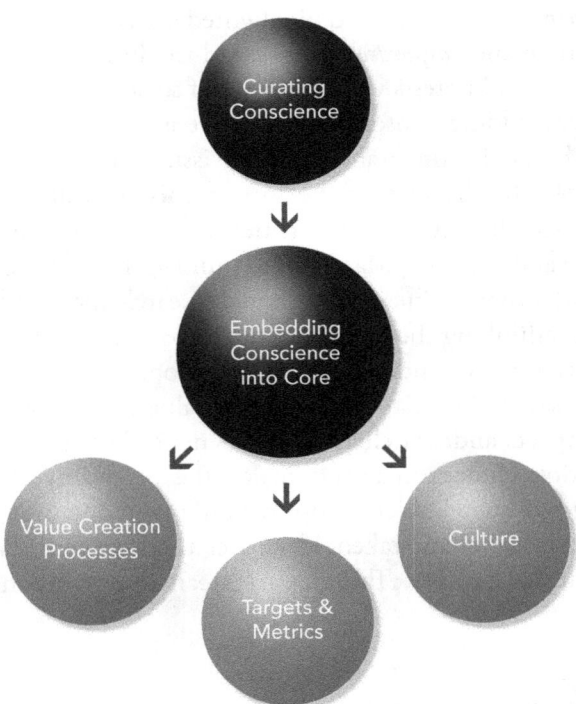

Fig. 5.3 Curating and embedding conscience

Embedding Conscience in Value Creation Processes

Rooting a business's conscience in value creation processes is an ongoing task and needs to encompass internal and external audiences. Internally, it is important both in terms of creating a desirable place to work and also in motivating employees to deliver value externally in a conscientious way to customers, partners and suppliers. Unfortunately, even if around three-quarters of businesses have specific environmental and social targets, there is still sometimes a lack of connection for employees, who while aware of the importance of their company's purpose, do not see its real impact.[14] This signals the need to ensure that the company's intentions have meaning for people. One argument here is that it is easier to realize if the process of articulating the conscience in the form of the purpose and principles is itself participative; people then discover for themselves the meaning of the conscience in the dialogue that leads to definition. Some companies—as we saw with Unilever—also then create the opportunity for employees to acquire self-knowledge and link it to the company's purpose. As a study of seven US and European companies recognized for their sustainability activities observed, 'most of the executives and managers we interviewed highlighted the close connection between *individual* purpose and *corporate* purpose and the importance of linking the company's long-term interests with the good of society'.[15]

Externally, embedding conscience involves ensuring that businesses build insights into the environmental and social issues and into the needs and desires of people. In the case of the former this typically means working together with research institutes, universities and NGOs such as the Rainforest Alliance, WWF and the Ellen MacArthur Foundation and in some cases joining together with other businesses to conduct research and build coalitions for change (e.g. in rethinking the use of plastics in packaging). In the case of the latter, the task is to better understand the way people think about sustainability (such as we saw with Oda) and to create value that enhances experience and reduces impacts and/or delivers social benefits. When conscience drives the value creation choices managers make, the perspective broadens away from satisfying one stakeholder group to thinking about, and trying to balance, the needs of different stakeholders over the long-term. Value creation then is an inclusive process. This doesn't mean that companies can avoid

---

[14] HSBC (2020). Navigator 2020: now, next and how for business. https://www.business.hsbc.com/navigator/report; Gast A., Illanes, P., Probst N., Schaninger B. and Simpson B. (2020). Purpose: Shifting from why to how. *McKinsey Quarterly*. April 22 2020.

difficult decisions over resource allocation and having to make trade-offs, but a conscientious approach to value creation calls for taking 'a broad range of constituent interests into account'.[16]

Embedding Conscience into Targets and Metrics

This involves setting long-term targets that are credible and motivating for stakeholders—as we saw with Paul Polman at Unilever, when he set out the 10-year Sustainable Living Plan—but it also requires shorter-term granular targets that show the progress (hopefully) towards targets and demonstrates the value of engaging with the issues. That word 'hopefully' is there to remind that progress can be uneven. For Unilever, four years into the plan, the company could report that it had reduced its Greenhouse Gas emissions by 40% and water usage by 31%, but that its overall progress to halving its environmental impact was stuttering, with Greenhouse Gas impacts per consumer having increased by 4%. Oda, too, has found that the better it gets at measuring impacts, the more it finds and Tesco notes that while it was improving energy efficiency and cutting emissions per square foot, the impact of expansion was increasing total emissions.

The challenge with long-term targets, such as Tesco's quest to become carbon neutral by 2035, is how to engage employees with such a numinous ambition. Umeasiegbu argues that you need to embed your actions in everyday procedures and processes that people can relate to. It's about helping people to make the connection between long-term desire and short-term activity, so that targets are defined by specifics such as renewable electricity usage, phasing down of GWP (global warming potential) refrigerants and switching to a 100% electric delivery fleet. The shorter time frames involved here also help to create the urgency that tends to be missing when people look to distant horizons. Alongside, the definition of specific targets for a range of social and environmental initiatives is the need for managerial engagement. Some managers may be committed simply because they believe in its societal importance, but others may be swayed more in their decisions by sales targets and margins and therefore see talks about climate change as an unwelcome distraction. Umeasiegbu notes that the real transition in Tesco took place when the targets were endorsed by the board and everybody's Key Performance Indicators (KPIs) started to include sustainability performance.

[15] Geradts, T. H., & Bocken, N. M. (2019). Driving sustainability-oriented innovation. *MIT Sloan Management Review*, *60*(2), 1.

Embedding Conscience into Culture

Conscience requires a company to move beyond words and to integrate purpose and principles into the fabric of the organization. Organizations can easily make gestures towards disadvantaged groups or towards the environment, but this will not create a more conscientious culture. It is only when a business really believes in its purpose and principles and is willing to re-align existing ways of working to embrace conscience that cultural change becomes possible. Everything from induction schemes to career development plans to supply chains needs to be thought through from the perspective of conscience. Thus, the embedding process takes time, not least because it requires allocating human and financial resources away from other areas towards environmental and social initiatives, whose value may take longer to realize. Enacting conscience comes with both moral and real costs. Yet, as we saw with Rabobank's approach to ethics, by making these issues open and discussing them on a regular basis, conscience can begin to permeate people's behaviour and shift the culture.

However, as the example of Rabobank and its use of an ethics committee suggests, employing critical thinking and encouraging consideration of conscience is only half the story. Companies need to create the structures to bring conscience to life (as we will see in the examples below of Unilever and its supply chain programmes and John Lewis with its Embedding Purpose initiative), but effecting cultural change also needs the commitment of leaders and the active participation of employees and ecosystem partners. It also means driving conscience into the approach to innovation and to the sharing of belief systems through internal and external communications.

Conscience and Ecosystems of Change

One of the characteristics, common to Tesco and Oda, is the recognition that conscience cannot be realized alone; it involves acting together with suppliers and partners. This requires companies to construct platforms that enable ecosystems to flourish and to encompass a common approach that is linked together by corporate purpose. By configuring flows across interfaces, processes, contracts and people, companies can shape the impacts of their ecosystems.[17] In 2017, Walmart, the world's largest bricks and mortar retailer, embraced this ecosystem approach by establishing ProjectGigaton with the

---

[16] Goedhart M. and Koller T. (2020) The value of value creation. *McKinsey Quarterly*. March 2020.

ambition of avoiding 1 billion metric tons of greenhouse gases by 2030, together with thousands of their suppliers (who contribute 90% of their carbon emissions). Focusing on five areas—energy, waste, packaging, nature and product use and design—Walmart has created a structure that enables it to constantly scrutinize its suppliers and includes a finance platform that helps fund environmental changes. Using finance from HSBC, Walmart provides its suppliers with credit lines and additional benefits, particularly for those that cut greenhouse gas emissions in alignment with targets established by the Carbon Disclosure Project.[18]

Walmart's commitment to relationship building, with suppliers and partners, is also mirrored by Unilever's approach. In S&P Global ESG ratings, Unilever is a top performer across Environment, Society and Governance scores at 89/100 (by comparison Kraft Heinz and Procter & Gamble are both 58/100). S&P note that it is ahead of its peers in terms of its focus on sustainability issues: 'Our ESG Evaluation of 89 for Unilever reflects the company's continuous commitment to embed sustainability principles across the organization and its value chain'.[19] In our own research into Unilever's ecosystem, we found evidence of Unilever's sustainability commitment and also that of its suppliers and partners. One supplier told us that sustainability was there in every conversation, every meeting and in all documents. While relationships are contractual, the approach is typified by the quest to also take care of the wellbeing of business partners. This allows Unilever to empower and upskill their partners so that they can contribute to bringing the purpose to life. As the quote from this Unilever manager indicates there is a commitment to helping farmers become more sustainable that includes financial support:

> On Unilever's Vega del Guadiana estate [Spain], the company is teaching farmers to adopt a more sustainable form of agriculture. How is this done? The approach is a respectful one, the farmers take part in seminars and are given the financial help they need to buy the technology required to adopt these farming methods. The new methods make less use of water and pesticides. Such efforts both shrink farming's CO_2 footprint and foster produce that is both healthier and more environmentally sustainable.

---

[17] Ramaswamy V. & Ind N. (2021) Company Brands as Purpose-driven Lived Experience Ecosystems. *European Business Review* May 4 2021. https://www.europeanbusinessreview.com/company-brands-as-purpose-driven-lived-experience-ecosystems/.

[18] Talman K & Tett G. (2021) Walmart turns attention to suppliers' emissions. *Moral Money, Financial Times.* 8 December 2021.

[19] S&P Global Ratings. Unilever: Environmental, Social and Governance Evaluation. 9 July 2021.

This approach clearly benefits Unilever's partners, but it should also be noted that Unilever benefits in terms of increased productivity and in innovating together with others. By using open innovation, Unilever and its partners work on the longer-term goals of developing a circular economy, helping to end plastic waste and attaining net zero, while also meeting shorter-term performance goals. Nor is this commitment to openness confined to relationships with partners, in that Unilever also works in a co-creative way with NGOs, intergovernmental organizations, activists and competitors, as a means of tackling the most significant environmental and social issues.

The factors that make the Unilever ecosystem effective is that it is linked in an explicit way to the purpose and the company's strategy and that it is also very structured. Unilever has a programme known as Partner to Win, which sets the criteria for assessing the alignment with, and commitment to, the purpose of Unilever. Two policy documents detail the criteria: the Responsible Business Partner Policy establishes the need for a partner business to be run ethically and with integrity, while meeting standards in terms of employment practices, human rights policies and sustainability standards; and the Unilever Responsible Sourcing Policy (RSP) that marries the need to build a positive business by mitigating risk and building trust with making a positive contribution to society and the environment. Once an initial assessment of a partner has taken place, supplier performance is monitored by Unilever and independent verification services, to ensure alignment with Unilever's purpose. This description might sound like a transactional arrangement, and the RSP does incorporate a set of mandatory requirements, but as hinted at before there is also a soft power alongside the contractual: 'we encourage our suppliers to move from the Mandatory Requirements to Good Practice, and onwards to Best Practice—Unilever is committed to work with our suppliers on this journey of continuous improvement'.

While Unilever is demanding of its ecosystem partners, it also nurtures their capabilities by using its well-established expertise in sustainability to inspire and empower others. This is a form of power *with* (a jointly developed power) rather than power *over* (a coercive power), that can be seen in some of the language of the Responsible Business Partner Policy, which talks about sharing and working together: 'Collective action is key to successfully upholding human rights and fighting corruption in all its forms'. This again shows the need for critical thinking and discussion as a means for a company and its partners to act and uncover the meaning of sustainability within an ecosystem.

The Power of Power *with:* Embedding Conscience Through Participation

The concept of power *with* derives from the pioneering work of the management thinker, Mary Parker Follett and is an essential element in a way of thinking that encourages stakeholder inclusivity, of which she was an early advocate. Follett argues against the idea of imposing a view by management fiat and instead argues at arriving at thought in common.[20] Citing the work of Follett, the philosopher Eugene Holland suggests that the essential feature of common thought 'is not that it is held in common, but that it has been produced in common'. In other words, power *with* relies on the acceptance and preservation of different viewpoints. This is essentially a democratic approach that encourages the participation of stakeholders internally and the provision of product and service experiences that meet the needs of diverse customers and partners.[21] Part of the argument here—as we saw in the case of La Casa de Carlota—is that such diversity can be valuable for an organization, but there is also another part of the argument that is based on a belief that businesses can contribute to the more socially oriented SDGs and enhance social justice and cohesion. Yet, getting to a more inclusive position does require the organization to reflect on the assumptions that underpin its conscience and to overcome the cultural blind spots that prevent managers from seeing the world from the perspective of others. As Warren Bennis notes in his eulogy to Follett, 'Followers who tell the truth and leaders who listen to it are an unbeatable combination'.[22] To better understand how an organization can become more inclusive we will look at UK retailer and pioneer of industrial democracy, the John Lewis Partnership and then how organizations can embrace diversity in the way they create value together with others.

The John Lewis Partnership, which comprises the John Lewis & Partners department stores, Waitrose & Partners supermarkets as well as associated businesses, is a different sort of retailer, in that it is a large-scale employee-owned business with near 80,000 partners, which through a structured system gives an active voice to them in the running of the business. The partnership model was the creation of John Spedan Lewis, who established it

---

[20] Graham P. ed. (2003) *Mary Parker Follett, Prophet of Management: A Celebration of her writings from the 1920s.* Beard Books, Washington DC.
[21] Holland, Eugene W. (2006) *Nomad Citizenship and Global Democracy* in Deleuze and the Social. Ed. Martin Fuglsang and Bent Meier Sørensen. Edinburgh: Edinburgh University Press. 191–206.
[22] Graham P. Ed (2003) *op cit.* p. 179.

in 1929 as a far-reaching experiment in industrial democracy that would 'limit the earnings of capital and divide the rest among the workers'. The driver for Spedan Lewis was his conscience and a belief in a human-centric structure which he saw as delivering justice and kindness. In the 294 page Constitution published at the founding of the business, there was an ultimate purpose that focused on the happiness of the partners, 'through their worthwhile and satisfying employment in a successful business' Sarah Gillard, Purpose Director, notes that while the Constitution was a comprehensive explanation of Spedan Lewis's advocacy for industrial democracy and how that should be practised, there was a tendency for some to become fixated on the happiness of partners as the one and only requirement. The danger of the ultimate purpose, taken in isolation, is that it encourages introversion. However, Gillard notes that there are also many partners who take the view that, 'the organization is an experiment in trying to find a better way of doing business and creating meaning for all stakeholders, for society, for the environment, for employees, for customers, and that our interpretation, therefore, ought to evolve as the environment changes'. This view argues that the conscientious core of fairness and justice has to be maintained as other aspects change and new challenges are met. This does inevitably create dilemmas which have to be discussed through an exegesis of the Constitution together with an awareness of broader social and environmental needs. When there are actions that are seen to transgress, such as paying selected bonuses to some employees in 2020 when the company recorded its first ever loss, then conscience frames the criticism. Equally, when partners discussed and voted to cut final salary pensions to help ensure the long-term viability of the business, the conscience was the touchstone in the process.

In 2020 John Lewis Partnership started work on a new Constitution to ensure the future relevance and success of the business (it had last been reworked in 1999). Aligning with its democratic structure there was a widespread consultation involving all stakeholder groups—suppliers, NGOs, community leaders, current and future customers and employees—in a large-scale listening exercise. In the case of customers and employees, there was also a deliberate decision taken to include atypical groups—diversity networks—who were often under-represented in normal insight work. Out of this engagement a new ambition emerged. Stakeholders wanted to see the partnership use its history and its conscientious business model to become a more active participant in helping to solve environmental and social issues, giving emphasis to equality, wellbeing and cutting waste and carbon emissions. In the new 2022 Constitution, Chair of the Partnership, Sharon White notes, 'Today, the Constitution remains one of the many things that make the Partnership truly unique, setting out the role the Partnership has in society and defining our responsibilities to Partners, customers, suppliers and communities'. The new Constitution then goes on to describe the Purpose as 'Working in Partnership for a happier world' and the responsibility that entails towards different stakeholders. The Purpose is the inspiration then for three detailed Principles, which come under three headings: Happier people, Happier business and Happier world.[23] The new Constitution clearly draws on the thinking and language of the past but also emphasizes the future relevance of John Lewis Partnership and the connectedness of its stakeholders. Of course, the Constitution has to be enacted and a programme has been implemented called, Embedding Purpose. Gillard says,

> So, how are we measuring happier people? How are we measuring happier business? How are we measuring our impact on a happier world? So, it's changed how we define success. That's having a knock-on to changing our commercial strategy, our financial strategy, our diversification strategy, our people strategy, how we recruit, how we induct, what we expect of leaders, how we measure people.

Power *with* Diversity and Inclusion

John Lewis Partnership exemplifies Follett's Power *with* concept by showing how to bring together diverse viewpoints to enhance the capacity of an organization to create value for different stakeholders and to build internal ownership. Inevitably Follett's approach has to overcome barriers in the form of inertia or (dis)interest. In the case of the former, there is an acceptance of the way things are and an inability to imagine how things could be different. As the philosopher Gilles Deleuze notes, 'Most cultures refuse to allow their own senses and values to be questioned—they become a set of incorrigible fictions'.[24] Inertia encourages a same old, same old view that is comfortable with things as they are, but is undynamic. In the case of the latter, self-interest inhibits empathy. Power *with* is only effective when people are able to see with new eyes what was previously obscured. This is particularly noticeable in the inability of people to see the reality of racial injustice. In a study of the systemic nature of racism in the US, researchers show that white people often cannot see the inherent disadvantages of other

---

[23] https://www.johnlewispartnership.co.uk/content/dam/cws/pdfs/Juniper/jlp-constitution.pdf).
[24] Deleuze, G. (1983) *Nietzsche and Philosophy*. Trans. Hugh Tomlinson. London: Athlone. p. 141.

ethnicities and engage in three different strategies to justify themselves: denial (which argues that race is not an issue), distance (separating themselves psychologically from white racial identity by stressing another aspect of their identity) and distortion (which recognizes the existence of racism but distorts the nature of racial inequity as a way to protect their own feelings, such that they often position racism as the action of specific individuals rather than systemic).[25] To overcome these blinkered views, the researchers suggest countering denial and distortion with data, so that people can see the facts of disadvantage and discrimination and countering distance and distortion through collaboration such that white people are engaged with developing solutions. Finally, the researchers note that distortion can be countered also by a vision grounded in justice. This last point urges managers to go beyond the view that diversity is simply good for business, because there is sometimes blowback when a company underperforms: 'We urge organizational leaders to instead base their case on widely held moral values of fairness and equity, with justice as their goal'.[26]

However, even if companies ought to be cautious about making claims for the business benefits of diversity and inclusion, a series of studies by McKinsey conducted in 2014, 2017 and 2019, show 'a positive, statistically significant correlation between company financial outperformance and diversity on the dimensions of both gender and ethnicity'. In the 2019 study the difference in financial outperformance is 25% between the bottom quartile and top quartile in terms of gender and 36% in terms of ethnicity. McKinsey argues that their research shows that diverse and inclusive companies 'make better, bolder decisions' and that diverse teams are better at radical innovation and in anticipating shifts in consumer needs and consumption patterns. Yet, while there are benefits to be derived from diversity, the studies also show that company commitment is divergent, leading to a widening gap between the leaders and the laggards. While one-third of the companies tracked since 2014 have achieved significant gains, about half have made little or no progress and some have gone backwards. Also, it should be noted that promoting diversity does not necessarily lead to a culture of inclusion.[27]

[25] Chow, R.M., Phillips, L.T., Lowery B.S., & Unzuetta M.M. (2021) Fighting Backlash to Racial Equity Efforts. *MIT Sloan Management Review.* Summer 2021: 25–31.

[26] Chow R.M. et al., (2021) ibid., p. 29.

[27] McKinsey & Company (2020). Diversity wins: How inclusion matters. May 2020.

HP's Commitment to Equality

One of McKinsey's core arguments is that to reap the rewards of diversity and inclusion, companies need to adopt a systematic, business-led approach. As an illustration of this, technology company, HP, which scores well on ESG ratings (35th out of 477 technology hardware companies)[28] has made fairness integral to its business success and has embedded it into its practices. To get there HP first went through a process of strategic reflection, which led the company to reformulate its purpose: 'To create technology that inspires ambitious and meaningful progress' and to state a vision that is explicit in the ambition to become the most sustainable and just technology company.

To ground the vision HP has set specific goals in terms of social justice, racial and gender equity. For example, it has set a target to achieve gender parity in the company's leadership by 2030—the first Fortune 100 technology company to do so. Already 30% of the company's senior managers are women, against an industry average of 16%. Furthermore, the aim is to have 30% women in engineering and/or technical positions. Also, HP has a highly diverse Board of Directors, with 61% of its members being drawn from minorities. This reflects the company's commitment to promoting racial equality through a host of initiatives that are focused on encouraging Black students to begin a professional career in technology and speeding up the recruitment and promotion of Black talent, not only within the company but also throughout its value chain, including distributors, suppliers and partners.

As part of its Human Rights focus, in 2021 the company launched the HP PATH project (Partnership and Technology for Humanity) to narrow the 'Digital Divide' in the world's most deprived communities. Investment in this acceleration programme works through collaborative agreements with a variety of organizations. The programme seeks to develop these communities by fostering digital education, creating economic opportunity and developing healthcare systems, especially for the four communities most likely to be hurt by the digital divide: women and girls; people with disabilities; marginalized communities (e.g. certain racial groups); and educators in underdeveloped societies. HP's CEO, Enrique Lores argument for this approach is that 'by creating technology in the service of humanity, we can create the conditions for business and society to thrive hand in hand'.[29]

---

[28] https://www.sustainalytics.com/esg-rating/hp-inc/1007987102.

[29] HP Sustainable Impact Report 2020. https://h20195.www2.hp.com/v2/getpdf.aspx/c07539064.pdf.

HP shows that a company can support through its actions the diversity that exists in the world. Whatever our gender, sexual orientation or ethnicity, each of us desires positive judgements about our worth and dignity and feels pride when we receive it and anger or shame when we do not.[30] When a company is inattentive to diversity in its work force, there is a likelihood that it also ignores the desires of its different stakeholders and misses the opportunity to create relevant value for them. In the next section Marianne Waite describes how companies can overcome their unseeing of disability and work together with disabled consumers to meet their expectations.

Inclusivity: From Passive to Purpose-Driven

Marianne Waite

Most of us negotiate the world on autopilot. We get dressed, we grab a coffee, we travel to work, we go for dinner etc., etc. No trouble at all. All part of a subconscious process we take for granted throughout our daily lives.

It is not like that if you have a disability. Imagine inhabiting a world that simply isn't designed for you. Each day being confronted with environments, interactions and experiences, that all present physical or attitudinal barriers.

These barriers aren't always related to explicit accessibility issues like whether there's a lift or not. They're often smaller, more discrete exchanges that knock confidence and hinder participation.

And it's this lack of consideration and provision that makes an experience exclusive. So, unless managers actively consider how to remove these barriers, companies disable by default.

Accessibility is the bedrock of improved experiences not only for this market but for nondisabled people too, as our collective desire for innovation, utility and simplification grows.

Because the reality is that we will all experience disability at some point in our lives—some sooner than others. This could be because of long-term illness or health challenges, temporary disabilities (poor mental health or short-term injury) or situational disability (exclusion experienced through lockdown restrictions).

Consider the Coronavirus pandemic; the brands that worked quickly to meet the needs of employees and customers confined to their homes did rather well. Whereas businesses that hadn't invested in accessibility and user experience to the same extent struggled. (Primark's profits plunged by 60% in 2020.)[31]

The historical hangover of our environments and infrastructures coupled with outdated ideals and a fear of disability has meant change has often been slow and hard.

(continued)

---

[30] Fukuyama F. (2018) *Identity: contemporary identity politics and the struggle for recognition.* Profile Books.
[31] https://www.retailgazette.co.uk/blog/2020/11/primark-profits-plunge-60-after-a-difficult-year-with-covid/.

(continued)

Whilst governments and associated organizations will never be replaced, their roles are limited. Increasingly businesses and their brands have become drivers for change, harnessing this generation's willingness to invest in those they believe will help fight for the causes they care about. Brands have become vehicles through which consumers can make their voices heard.

This accelerated rate of change over just a few years has helped break down barriers that have been holding people back for centuries. But significant challenges remain. Challenges that go deeper than representation and recruitment. It's now crucial to focus on how we address disability in all aspects of business, including the customer journey. This is how companies can create truly enhancing experiences: from retail access and product development to cultural engagement.

The global spending power of disabled people, their carers and families has been calculated at $13 trillion. 73% of consumers are touched by disability, yet 75–80% of consumer experiences are deemed to be a failure by disabled people.[32]

Catering to the needs of disabled people is not just about doing the right thing as decent human beings—although providing human rights through consumer rights seems like a pretty strong reason in itself. Inclusivity is becoming an increasingly important business driver.

So far, most efforts to tackle disability have been superficial and at times, tokenistic. A few, however, have become shining beacons of hope; demonstrating how businesses can create impactful change. Their success demonstrates any efforts must go beyond regulatory box-ticking and trend-following.

Rather than one-off projects, or quick-fix 'firework' efforts, businesses need to invest in longer-term efforts to remove barriers. This is about embarking on a journey, not to reach the end, but to make a continued commitment to learning and evolution.

Companies such as Apple, Amazon, P&G and Netflix are proving that inclusivity provides sustainable growth opportunities as they demonstrate the vast number of benefits including stronger brand loyalty, greater distinction, enhanced credibility, innovation opportunities, improved talent retention and higher brand engagement.

For instance, Apple is the tech brand of choice for many disabled and nondisabled people. This has as much to do with the seamless nature of communications as it does with the accessible features.

The Gillette Treo razor was designed to enhance assisted shaving, inspired by the need to make caring for loved ones easier. This iconic move was launched with online tutorials from carers which provided extra guidance around safe shaving.

From the Amazon Echo to the Fire TV Stick and One Click, Amazon has cut through user and purchasing barriers to create technology that makes life easier for disabled and nondisabled people.

Putting Inclusive Design at the Heart of the Business

Over recent years, Interbrand has observed a correlation between accessibility and its Best Global Brand rankings.[33] It's becoming clear that by putting accessibility

(continued)

---

[32] https://www.rod-group.com/insights/rod-research.

[33] https://interbrand.com/best-brands/.

(continued)

lity at the heart of their business strategy, brands can positively impact their brand strength and improve their value. This is especially true of the three most crucial levers of brand strength: Agility, Affinity and Empathy.

Becoming a purpose-driven inclusive business involves a process of awakening which requires having new and different conversations with disabled and older consumers on an ongoing basis.

By having these conversations and by using key insights from this audience to understand what needs to change, companies can ensure that no one is left behind and can start embedding repeatable processes and models that remove barriers and make customer journeys equitable and seamless.

Just as environmentalism is now firmly in our individual and community conscience, business objectives and international political agendas, so disability inclusivity should be treated in much the same way. This means strong strategies, board-level investment, commitment and ongoing measurement.

It takes time and perseverance. But the time is now and the only real risk is being left behind. On behalf of the 73% (and your future selves), consider hardwiring inclusive design at the heart of your strategy to help create a world that works for everybody.

Where are You on the Journey?

Interbrand's Inclusive Brand Experience Maturity Model examines performance across four quadrants of brand experience, categorizing efforts in four stages. We can use this to gauge where businesses are in their inclusive design journeys and use it as a basis for designing and implementing new more inclusive approaches and experiences.

Stage 1: Passive

- The majority of brands only just meet the minimum mandated requirements for catering to the needs of disabled people.
- Most see disability inclusivity as complicated and unnecessary.
- Those who do not actively attempt to remove barriers disable by default.

Stage 2: Progressive

- These brands are enlightened about the issue and look to raise the profile of disabled people through media representation.
- Success relies on insight from and collaboration with disabled talent.
- The output may be campaigns or communications which attempt to champion and connect with the 1 billion disabled people and their families worldwide.

Stage 3: Pioneering

- Pioneering brands invest beyond campaigns to provide augmented products and services for disabled consumers.

(continued)

(continued)

- They invest heavily in becoming aware of any strengths or weaknesses across the customer journey, before innovating in a way which makes a tangible difference to the day-to-day lives of disabled consumers.
- When done successfully, this activity drives brand differentiation, loyalty and awareness.

Stage 4: Purpose-driven

- A select few brands have placed inclusivity so much at the heart of their business that there is no distinction in the provision for disabled and nondisabled consumers.
- The ambition of these brands is deeply embedded in their business functions and strategy. It is also evidenced in their brand definition and purpose.
- The commitment to, and responsibility for, radical and sustainable innovation is shared in every area of the organization.
- Campaigns are backed up with the certainty that the entire customer experience has been reviewed and enhanced.

Marianne Waite is Director of Inclusive Design at Interbrand, UK Disability and Access Ambassador for Advertising and a Trustee of the Disabilities Trust.

Conclusion

As employees, partners, investors and customers put pressure on business to act in alignment with their values, so companies have to consider what they should focus on and how they should embed it in the organization. This means organizations have to look outwards to the world and the issues that resonate and inwards to determine where they have the capabilities to make a significant impact. They then have to think critically and use their purpose and principles to determine an appropriate strategy and act on it in such a way that they maximize their impact. By embedding conscience into the core of the business, companies can overcome the challenge of gestures in favour of tackling systemic problems associated with such issues as climate changes, biodiversity loss and discrimination. Our argument in this chapter is that this should be a participative process—a power *with*—that involves internal and external stakeholders in delivering change.

6

Fostering Conscientious Innovation

Innovation is a two-edged sword. It drives new technologies and growth yet spurs a hyper-consumerist economy by exponentially increasing the offering across business sectors. Furthermore, the innovation undertaken in recent decades has promoted a 'throw-away' society that over-exploits natural resources and has also brought increasing levels of social inequality. In the view of the economist Theodore Levitt, the great challenge for the coming decades is to foster innovation that creates real prosperity. This means that innovation must not only create consumer value but also encourage social progress and help meet the pressing environmental challenges facing mankind.[1]

Sustainable investments, which are governed by environmental, social and ethical governance criteria, reached 4 trillion dollars globally in 2021. While it is true that 77% of sustainable funds worldwide are still concentrated in Europe and that the US accounts for an additional 14%,[2] we are now at a tipping-point in the exponential growth in sustainable investments. The forecast for 2025 is that such investments will make up over 50% of European Funds.[3] This deep change in the financial sector is a golden opportunity to promote more conscientious innovation for tackling climate change,

---

[1] Kurtmollaiev, S., Lervik-Olsen, L., & Andreassen, T.W. (2022) Honey or condensed milk? Improving relative brand attractiveness through commercial and social innovations (211–227). In The Routledge Companion to Corporate Branding. Edited by: Iglesias, O., Ind, N., and Schultz, M.

[2] www.credit-suisse.com/about-us-news/en/articles/news-and-expertise/coronavirus-brings-esg-invest-ing-to-the-fore-202005.html.

[3] www.ft.com/content/5cd6e923-81e0-4557-8cff-a02fb5e01d42.

© The Author(s), under exclusive license to Springer Nature Switzerland AG 2022
N. Ind, O. Iglesias, *In Good Conscience*, https://doi.org/10.1007/978-3-031-09338-8_6

decarbonizing the economy, building more sustainable business models and helping society progress. As Larry Fink, the CEO of BlackRock, the world's leading financial investment firm, argues:

> The next 1,000 unicorns won't be search engines or social media companies, they'll be sustainable, scalable innovators—start-ups that help the world decarbonise and make the energy transition affordable for all consumers.[4]

Yet this is not only a challenge for start-ups since any company wishing to compete successfully over the coming decades must innovate and develop new, distinctive skills that make it more sustainable and to create value in a more balanced way for its stakeholders. In the same vein, Fink states:

> And it's not just start-ups that can and will disrupt industries. Bold incumbents can and must do it too. Indeed, many incumbents have an advantage in capital, market knowledge, and technical expertise on the global scale required for the disruption ahead. Our question to these companies is: What are you doing to disrupt your business? How are you preparing for and participating in the net zero transition? As your industry gets transformed by the energy transition, will you go the way of The Dodo, or will you be a Phoenix?

Both start-ups and consolidated companies face an extraordinary challenge demanding more conscientious innovation strategies inspired by corporate purpose and principles. These innovation strategies must create value for various stakeholders, more sustainable business models and spur social progress. The good news is that research in this area suggests that companies whose innovation is inspired by a transformative purpose are better at identifying new business opportunities. The reason for this is that such firms take a multi-stakeholder approach, giving them a much broader perspective. Furthermore, it is easier to build co-operation and collaborative innovation strategies in these companies—features that are the key to developing new capabilities[5] and that facilitate faster transformation. Last but not least, companies that prioritize responsible innovation are seen as more credible and are able to build stronger, more reputable brands.[6]

---

[4] https://www.blackrock.com/corporate/investor-relations/larry-fink-ceo-letter.

[5] Henderson, R. (2020) *Reimagining capitalism in a world on fire: how business can save the world.* Perseus Books.

[6] Kurtmollaiev, S., Lervik-Olsen, L., and Andreassen, T.W. (2022) *op cit.*

Bringing Rest to the World: Conscientious Innovation at Auping

Royal Auping is a B Corp that produces and sells top-quality beds and mattresses, mainly in Europe. The company is still 80% owned by the Auping family, while the remaining 20% is owned by Wadinko, an investment fund committed to a long-term view of business. The company's strategy is based on the creation of a circular product range and a sustainable business model to combat society's current wastefulness. The strategy seeks to cut waste in production processes and to foster recycling. In fact, ten years ago, Auping was the first company in its industry to produce a 'cradle-to-cradle' bed and a fully recyclable mattress.

Auping's approach is articulated through its purpose: 'Auping brings rest to the world'. The purpose has three nuances: (1) it suggests that Auping provides its customers with rest by producing high-quality, functional products that allow them to sleep soundly; (2) it means that Auping gives the world 'a rest' (in the sense of a respite) by pursuing a circular economy and an environmentally sustainable business model; (3) it means that Auping helps provide mental rest which is important in enabling people to be social and creative. Additionally, the firm works with the Sheltersuit Foundation in providing rest for the homeless by providing upcycled sleeping materials for Shelterbags. Auping's purpose thus combines a business dimension with environmental and social ones, which in turn inspires and guides the company's conscientious innovation strategy and policies.

From a consumer and business perspective, Auping's innovation strategy sets out to discover why people sleep badly. The firm's research reveals that temperature, noise, pain (mainly backache), light and stress are the main causes of sleeplessness. Auping is working on innovative solutions to each of these problems. For example, Auping worked with a start-up involving students from The Technical University of Delft to develop Somnox, a robot that lessens stress and the risk of insomnia. Somnox is a small device that people hold close to their chest when they go to sleep. It helps them slow down their breathing, facilitating relaxation. Somnox has been shown to help one sleep more soundly and wake up calmer.

From a sustainability standpoint, Auping's goal is to build a business model and a 100% circular product portfolio by 2030. This means innovating to develop more sustainable materials, produce high-quality products that have a longer useful life, as well as recycling and re-using the materials of those products that are no longer fit for use. Within this strategy, one of the company's main priorities has been to work on its mattress line. Most mattresses are dumped by their users once they decide to buy a new one. As a result, old mattresses end up being incinerated—something that is bad for the environment. For example, in The Netherlands alone (the first market in which the company operated) around one-and-a-half million mattresses are dumped and incinerated every year.

To tackle the problem, Auping came up with a scheme in which when a customer buys one of its mattresses, the company picks up the old one (whether made by Auping or not) and does its best to reuse the materials. For example, some of the mattress materials are reused as sound-proofing for buildings. Although this is a step forward in building a more conscientious, sustainable business model, not all old mattress materials can be reused because they come from many different sources, which can prove hard to separate. The business model is thus not wholly circular. Thus, only one strategy can be applied (namely, 'downcycling'), which is less than ideal. Downcycling is a kind of recycling of used materials that produces a new material that is of lower quality than the starting one. To try to find a solution to this problem, Auping worked with Niaga®, a company that had already come up with pioneering solutions for making carpet manufacture more environmentally sustainable. This joint innovation project led to the design of a new kind of mattress consisting of just two materials: the steel of the pocket springs and the polyester for the rest of the mattress. Although polyester is man-made, once it has been produced, it generates a very clean manufacturing chain because it can be wholly reused while keeping all the original product's functionality and quality. Thus this new mattress technology fully meets the requisites of the circular economy. Here, one should note that Auping decided not to hog this new technology but rather chose to share it with other companies in the sector to speed up the whole bedding industry's switch to more sustainable business models.

Four Conscientious Innovation Strategies

The post-industrial (hyper) consumerist economy has spurred innovation strategies based on both fast-consumption business models and planned obsolescence. Take, for example, the fashion industry. In recent decades, it has been dominated by a fast-fashion business model, which encourages consumers to buy cheap clothes, and to discard and replace them with new ones shortly afterwards. This business model is complemented by planned obsolescence. Here, the garments are deliberately designed and manufactured so that they fade after a few washes and wear quickly. As the book *The Waste Makers*, written by the North American journalist Vance Packard argues, it is a question of both functional and psychological obsolescence, leading to unbridled mass consumption. This business model has spawned the 'waste-society' and produced shocking environmental impacts. The fashion industry produces 92 million tonnes of textile waste a year—which works out at roughly 11 kilos a year for every man, woman and child on the planet.[7] In addition, the fashion industry generates 10% of global carbon emissions and accounts for 20% of water use. It also pollutes the oceans with half-a-million tonnes of microplastics a year.

Clearly, we need to foster a more conscientious, sustainable and socially responsible approach to innovation. How can this be achieved? Innovation research conducted in Norway, Sweden, the US, Finland and Denmark, based on extensive consumer input, argues that companies that embrace social and commercial innovation strategies are more likely to generate consumer preference and loyalty. In a quirky quote, the researchers note, 'Commercial and social innovations are like Winnie-the-Pooh's honey and condensed milk, with consumers preferring to have both'. To deliver on this duality, companies can adopt one or more of four different strategies. As to which strategy is most appropriate we see that companies tend to naturally start with the one that better resonates with their identity and/or that better leverages on their distinctive capabilities. However, to develop a conscientious approach to innovation, managers should become familiar with each one of the four strategies and explore the potential synergies between them (Fig. 6.1).

Built to Last: Slow but Agile Business Models

'Slow but agile' sounds counter-intuitive, but in practice involves developing innovation strategies that avoid waste by better matching supply and demand, and making higher-quality, longer-lasting products that encourage consumers to be less impulsive and thoughtless in their shopping habits.

With a view to matching supply and demand, IKEA has an Artificial Intelligence (AI) tool that enhances forecasting. IKEA has some 500 stores in 54 countries, as well as an e-commerce platform and sells some 2 billion products a year. Given the massive volume of its operations, demand-forecasting

---

[7] https://www.fastcompany.com/90596456/hm-is-one-of-fashions-biggest-polluters-now-its-on-a-100-million-quest-to-save-the-planet.

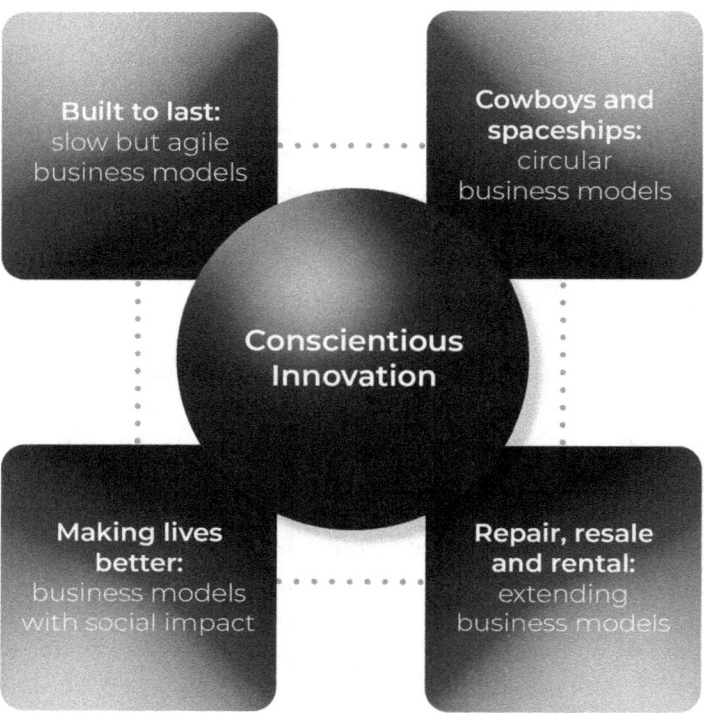

Fig. 6.1 Conscientious innovation business models

inaccuracies can lead to either product shortages (making customers dissatisfied) or over-stocking and waste. The AI tool can tap over 200 data sources for each of the products in the IKEA portfolio. Factors such as changes in consumer preferences, and weather forecasts are used to come up with more accurate estimates of trends in demand. The AI tool also makes day-by-day estimates for up to 4 months ahead, globally, regionally and for each of the stores. It is a remarkably precise, easy-to-use tool that lets the company tweak its production and logistics chain the whole time. In short, the AI tool lets IKEA serve its customers better, cutting stocks, waste and CO_2 emission levels while optimizing the supply chain and increasing the company's agility.

The shift from 'fast' business models to 'slower' but more agile ones makes for better-designed, longer-lasting products. For example, IKEA has designed versatile, multifunctional products that can be used in different ways, thereby extending life cycles. For instance, some of its sofas, such as the VIMLE, have covers that can be changed to extend the product life. Its modules can also be recombined to create new designs and thus redecorate the room using the same base piece, again extending its useful life. This same approach is also used by IKEA to design its cabinet storage modules.

Similarly, the British fashion company Deploy London's goal is to 'deploy' its customization expertise to make fashion more sustainable. The fashion firm is fully committed to the generation of zero waste. One of the ways in which it achieves this goal is through its approach to design and production. The result is garments that are high-quality, functionally versatile, timeless and durable. This manufacturing philosophy lets the company develop longer consumption cycles. The multi-functionality of the firm's garments is another main plank in the corporate strategy. This means, say, that a dress can be quickly turned into a blouse, a coat or a jacket. Each garment can be used in several different ways, on many different occasions, and thus for longer. The company's approach yields maximum value for its customers, while reducing environmental impact. Deploy London states that; 'We are convinced that slow fashion is the only authentic way of making fashion'.

It is worth analysing how 'quality' lies at the core of 'slow business' models. Quality is seen as a feature that not only gives consumers greater value but that also lessens a product's environmental impact. This is because there is a direct link between a product's quality and how long consumers will use it. This is relevant because the longer a product lasts, the lower the energy and materials consumed by its manufacture, and the less waste is generated—hence the need to design and produce quality products. Yet this leads us to ask how quality should be defined and measured. In 2005, these issues led Patagonia to come up with an index built from a set of attributes, which detail and specify what the company understands by quality. Some of the questions that Patagonia asks itself to measure the quality of its products are: Is the product functional? Is it multifunctional? Is it durable? Is it repairable?

Patagonia uses a specially designed algorithm to take these attributes into account and rate the quality of its products on a scale from one to ten. Until the beginning of 2020, this index was drawn up manually and therefore the company could only analyse those products that were redesigned at the time. Today they use computational models that give instant, objective analyses of their whole product line. Currently, the average portfolio score is 8.87. Any product that scores lower than 8 will not be manufactured unless or until the organization manages to innovate and thus improve its score to the minimum required. This exhaustive analysis of each product's quality (which helps Patagonia ensure that its products will have lengthy lives) cuts waste and lessens the firm's environmental impact.

In short, conscientious innovation must spur slow but agile business models. This means innovation has to boost the quality, versatility and longevity of products and the better matching of supply and demand to cut both stocks and waste. AI, among other IT technologies, has a key role to play in this field.

Cowboys and Spaceships: Circular Business Models

The first definition of the circular economy was formulated in 1990 by David W. Pearce and R. Kerry Turner, in their book *Economics of Natural Resources and the Environment*. Although Turner and Pearce coined the term 'circular economy', it was the British-born American economist Kenneth E. Boulding who, in 1966, published an article[8] outlining many of the central ideas of what would later become today's theory and practice. In his influential article, Boulding draws a distinction between what he calls 'cowboy' and 'spaceship' economies. In cowboy economies, natural resources are exploited as if they were limitless. Therefore, cowboy economies are extractive by nature and are blind to limitations. By contrast, spaceship economies understand resources as finite. From the latter standpoint, it behoves us to foster a cyclical ecological system in which materials and products are in continuous use. Interestingly, Boulding also questions the 'progress' metrics used by cowboy economies, such as 'productivity' or Gross Domestic Product (GDP). He argues that such metrics do not take into account the negative externalities arising from the system (such as environmental degradation).

Even if the idea of the circular economy had been around a while, it was only in 2013 that it really began to gain traction when the Ellen MacArthur Foundation (EMF) in collaboration with McKinsey and a small group of large companies (including IKEA) published *Towards the Circular Economy*. The publication defined the circular economy as:

(...) an industrial system that is restorative or regenerative by intention and design. (...) It replaces the 'end-of-life' concept with restoration, shifts towards the use of renewable energy, eliminates the use of toxic chemicals, which impair reuse, and aims for the elimination of waste through the superior design of materials, products, systems, and, within this, business models.[9]

---

[8] Boulding, K. (1996) *The economics of the coming spaceship earth*. In H. Jarrett (ed.) 1966. Environmental Quality in a Growing Economy, pp. 3–14. Baltimore, MD: Resources for the Future/Johns Hopkins University Press. EMF (2013), Towards the Circular Economy, Vol. 1, (Ellen MacArthur Foundation), Cowes, Isle of Wight, p. 7.

[9] EMF (2013), *Towards the Circular Economy*, Vol. 1, (Ellen MacArthur Foundation), Cowes, Isle of Wight, p. 7.

In a circular economy, companies must both conserve natural resources and make continued use of materials by regenerating them at the end of their life cycles. This approach questions the traditional use that has been made of resources, and instead considers waste as a key input in production processes. Conscientious innovation should promote the development of circular business models. First, by innovating in the design of new materials that consume fewer resources and that are potentially recyclable and more sustainable. Second, by recycling all the materials used in production processes and, whenever possible, investing in their 'upcycling' (the reuse of materials or products to generate a new product that has a higher quality than the original), which not only keeps the materials in use but can create greater added value. Third, by investing in systems that allow used products to be repaired to restore their functional and/or aesthetic value.

Ecoalf, whom we met briefly in Chap. 2, is a fashion company that is a pioneer in the circular economy. From the beginning, the company has questioned the 'fast-fashion' model and its appalling impact on the planet in terms of the vast use of natural resources and energy, and pollution. Thus, Ecoalf defends a slow fashion model based on sustainability, innovation, quality and timeless design. This involves matching supply and demand to minimize over-production and over-stocking (both of which generate waste) and fostering responsible consumption by helping consumers buy fewer but higher-quality products.

Up-cycling is also a main plank in Ecoalf's business model. For example, some of the company's products are made from plastic waste gathered from the seabed. Ecoalf calls this initiative 'Upcycling The Oceans'. Since starting the project in 2015 in Spain, it has expanded across the Mediterranean and also to Thailand. Ecoalf, together with its network of fishermen (some 4000 of them in 2022), recover rubbish from the sea and use the plastic they find to produce top-quality clothing and textile products.

In parallel, Ecoalf invests strongly in innovation to create new, more sustainable materials. Thanks to this conscientious innovation strategy and the firm's new technologies, Ecoalf now produces nylon from discarded fishing nets (25%), carpet scraps (25%) and nylon waste (50%). The firm uses this waste to produce a new regenerated nylon yarn that has the same characteristics as virgin nylon. In addition, the production process of this nylon requires fewer steps than that of traditional nylon, greatly cutting water consumption and CO_2 emissions. Furthermore, the regenerated nylon can be recycled again when the garments reach the end of their useful life. Using a similar approach, Ecoalf has also incorporated recycled polyester, wool and cotton into its garments. The company has also used its conscientious, circular innovation strategy to develop new materials, such as imitation leather (produced from grape waste), and a water-resistant fabric made from maize waste.

In reviewing fashion businesses it could be argued that expressing conscience is easier for start-ups or companies built upon sustainability-based value propositions from the outset (Ecoalf, Deploy, Patagonia). But what about those big fast-fashion companies? As Larry Fink stated, large corporations also have to meet the challenge of innovating and of transforming themselves to become more aware sustainable. This is a complex task. Take H&M, a company that in 2020 appointed Helena Helmersson as its new CEO—a statement of intent given she had led the company's sustainability strategy for eight years before being given the top job.

Not only has she questioned the company's traditional business model, she has also advocated re-invention of the fast-fashion concept and stressed the need for a root-and-branch transformation of H&M.[10]

> If we are talking about a model that provides an agile and rapid response to consumer demands, and that allows access to a more sustainable lifestyle for a greater number of people, so I do identify with the term (fast-fashion). But if we understand it as a way of offering the buyer garments that favor a throwaway attitude, then no.

Achieving this change is a remarkable challenge for a company that makes and sells 3 billion garments a year. Given the huge volume of the company's operations, a deep transformation of H&M would lead to cascading transformation through H&M's whole ecosystem of suppliers. Here, one should note that many of H&M's suppliers also work for other leading brands in the sector. This is why the transformation of the dominant players in the fashion industry (or any other industry) is vital for getting all the other companies in the garment ecosystem to join the circular economy.

In another interview,[11] Helmersson highlights that the first step in this transformation involves better matching of supply and demand to slash both stocks and waste:

> We need to make sure that we produce what we can sell. [...] How can we forecast customer demand in better ways through tech and AI, so we don't produce unnecessary volumes?

---

[10] https://elpais-com.cdn.ampproject.org/c/s/elpais.com/eps/2021-12-06/helena-helmersson-la-mujer-que-quiere-ralentizar-la-moda-rapida.html?outputType=amp.

[11] https://www.fastcompany.com/90596456/hm-is-one-of-fashions-biggest-polluters-now-its-on-a-100-million-quest-to-save-the-planet.

This strategy is similar to that of IKEA, yet Helmersson is also trying to foster a more circular economy and a sustainable business model at the same time. H&M has announced very ambitious goals. The CEO wants 100% of its materials and fabrics to be recycled or sustainably sourced by the year 2030, and to turn H&M into a climate positive company by 2040. To achieve these goals, the firm has launched many initiatives, such as 'The Circulator', a tool that lets designers of new products analyse the quality, durability and recyclability of their projects so as to better align their products with the new company strategy.

Similarly, several of H&M's brands have recently launched up-cycling initiatives through the work of The Laboratory—the name given to the firm's innovation department. An example is the Re-Made collection of denim clothing, developed for the Weekday brand. The company is also investing in developing new, more sustainable materials and in new recycling and up-cycling technologies. For example, the Persson family, the company's founders and owners, invested $100 million almost a decade ago through the H&M Foundation in an innovation project called the Green Machine, a new technology for recycling clothes. This is another joint innovation project in which H&M is working with Ehime University and Shinshu University (both in Japan) and the Hong Kong Research Institute of Textiles and Apparel (HKRITA). The Green Machine uses hydro-thermal technology to break down fabric into fibres that can then be reused more efficiently and profitably. In view of the strides being made by the new technology, H&M Foundation has decided to invest a further $100 million in the project to scale up the technology more quickly. The company has decided to open up the intellectual property of this new technology so that HKRITA can sell the machine to competitors at a lower cost.

Overall, investing in innovation aimed at promoting circular business models allows companies to reduce their use of natural resources and to keep the materials in use for a longer time, thus reducing waste. Consequently, circular business models bring great benefits from an environmental perspective. Additionally, circular business models also help to spur change in consumer attitudes and behaviours. Here, it is also worth noting that research shows that these circular innovations translate into cost savings due to waste reduction, bring higher efficiency into a company's operations and supply chain management and enable longer and better relationships with customers.[12] Furthermore, specific strategies, such as upcycling, have the potential to create additional value and increase margins.

---

[12] Lahti, T.; Wincent, J; and Parida, V. (2018) A Definition and Theoretical Review of the Circular Economy, Value Creation, and Sustainable Business Models: Where Are We Now and Where Should Research Move in the Future? *Sustainability*, 10 (8), 2799.

Repair, Resale and Rental: Extending Business Models

Conscientious innovation must also extend traditional business models to enable consumers to either buy second-hand products or rent items only when they need them. Both alternatives decouple growth from manufacturing volume, greatly lessening business's environmental impact.

All the signs are that the market for the resale of used products is soaring. In the US, the market for second-hand goods is expected to grow 153% in the period up to 2030[13] and the global market for second-hand clothing will rocket from $27 billion in 2020 to $77 billion by 2025.[14] This is eleven times the growth estimated for the retail clothing market during the same time frame. A study by Boston Consulting Group[15] argues consumers find this market alluring because it lets them buy cheaper products. Moreover, in 70% of cases, consumers see such purchases as being more environmentally sustainable.

Another sign of the boom in this sector is the host of used clothing resale platforms that have sprung up, such as Thred Up, The RealReal, Tradesy and Depop. As Julie Wainwright, CEO and founder of The RealReal (TRR), says:[16]

> We have to get people thinking about the life cycle of what they buy. One garbage truck's worth of textiles is landfilled or burned every second. Fashion can't continue to be disposable—we have to buy things that are well made and resell [them] when we're done with them.

Most of these platforms such as TRR and the market leader—thredUP—have built their value proposition around a more sustainable vision of the fashion business. ThredUP was founded by co-CEO James Reinhart in 2009, when he was still a college student, and since then the thredUP marketplace has handled over 125 million transactions. ThredUP has also forged many agreements with leading brands in the fashion sector, such as adidas. Through this agreement, adidas and thredUP have launched a programme called 'Choose to Give Back', whereby adidas consumers can send their used products to the thredUP platform, where they can then be resold. Consumers

---

[13] https://www.globaldata.com/americans-projected-spend-160-1-billion-secondhand-items-2021-according-mercari-globaldatas-inaugural-reuse-report/.

[14] https://www.statista.com/statistics/826162/apparel-resale-market-value-worldwide/.

[15] https://www.bcg.com/publications/2020/consumer-segments-behind-growing-secondhand-fashion-market.

[16] https://www.vogue.com/article/gucci-the-realreal-partnership-secondhand-consignment.

currently receive points, based on the quality and wear of each product they send to thredUP. The points can then be redeemed within a benefits programme, which adidas is gradually expanding. The long-term goal of this initiative is to extend the life cycle of products and lessen their environmental impact.

In a similar vein, Gucci and The RealReal (TRR) have a scheme whereby Gucci encourages customers to buy used clothing and accessories in the TRR Marketplace. In addition, for each Gucci product sold on the resale platform, TRR will plant a tree through One Tree Planted, an NGO that undertakes reforestation.

As to the online clothing rental market, its global value is expected to grow to over $2 trillion by 2027, rising 10.2% a year in the period 2020–2027.[17] This is therefore another very attractive market, although for manufacturers it is a much tougher business model to manage. Here, they need to meet two challenges: (1) the possible deterioration of the rented garments; (2) the need to efficiently manage the logistics of washing clothes, delivery and returns. On the bright side, this business model facilitates real-time information on consumer preferences and therefore gives invaluable feedback on anticipating future demand and for planning and developing designs for the next season.

One of the first companies to extend its traditional business model and commit to renting has been Ralph Lauren. The company now has its own platform— 'The Lauren Look'. This is a subscription business model where customers pay $125 a month to access four garments from the brand's catalogue. When the client has made use of the garments (there are no time commitments or limitations), she returns them to Ralph Lauren. She may then choose and receive four new garments. The customer can also decide to keep one or more garments, paying a discounted price for each of them. Once the garments have reached the end of their lives and can no longer be rented out, Ralph Lauren donates them to the NGO, Delivering Good, which distributes them to the needy.

Investment in rental business models fosters sustainability and anticipates consumer trends. This is a business in which traditional brands share the stage, together with new emerging digital players in the fashion industry such as Cocoon, Onloan, Rotaro and Rent the Runway (RTR). This last company (RTR) was founded in 2009 by Jennifer Hyman and Jennifer Fleiss, two entrepreneurs who wanted to disrupt the traditional fashion business model and develop a more sustainable approach that cuts waste and energy

---

[17] https://www.coherentmarketinsights.com/market-insight/online-clothing-rental-market-1446.

consumption. The company's pitch is the self-explanatory marketing slogan *Buy Less, Wear More*. If consumers take the idea on board it would obviate the need to raise manufacturing volume. According to an internal study carried out by the company, when a client rents a garment in RTR instead of buying new, there is a saving of 24% in water consumption, 6% in electricity consumption and 3% in CO_2 emissions. Furthermore, renting lengthens the life cycle of the product and eliminates the waste generated by traditional fast-fashion business models. As another way of extending product life, as of 2021 RTR has carried out over 4.1 million repairs on garments.

In H&M's case, the third plank in the CEO's strategy is to broaden the firm's traditional business model through reselling its products. H&M already took the first step in this field in 2015 when it acquired a first block of shares in Sellpy, a Swedish online reselling platform. H&M has raised its investment to $25 million, giving it 70% of Sellpy's share capital. In May 2021, H&M decided to expand Sellpy's operations to 20 more countries in Europe. A second step came in September 2021 with the launch of the Rewear pilot project in Canada. Rewear is a resale platform where customers can buy H&M products and those of other brands. Once a customer resells one of her garments on the platform, H&M offers her the option of getting cash or receiving an H&M gift card worth 20% more.

François Souchet, the Fashion Lead at the Ellen MacArthur Foundation, sees this as a golden opportunity for fashion brands:

> The solution to the environmental crisis is to change your business model so you don't rely on increasing volume to sustain your financial targets. [...] You need to figure out how to decouple your economic growth from volume.[18]

Such an approach though is only made possible through innovation and by fostering new business models that do not require the manufacture of yet more clothes but that instead are based upon the resale or rental of existing ones. In the first stage, this can allow companies to extend and complement their traditional revenue streams. However, the challenge is to reach the second stage, where traditional business models based on ownership are displaced by new models based on liquid consumption (usage through rental-lease). Ownership comes with certain virtues in that it can express social status and provide an emotional connectivity to objects, especially when we invest them with meaning, but it also encumbers us. Ownership can come with obligations and can

[18] https://www.fastcompany.com/90596456/hm-is-one-of-fashions-biggest-polluters-now-its-on-a-100-million-quest-to-save-the-planet.

reduce freedom and mobility. In its place, we can think of consumer benefits connected to sharing, community and making better use of our time. The researchers, Giana Eckhardt and Fleura Bardhi, have studied this idea of liquid modernity (which draws on the work of the sociologist Zygmunt Bauman) to look at the way consumption is becoming more ephemeral, access-based and dematerialized. In this context identity is less about the goods we own and more about the experiences we share and the communities we build.[19]

Making Lives Better: Business Models with Social Impact

Conscientious innovation should also make society better. This means stimulating social innovation that drives progress in the communities in which a company operates and in fostering fair, trustworthy relationships with its external value creation ecosystem. The term 'social innovation' can be traced back to the work of the nineteenth-century French sociologist, Gabriel Tarde.[20] He came up with the idea that innovation was the key to driving social change. However, the term 'social innovation' only took hold in the late twentieth century, when authors such as Gershuny[21] delved into the relationship between technological innovation and social development and both the spin-off from and side-effects of their interaction. More recently, social innovation has been defined as:

> (…) new ideas (products, services and models) that simultaneously meet social needs and create new social relationships or collaborations. In other words, they are innovations that are both good for society and enhance society's capacity to act.[22]

Social innovation creates business opportunities and social value at the same time. It involves transforming social structures and altering the power relationships found within a community.[23] M-Pesa provides a fascinating example of this dynamic. The project began in Kenya and later expanded to

---

[19] Bardhi, F., & Eckhardt, G. M. (2017). Liquid consumption. *Journal of Consumer Research*, 44(3), 582–597; Eckhardt, G. M., & Bardhi, F. (2020). New dynamics of social status and distinction. *Marketing Theory*, 20(1), 85–102.

[20] Tarde, G. (1899), *Social Laws: An outline of sociology*, New York: Macmillan. End Note Eighteen.

[21] Gershuny, J. (1983), *Social Innovation and the Division of Labour*, Oxford: Oxford University Press.

[22] Murray, R., Grice, J. C. and Mulgan, G. (2010), *The Open Book of Social Innovation*. The Young Foundation & NESTA, p. 3.

[23] Choi, N., Majumdar, S. (2015). *Social Innovation: Towards a Conceptualisation*. In: Majumdar, S., Guha, S., Marakkath, N. (eds) Technology and Innovation for Social Change. Springer, New Delhi. https://doi.org/10.1007/978-81-322-2071-8_2.

many other African countries. One of the main weaknesses of African economies is that so few people have bank accounts (under 20% in most African
nations). Low levels of banking make economic transactions much harder,
raise the credit risks involved, limit access to credit and generally hinder economic growth. By contrast, access to cell phones has soared over the last few
years. In fact, almost 50% of the population of Sub-Saharan Africa has a
mobile phone contract.[24] Given this situation the Vodafone telecom company
launched its M-Pesa app in Kenya in 2003. The app lets users transfer money
to other M-Pesa users and to pay invoices. The app also allows deposits and
cash withdrawals through a wide network of retail outlets and the issue of
micro-loans. In Swahili, the name 'pesa' means 'money' and the app's name—
M-Pesa—refers to accessing money through one's mobile phone.

M-Pesa is therefore a social innovation because it creates social value and
transforms existing social structures. M-Pesa fosters secure transactions, forges
trust in the economy and cuts management costs because app users do not
have to go to the bank. It also encourages saving, allows swift access to micro-
loans and facilitates their management, which evidently stimulates micro-
entrepreneurial activity, social progress and the economy in general.
Furthermore, over 160,000 people act as M-Pesa agents through a network of
retail outlets, most of which also offer maintenance of users' terminals.

The success of Vodacom's initiative in Kenya (the African company is a
Vodaphone subsidiary) led it to expand its app to seven African countries in
which it now serves over 50 million users. Vodacom has recently taken the
leap into the Indian and European markets (in the latter case, through its
operations in Romania).

The first step in fostering social innovation is to open up the company to
the outside world to get a better grasp of stakeholders' problems and expectations. Once this hurdle has been overcome, the next step is to develop business solutions that are profitable but that also drive social progress. To ensure
relevance and viability, stakeholders need to take part in developing solutions—an approach that is rooted in the philosophy and methodology of
Open Innovation and co-creation.[25]

In tandem with openness to the world, there is value in being open inside
the organization by encouraging social intrapreneurship. This involves embedding conscience and taking a multi-stakeholder approach to nurture a culture
where ideas are valued and creativity can be expressed. It also calls for building

---

[24] https://www.gsma.com/mobileeconomy/sub-saharan-africa/.
[25] Chesbrough, H. and Di Minin, A. (2014) *Open social innovation*. In: New frontiers in open innovation.
Edited by: Chesbrough, H; Vanhaverbeke, W.; and West, J.

internal communication channels so that intrapreneurship ideas can emerge and reach decision-makers. Last but not least, it is worth noting that in many cases social innovation projects stem from linking and taking extant services and/or processes in one of the company's business units or departments to cater to the needs of another stakeholder. Thus, intrapreneurship requires the promotion of collaboration within the firm.

By way of illustration, an employee of the Octopus telecom company, a leading firm in its field in Australia—realized that many homeless people bought call plans at $2 a day which had originally been designed with students in mind. This insight made the company realize that it could modify a service originally designed for another target market in a way that would benefit the homeless. As a result, it drew up a special plan that would allow the homeless to make free calls to the Social Services and other entities with their welfare at stake.[26] This scheme ensured that Australia's homeless are now permanently connected with those institutions in a position to help them.

The Three Enablers of a Conscientious Innovation Strategy

It's one thing to have a conscientious innovation strategy and another to execute it effectively. To improve the likelihood of success, the above four strategies can adopt three key enablers: (1) digitalization of business models and innovation processes; (2) servitization of the business model; (3) adoption of a collaborative approach to innovation, based on co-creation.

Digitalization

Digitalization, which has been the main driver of business transformation over the last decade, is an innovation process based on information technologies that allow the development of new products, services, operating systems and business models.[27] Although both digitalization and sustainability are both planks in most companies' strategies, a 2021 Accenture study[28] shows

---

[26] https://sloanreview.mit.edu/article/social-intrapreneurship-unleashing-social-innovation-from-within/?social_token=0cc68ab5596dbc640234c3fe74b49f73&utm_source=twitter&utm_medium=social&utm_campaign=sm-direct.

[27] Fichman, R. G.; Dos Santos, B. L.; and Zheng, Z. (2014) *MIS Quarterly*, 38, (2): 329–354.

[28] https://www.accenture.com/ch-en/insights/strategy/european-double-up.

that only 5% of firms are tackling both challenges in a co-ordinated fashion. Similarly, recent academic research in this field suggests that while most companies are drawing up sustainability strategies and plans, few of them link these to their digitalization strategies. This situation has led a team of researchers led by Professor Shivam Gupta to coin the term *digitainability* to refer to the scope for 'cross-fertilisation between the processes of digitalisation and sustainable development'.[29] Thus, one of the great challenges most companies will face is how to carry out a 'twin transformation' that fully exploits the huge scope offered by new technology and digitalization to pave the way to more sustainable business models, processes, products and services.

Among other things, the digital ecosystem of the future will include the Internet of Things (IoT), Big Data, Artificial Intelligence (AI) and machine learning. For example, IoT lets companies gather huge amounts of data in real time on their energy consumption—information that is invaluable for more efficiently planning and managing energy use. As to AI, we mentioned earlier in this chapter how companies such as IKEA and H&M are using it to better match production with demand, cutting waste, over-stocking and logistics' CO_2 emissions. Unilever is also pioneering the use of new technologies to realize its purpose and sustainability strategy. For instance, the company has forged a strategic collaboration agreement with Orbital Insight, a North American company specializing in geo-spatial analytics. The collaboration will ensure that soya bean and palm oil cropping do not lead to deforestation. AI analysis of satellite images lets Unilever monitor its suppliers' cropping practices. The technology precisely locates the areas where its suppliers grow their crops and pinpoints any negative environmental impacts. This allows Unilever to take any remedial action it deems fit.

The interaction between sustainability and digitalization strategies offers companies a great deal of scope. Nevertheless, one needs to avoid taking a Utopian view of technology's promise in dealing with environmental problems. One needs to be wary of undesirable side-effects of digitalization strategies. New digital infrastructures, such as the IoT and Blockchain, consume large amounts of energy and also over-exploit certain natural resources. Recent research by the French Think Tank *Shift Project* (which seeks to foster companies' shift towards a decarbonized economy) suggests that the global CO_2 emissions arising from the viewing of online videos is equivalent to the whole

---

[29] Lichtenthaler, U.C., (2021). Digitainability: The Combined Effects of the Megatrends Digitalization and Sustainability, *Journal of Innovation Management*, 9(2), 64–80. https://doi.org/10.24840/2183-0606_009.002_0006.

of Spain's annual CO_2 releases. That is why Professor Ulrich Lichtenthaler (an expert in the innovation, digitalization and sustainability fields) argues that companies should pursue 'digital efficiency' to slash their energy consumption and to minimize the negative impact of digital technologies. Here, one should note that Google is using its *Deep Mind* AI system to boost the efficiency of its data centres and has managed to slash its energy consumption by 40%.[30]

Servitization

Although digitalization and digital efficiency can do a great deal to foster a more sustainable economy, many authors argue that these contributions will not be enough unless developed societies drastically cut their consumption over the next few years. One of the main levers companies can use to achieve this aim is through the *servitization* of their business models.[31] The term 'servitisation' was coined in 1988 by Imperial College London's Professor Sandra Vandermerwe and Professor Juan Rada of the International Management Institute in Geneva. Servitization is a process by which companies bundle their product offerings with services, or else transform their business models to sell services. A classic example is Rolls-Royce, a pioneering company in this field. Back in 1962, it started offering airlines service contracts based on the number of flight hours logged by their engines. Now, the company offers its customers a Total Care Service package, under which customers only pay Rolls-Royce for flight hours' time. This means Rolls-Royce has strong incentives to undertake detailed monitoring of engine flight data with a view to avoiding faults, boosting efficiency and optimizing maintenance schedules. This approach maximizes flight hours—something that is in both Rolls-Royce's interests and those of its airline customers. Thus, servitization is '(…) the transformational process of shifting from a product-centric business model and logic to a service-centric approach'.[32]

Traditional business models are being steadily servitized for three interlinked reasons: (1) the emergence of new digital platforms allows traditional product-oriented value propositions to be turned into services (e.g. Netflix), and to maximize the use/value of a given asset (Uber, Airbnb); (2) it is cheaper

---

[30] https://deepmind.com/blog/article/deepmind-ai-reduces-google-data-centre-cooling-bill-40.

[31] https://sloanreview.mit.edu/article/sustainability-through-servicizing/.

[32] Kowalkowski, C., Gebauer, H., Kamp, B., and Parry, G. (2017) *Industrial Marketing Management*, 60, 4–10.

to use a service when needed than to pay to own a product. This trend explains the rise of new business models, such as car-sharing; (3) a growing number of environmentally aware consumers grasp that it would be better if they only used a service when they need it. They realize that the alternative of buying mass-produced consumer goods to meet the same need is one that is environmentally unsustainable.

Servitization can boost the sustainability of business models because the company that makes the product does not sell it, but instead keeps ownership of it and rents it out. A company adopting this model has a vested interest in extending a product's life cycle with a view to maximizing rental income. This contrasts with the short-term transactional approach taken by firms pursuing the old consumerist model. Thus servitization fosters more intensive use of products without raising raw material inputs. The advantages of the new approach are lower resource consumption and CO_2 emissions. Furthermore, since the producing company owns the product, it has greater incentives to not only extend its life cycle but also to recycle it at the end of its useful life. Thus, servitization also helps drive the circular economy. Last but not least, research[33] suggests that servitization business models pay more attention to stakeholder needs because they are based on building long-term strategic relationships. This is why servitization also tends to foster social innovation strategies boosting the wellbeing of a firm's stakeholders.

Earlier in this chapter we introduced servitized business models, such as Ralph Lauren's *The Lauren Look*. Another example is the agreement between Signify (formerly Phillips Lighting) and Schiphol Airport (Amsterdam). Under the accord, the airport pays a fee for the use of the lighting service while Signify retains ownership of all of the equipment and does its utmost to ensure maximum lighting performance and durability. Since Signify owns the equipment, it has a vested interest in ensuring maximum system efficiency, and in recycling equipment once it has reached the end of its life. This kind of agreement (which is based on servitized business models) promotes both the circular economy and environmental sustainability. Schiphol has recently taken the model one stage further to servitize many other parts of its extended product, such as for instance the management of the airport's information panels.

---

[33] Zhang, J., Qi, L., Wang, C. and Lyu, X. (2022), "The impact of servitization on the environmental and social performance in manufacturing firms", *Journal of Manufacturing Technology Management*, Vol. 33 No. 3, pp. 425–447. https://doi.org/10.1108/JMTM-11-2020-0451.

Any company setting out on the servitization path faces two major challenges.[34] The first is the need to foster a risk-taking corporate culture willing to self-cannibalize its own products. Many car companies are now trying to pull off this tricky transition. Autonomous vehicles are the industry's future. Yet once safe, efficient self-driving vehicles are available, selling cars will no longer make business sense. This is because several users will then be able to share the same car thus maximizing use of this asset. That means auto companies not only need to develop the technology for making self-driving cars but must also servitize their business models. That is why Volkswagen launched MOIA in 2016—a group company experimenting with ways to transform the industry by shifting from selling cars to the provision of personal transport services.

The second challenge is to disrupt traditional pricing systems. The servitization of business models creates a need for payment schemes in which customers pay a given fee to access a service for a specified period of time (pay-per-time). These are the pricing schemes used by businesses such as Netflix and Disney+ but also by *The Lauren Look,* where customers pay a fee for each month that they want to have access to the service. Servitization can also opt for pricing schemes of the pay-per-use kind, in which the amount customers pay is based on how much they use a given resource. Finally, as ESADE's Professor Marco Bertini (an international expert on pricing) argues in his book *The Ends Game,* servitization will also lead to growth in pricing models based on 'pay-for-outcomes'.[35] In these cases, customers pay for the value stemming from the use of a certain product or service.

Co-creation

As we discussed at the beginning of this chapter, innovation can be a two-edged sword. Thus, for innovation to drive real progress, it is vital to focus on balanced value creation for stakeholders. From this standpoint, conscientious innovation should not only be promoted within a company. It is also about

[34] González Chávez; C. A., Holgado, M; Öhrwall Rönnbäck, A.; Despeisse, M; and Johansson, B. (2021) Towards sustainable servitization: A literature review of methods and frameworks, *Procedia CIRP*, 104: 283–288.
[35] Bertini, M and Koeninsberg, O. (2020) *The Ends Game. How Smart Companies Stop Selling Products and Start Delivering Value.* Cambridge, MA: MIT Press.

opening the firm up to the outside world to incorporate stakeholders' expectations and ideas. In parallel, conscientious innovation requires distinctive new capabilities that encourage circular, servitized business models with a positive social impact. Yet developing such capabilities poses a big challenge for firms because it calls for many kinds of investment and the shouldering of major risks. Research points to collaborative innovation strategies as the best way to minimize the risks stemming from the creation of new capabilities and the speeding up of innovation processes.[36]

Co-creation is an approach through which a company forges strategic collaboration agreements to spur innovation together with external partners. Conscientious companies often promote co-creation strategies at three levels, which are discussed below.

First, conscientious companies forge co-creation strategies with partners (such as suppliers or distributors) in their value chain. Unilever is an excellent example of a company that has strongly committed to co-creation. In fact, in 2020 the company launched its Unilever's Partner with Purpose (UPWP) programme, through which it seeks to promote strategic collaboration agreements with some partners in its value chain. The goal here is to come up with innovations that can then be scaled up to the whole industry and that both conserve and restore the environment. On these lines, Unilever signed a strategic collaboration agreement both with Viridor (a British company specializing in waste management and recycling) and with Nextek (a consultancy specializing in resource management). Their joint aim was to invent a new kind of black plastic. The problem with black plastic is that it is not detected by scanners at recycling plants and so ends up in landfill. The three partners' co-creation led to the manufacture of a new sort of black plastic that can be detected by plant scanners, allowing some 2500 tonnes of plastic containers to be recycled that would otherwise have ended up as waste.

Second, conscientious companies also promote co-creation strategies with their competitors. Here, the end goal is to make industry adopt more sustainable practices and thus drive positive social change. Here, one should note the Sustainable Apparel Coalition (SAC). This is an initiative initially developed by Patagonia and Walmart to promote sustainability that has managed to bring together more than 250 companies with combined revenues of €845 million (2021), while more than 10,000 manufacturers use its main tool, the Higg Index, for measuring sustainability.[37]

[36] Ind, N., Iglesias, O. & Markovic Markovic, S. (2017). The co-creation continuum: From tactical market research tool to strategic collaborative innovation. *Journal of Brand Management*, 24 (4), pp. 310–321. https://doi.org/10.1057/s41262-017-0051-7.

[37] http://apparelcoalition.org/wp-content/uploads/2021/02/SAC-A-Decade-in-Review.pdf.

Third, environmentally aware companies establish co-creation strategies jointly with other activist stakeholders, such as NGOs, or with other conscientious companies operating in other fields. For example, Samsung and Patagonia are working together to co-create a solution to tackle the micro-plastics released when washing certain textiles. Several scientific studies estimate that the oceans are home to over 14 million tonnes of micro-plastics. These studies also reveal that no less than 80% of the world's tap water contains traces of these harmful substances. According to a WWF study, humans consume the plastic equivalent of a credit card every week. Micro-plastics are generated in various ways but recently there has been compelling evidence that washing garments made from certain synthetic fabrics is a major source of such pollution.[38] That is why many companies already recommend add-on filters for washing machines and the use of washing bags. The new collaborative innovation project jointly promoted by Patagonia and Samsung seeks to develop a more efficient solution to the burgeoning problem.

How Shifting Consumer Behaviour Is Driving More Conscientious Innovations

Sandro Kaulartz

Without a doubt, the ability to innovate in an agile and sustainable fashion has never been more essential to survive. Yet, in the current volatile business era, constantly disrupted by technological shifts, new 'out of the box' business models, and rapidly changing consumer culture, the innovation failure rate continues to rise.

Traditionally the corporate innovation growth engine was fuelled by exploiting scale effects from products that targeted the market majority with high efficiency and profitability. Over the last century the need for speed to market increased dramatically and the idea of 'breakthrough innovations' turned into 'shortcut innovations' that built on past successes with minor adjustments to existing products or line extensions. Today our economy is driven by technology, AI algorithms, the data explosion and the shift towards more conscientious consumerism. Within this new set-up and the removal of the historic hurdle of scale, challengers can enter the stage more easily. The first wave of category disruptors, such as Spotify, Uber and Airbnb, transformed markets at tremendous speed with business models that focused on higher convenience thanks to instant access enabled by technology and new subscription models. The second wave of challenger brands is rethinking established markets with products that

---

[38] Tekman, M. B., Walther, B. A., Peter, C., Gutow, L. & Bergmann, M. (2022): Impacts of plastic pollution in the oceans on marine species, biodiversity and ecosystems, 1–221, *WWF Germany*, Berlin. https://doi.org/10.5281/zenodo.5898684.

(continued)

address the rising value-based, conscientious consumer. Their value proposition to consumers is grounded in innovations that bring guilt-free products, carbon-neutrality and a transparent sustainability agenda. They leverage the advantage of a credible brand purpose with a focus on the planet.

Conscientious Consumerism

Conscientious consumerism is not new but is growing rapidly. The hopes are high that a more ethical consumer will mark our current century. What started as a slow motion avalanche in frequent purchase categories such as fashion or foods has become an ever-accelerating carousel across all major industries. Today we see seismic shifts towards more ethical consumption in the fight against the human-caused climate crisis, collapsing ecosystems and rising inequalities. This behavioural change manifests itself in shopping for green cleaning products, drinking fair-trade coffees, boycotting unsustainable fast-fashion brands and adopting low energy demand habits. The Ipsos Global Trend Survey, which covers 25 countries, in 2021 identified the climate emergency as the one global issue that unites us all.[39] Across the markets surveyed, 63% of people expect companies to do as much as they can to protect the environment. This demand for more ecological corporate actions is highest in emerging countries such as Columbia (82%), Brazil (78%), China (78%) and Mexico (77%) in contrast to the US (45%) and Great Britain (47%).

Gen Y and Z are teaching older generations that buying products, if it is necessary in the first place, shouldn't be a neutral act, but a statement. The survey revealed an imbalance across generations when it comes to the role of organizations in reducing environmental damage. In the UK 64% of Gen Zers say it is important to them that firms do as much as they can to protect our planet, compared to 49% Millennials, 42% Gen Xers and 42% Baby Boomers. It becomes evident that young generations in particular will force brands to take a stance and put their skin in the game in the quest for a more sustainable future.

However, the question remains how such good intentions towards more conscientious consumption translates into behavioural change and adapted lifestyles.[40] In a global study conducted in September-October 2021, 56% of consumers claimed they had modified their consumption habits due to their increasing concern about the climate crisis. Notably, though, the proportion of people saying they changed their lifestyle declined by 13 percentage points compared to January 2020. The pandemic slowed down climate positive behavioural change as consumers became preoccupied with adjusting their daily lives to combat the health crisis.

The divide between emerging and developed economies sheds an interesting light on behavioural change across the globe.[41] In India, Mexico, Chile, Columbia and China more than 70% of consumers say they made changes due to concerns

(continued)

---

[39] https://www.ipsos.com/en/climate-change-consumer-behaviour-2021.

[40] https://www.ipsos.com/sites/default/files/ct/publication/documents/2021-07/Ipsos-Views_Addressing-the-Sustainability-Say-Do-Gap.pdf.

[41] https://www.ipsos.com/sites/default/files/ct/publication/documents/2020-11/the-sustainability-imperative-ipsos-2020.pdf.

(continued)

about the climate crisis. In the US, Norway and the Netherlands, less than 50% claim they changed their purchase habits in recent years. The strongest decrease from 2020 to 2021 in more conscientious consumption was in Malaysia (-23 points), Spain (-23 points), Poland (-23 points) and France (-21 points). The range of actions that drive a more conscientious lifestyle diverge across the globe. Canada and Sweden lead the list when it comes to an overall reduction of consumption. Columbian, Mexican and Turkish consumers are most focused in reducing energy consumption at home. People in South Korea and Belgium are leading when it comes to avoiding over-packaging. Reducing meat consumption is strongest in Italy and the Netherlands. And Chinese and Mexican consumers show the highest values in environmentally friendly mobility by using public transportation, cycling or walking.

Beyond the difference between emerging and developed economies, we also see a considerable gender divide with regard to conscientious consumption. Our analysis shows that women took stronger climate positive actions across most all criteria: avoiding food waste (+10 points) and packaging (+8 points), saving water (+10 points) and buying fewer things (+10 points).

Overall we see a growing demand from consumers for sustainable products and services and a continued increase in the alertness towards more climate positive consumption. However, the stated actions that would indicate concrete behaviour lag behind. Despite increasing public concern, the desperately needed significant shift in behavioural change fails to materialize. Our deeper analysis of the barriers behind real change reveals a mix of factors that could explain the gap between public concern and corresponding actions. 75% of consumers in the UK think that the government should take action compared to 50% for citizens and 49% for private companies. While consumers have a sense of urgency, they don't feel they are primarily responsible for taking actions. Another hurdle for behavioural change is related to the lack of knowledge or misunderstanding of actions that have the highest impact on sustainability. We found that consumers tend to believe the consumption of local meat has a stronger climate positive effect than adopting a vegetarian or vegan diet sourced from imported plants. It doesn't.

Lead Users and the Drive to Sustainable Innovation Ecosystems

Looking to the future a real—and under-explored—opportunity is the role consumers can play in initiating and implementing sustainable innovations. Rather than seeing consumers as passive adopters of novel solutions, they should be thought of as active contributors and agents of change within corporate innovation design process. Academic innovation research has long shown that consumers themselves are often the real pioneers behind breakthrough innovations. Those forerunning users adopt trends earlier than the majority and therefore set the horizon for the distant future. Those most engaged in a particular field—the 'lead users'—have an inherent motivation to develop novel solutions and do regularly create radically new products and services ahead of market demand. Today, the ideas, hacks and prototypes of innovating users are an untapped resource within sustainable innovation.

User innovations are omnipresent, and it is hard to imagine our life without pioneering users. The first personal computers were developed by lead users. So were the first personal 3D printers and disposable diapers. Trends in hair styles, from mohawks to bright colours (or most recently grey), exist because users, not

(continued)

firms, dared to try something new. Think also of the new medical apps being built into smartphone and smartwatches today—done first by hackers. In order for sustainable corporate innovation to materialize, users will play a key role as they adopt innovations in their daily practices and create (more) sustainable lifestyles. Collaborative innovation ecosystems that involve lead users at the early stage of the innovation process will give firms the earliest possible access to the future needs of the market majority with corresponding ideas and solutions to address these unmet needs. Eventually, these bi-directional sustainable innovation ecosystems will help companies and societies to overcome the current barriers to adopting sustainable solutions and drive behavioural change on a significant scale.

The idea of searching for Lead Users to develop collaborative innovations is not a new concept. In fact, Lead User Innovation methods were pioneered by Professor von Hippel from MIT over 30 years ago. Since then, the underlying motivation and social dynamics that turn a consumer into an innovating prosumer have been studied by hundreds of academics and practitioners. However, innovating users are hard to find and for that reason, the practical value of Lead User methods has long suffered from the time and cost required to identify them. In partnership with Eric von Hippel, we established a new user innovation discovery method that is grounded on Semantic AI for Natural Language Understanding applied to the enormous universe of digital user generated data that is available to most organizations today.[42] The development was grounded on the simple vision that giving firms early access to critical user innovation insights rooted in big consumer data would eventually lead to better and more purposeful innovations. The latest advancements in machine learning have made it practical to discover early signals of changing consumer need patterns with corresponding solutions from innovating users on a massive scale. After exploring Sematic AI applied to data from millions of consumers over the past ten years, there is no doubt left that the web is an incredibly rich user innovation ecosystem. Corporations now have access to the needed analytic instruments to turn Big Data into an ongoing innovation cornucopia for more sustainable innovations in a truly consumer-centric manner.

Sandro Kaulartz is Chief Research Office, Social Intelligence Analytics at Ipsos

Conclusion

Innovation is the driver of social progress—as long as it: (a) creates value that strikes a reasonable balance among the company's stakeholders; (b) fosters sustainability and helps to regenerate the planet (insofar as this is possible); (c) delivers social impact. This means promoting innovation strategies that are driven by corporate purpose and principles—something we have seen in the

---

[42] von Hippel, E., & Kaulartz, S. (2021). Next-generation consumer innovation search: Identifying early-stage need-solution pairs on the web. *Research Policy*, *50*(8), 104056.

cases of Auping, Ecoalf and Deploy London, to name but three. There are also huge opportunities for creating and developing new business models based upon conscientious innovation processes, as start-ups such as thredUP, The RealReal and Rent the Runway show. Yet as Larry Flink suggested, this is a challenge that big corporations must also embrace. If they want to stay competitive, they will need to invest in more conscientious innovation strategies of the kind drawn up by IKEA and H&M.

Promoting more conscientious innovation strategies means replacing fast-business models and planned obsolescence with new, slower but more agile business models. This shift is partially made possible by exciting new technologies such as AI. Conscientious innovation must also promote circular business models, as well as extend traditional business approaches to include resale and rental schemes. Last but not least, it must nurture social innovation projects. Managers can speed up this transformation by taking advantage of the huge scope offered by digitalization, servitization and co-creation. As we shall discuss in Chap. 8, this transformation also requires new styles of leadership.

7

Communicating and Demonstrating Conscience

When a company makes a significant investment in conscientious acts, should it tell others about it? If we abide by Friedman's dictum on the role of the firm, then the answer would clearly be 'yes', because the only valid reason for investing in social responsibility in the first place is to benefit the business in terms of its corporate reputation. Equally, if we listen to those companies who couch doing good in terms of corporate philanthropy, the answer would be 'yes', because the concern is to maximize the business benefits through effective communication. Without economic advantage, the argument is that philanthropy will not be maintained in difficult times.[1] Our answer is less clear-cut, for both moral and practical reasons. The moral argument is that, if actions are always driven primarily by a desire to enhance corporate reputation, this will encourage some companies to over-claim, leading to greenwashing and wokewashing, while some important and complex social and environmental issues may be ignored—especially if they are contentious or divisive, such as gay marriage, abortion rights or policing laws. Companies in recognizing their societal role, should sometimes engage with an issue, without taking advantage of it through communication, simply because it is the right thing to do. From a Kantian perspective, it is these disinterested acts that are done for themselves that are truly moral.

---

[1] Bruch, F. W. H. & Walter F. (2005). The keys to rethinking corporate philanthropy. *MIT Sloan management review*, 47(1), 49.

Electronic Supplementary Material The online version of this chapter (https://doi. org/10.1007/978-3-031-09338-8_7) contains supplementary material, which is available to authorized users. The videos can be accessed by scanning the related images with the SN More Media App.

The practical argument has two aspects to it. First, expressions of conscience may not be the dominant factor in the minds of some stakeholders. For example, consumers of a fashion brand, which has a strong emphasis on sustainability, may be primarily motivated by the design and feel of the clothing, rather than the use of sustainable materials and the brand's environmental ethos, while purchasers of an electric vehicle may put sustainability credentials, well below styling and driving experience. This does not negate the point of communicating sustainability, but a company should recognize that sustainability is likely to be only one factor among many in creating value. Second, as the context around consumption becomes increasingly politicized, companies need to be confident that what they say is authentic and can be backed up by evidence. They need to be sure as they can be that they have been consistent over time in their actions and that within their business ecosystems there are no failings in sourcing materials, labour rights and environmental policies that can come back to haunt them. Without clear support for claims and consistency of action, companies may be well advised to steer clear of communicating their achievements. As the Scottish brewer, Brewdog, discovered with its high-profile advocacy of various social issues, followed by widespread criticism of its toxic work culture, communications can impact back negatively on a corporate reputation if conscience is forgotten.

In this chapter, we will look at the factors that companies should consider when making a decision on whether to communicate their environmental and social commitments. We'll look at the process involved in creating communications and how companies can best bring stories to life for consumers and other stakeholders through what they say and do, in a credible way.

Helping Stakeholders Make Good Choices

Here's an assumption: many consumers will make good choices when they are well informed about the products and services they buy. Of course, 'good' is problematic in that consumers' understanding of the term is variable, but in this context, we mean choices that meet consumer's functional, emotional or self-expressive needs and that promote social and/or environmental benefits. It's not a hollow assumption. Research by Ipsos shows that 31% of people actively seek out products with fair trade, sustainable and organic labels and they are willing to pay a 10% premium for them,[2] while research by Fidelity

---

[2] Lacey N & Long J. (2020). The Sustainability Imperative: the case for building sustainable businesses has never been stronger. *Ipsos Views*. November 2020.

shows that 65% of Millennials buy from socially responsible companies.[3] The challenge here is that in spite of the rapid growth in sustainable consumption—for Consumer Packaged Goods in the US, sustainability marketed goods have grown seven times faster than conventional products since 2015[4]—even more people would purchase sustainable products if such products were easier to understand. Consumers often struggle to 'identify more or less virtuous firms',[5] so companies need to act as change agents by leading consumers on their journey to becoming conscientious. Here we will outline three factors that companies need to address in determining how they lead people through communication.

Know Your Audience

Having made an argument in support of the growing appeal of sustainability in the previous paragraph, we should now temper it with two qualifications. First, while growth has been rapid in the persuasive power of sustainability claims and products that have sustainability features, Ipsos's research also found that 33% of consumers are 'reluctant' and don't believe that buying sustainable products makes any real difference to the state of the environment and/or they don't believe the truth of the labels. Second, while figures show that consumption of sustainably marketed products is growing, we also know that often the real impacts are not in the composition of the product, but the way it is used by the consumer. These factors mean that a company cannot simply start out with the belief that their actions on social or environmental issues will find favour with consumers or have a significant impact on total emissions. Rather they have to spend time seeking insights into consumer's motivations and behaviour to understand (1) how to effectively communicate their sustainability initiatives and (2) how to persuade and nudge customers into becoming more conscientious and sustainable.

There are many ways that such insight work can be done, but two are of particular relevance here: ethnography and netnography. We focus on these

[3] Fidelity Charitable (2021) The new definition of philanthropy includes any act of social good. https://www.fidelitycharitable.org/insights/2021-future-of-philanthropy/new-definition.html.

[4] Kronthal-Sacco R. & Whelan T. (2021) Sustainable Market Share Index. NYU Stern Center for Sustainable Business. 21 March 2021. https://www.stern.nyu.edu/sites/default/files/assets/documents/Final%202021%20CSB%20Practice%20Forum-%207.14.21.pdf.

[5] Vogel, D. (2007). *The market for virtue: The potential and limits of corporate social responsibility.* Brookings Institution Press. p. 60.

because we need to aim for depth of insight; to dig beneath the surface of what people say to uncover their latent beliefs and to understand their actions. The reason for this is that social and environmental issues are complex, and it can be difficult for people to explain and to express their feelings. Also given environmental impacts occur in the usage of products and services over time, we need some sort of longitudinal perspective. The value of these immersive forms of research is that because they look at people in context in their own homes or out shopping or socializing, they provide us insight into what people really do, rather than what they say they do. As a research method, ethnography, which is a branch of social anthropology, is different from other more positivist approaches in that it adopts a naïve, open philosophy that aims to experience the world as others see it, rather than from the blinkered view of a corporate culture. Instead of defining a research question based on existing knowledge, ethnography is more like a quest to explore an issue that involves following where the situation takes the researcher. In this sense it is an inductive method which allows theory to emerge from observation and discussion. As Ken Anderson of Intel notes of ethnography, 'Unlike traditional market researchers, who ask specific, highly practical questions, anthropological researchers visit consumers in their homes or offices to observe and listen in a nondirected way. Our goal is to see people's behavior on their terms, not ours. This observational method enlightens us about the context in which customers would use a new product and the meaning that product might hold in their lives.'[6]

Ethnography does not aim to quantify and consequently sample sizes can be small, but it does aim to share life experiences over time. As an illustration of this approach, IKEA is a regular user of ethnography as a method, visiting people in their homes around the world and observing the consistencies and inconsistencies of the way people live in different cultures and the way they use space and furniture. In 2015, they also extended this into a form of action research, where together with a consultancy, Hubbub and the University of Surrey's Centre of Environment and Sustainability, they conducted a three-year long social experiment, called Live Lagom on sustainable living, where for each year of the project, 120 participants took part in exploring ways of cutting waste and improving efficiency. The use of the Swedish word, Lagom, which comes from the phrase *Lagom är bäst* (the right amount is best) was designed to reflect a belief that people should not deny themselves what they

---

[6] Anderson, K. (2009) Ethnographic research: a key to strategy. *Harvard Business Review* 87(3), 24.

love, but that they should also not take more than they need from the planet. At the start of the project only 25% of IKEA customers felt that sustainable living was 'easy, affordable and desirable'. By spending time together and creating a community, could that belief be changed? IKEA learned that by creating a safe environment, which was non-judgmental and where there was sufficient freedom to explore new ways of living, people were willing to try new behaviours that they hadn't previously considered and were able to maintain them, rather than regressing. The participants realized both environmental and economic benefits, reducing, on average, their CO_2 emissions per household by 317 kg and saving £1440 by reducing energy bills, spending less on food and reducing waste.[7]

Ethnographic research is mirrored in the online world by netnography, which is 'the use of various qualitative research methods to study social media in a way that maintains the complexities of its lived experience and cultural qualities'.[8] Netnography is concerned with providing insight through immersion in personal experiences as individuals encounter each other on social media. Robert Kozinets, who is a pioneer of the field, argues that it is particularly valuable in identifying lead users—those individuals who generate ideas ahead of others and provide the basis for future innovations—and uncovering together with them subtle and sophisticated needs.[9] This ability to 'discern the shady shapes of the future a little bit before they actually take form' is attributed to the way in which a collective intelligence emerges through interaction and amplification as ideas unfold.[10]

These inductive research methods are of particular value in defining attitudes and behaviour, because they take sufficient time to explore issues together with consumers. Instead of simply learning that consumers cannot distinguish a virtuous firm from an unvirtuous one, we can begin to see why that might be the case and to explore what it would take for a virtuous firm to get its message across in a credible way. We can also find out through observing consumer behaviour, the barriers that prevent people from changing their ways of living and the nudges that can help people to adapt to new contexts.

---

[7] IKEA (2018) Live Lagom Impact Report 2015–2018.

[8] Kozinets R.V. (2019) 'Netnographies of the Future' in Ind N. and Schmidt H.J. Co-creating Brands. London: Bloomsbury p. 144.

[9] Brem, A., & Bilgram, V. (2015). The search for innovative partners in co-creation: Identifying lead users in social media through netnography and crowdsourcing. *Journal of Engineering and Technology Management*, 37, 40–51.

[10] Pierre Lévy writes in his book 'Collective Intelligence' (1999), 'the collective intellect is its own formal cause. Its appearance is not conferred upon it by some external entity. It emerges continuously from the multitude of free relations that are formed within it.' p. 114. Lévy, P. (1999) *Collective Intelligence: Mankind's Emerging World in Cyberspace*. Ed. Robert Bononno. Cambridge, Mass: Perseus Books.

These methods do not exclude other forms of research, especially as a means of validating the findings from ethnography and netnography. What we should seek to glean from different methods is what consumers understand about an issue and their receptivity to attitudinal and behavioural shifts. When such issues as racial justice, immigration and climate are potentially so divisive, it's valuable to know the sources of acceptance and resistance, before starting to communicate.

Own the Issue

Latia Curry of communications consultancy, Rally, writes 'Navigating the waters of social advocacy is far more difficult for brands than they may want to acknowledge, and the price of getting it wrong can be extreme'. She goes on to argue that companies need to engage in a meaningful and consistent way if they are to become issue fluent.[11] Curry points out that a company must 'infuse equity' into their operations and values before taking a stance. This echoes the work of the researcher, Douglas Holt, who argued from the perspective of brand culture that a company needs to have both literacy (an understanding of the codes and idioms of an issue) and fidelity (a willingness to stand up for one's beliefs).[12]

Taking these one at a time, where does literacy come from? Holt notes that brands cannot simply co-opt the elements of an issue and re-package them. Rather they need to learn the idioms and understand how they connect with the meaning of the brand. This cannot be done by sitting in a board room. Companies need to encourage their managers to get out and connect with the NGOs and advocacy groups that may be criticizing them, not from a defensive position, but from a desire to share knowledge and to learn from others (see the boxed section below on the Dutch co-operative bank, Rabobank for more on this issue). This process of engagement enables a company to be critically reflective of its own position and to evolve it to meet the needs of groups that it might previously have ignored or rejected. For example, adidas has learned how to become more issue fluent on environmental issues by working with sustainability advocate, Stella McCartney, who has challenged its design practices and sourcing policies, Greenpeace, who confronted adidas over its

---

[11] Curry L. (2020). How brands can follow through on the values they're selling. *Harvard Business Review.* https://hbr.org/2020/08/how-brands-can-follow-through-on-the-values-theyre-selling.

[12] Holt, D. B. (2004). *How brands become icons: The principles of cultural branding.* Cambridge Mass: Harvard Business Press.

use of polluting polyfluorinated chemicals (PFCs) and challenged it to improve (it subsequently lauded adidas as a fashion detox leader) and Parley for the Oceans, with whom adidas has partnered to produce a range of products made from upcycled marine plastic waste.

What should be noted with literacy is that it takes time to achieve. A company such as adidas has had to learn how to articulate its message through participation in environmental issues. This also links to the point about fidelity in that conscience not only requires critical reflection, but action over time. For example, a company cannot simply declare a commitment to diversity without ensuring diversity is reflected in the make-up of its leadership team and its workforce. Similarly, making an environmental claim requires a company to align and validate its supply chain. This means building a network of relationships where the partners learn to trust each other by establishing protocols, sharing best practice, building communities and developing training programmes. However, such processes are also more resilient if they are validated by independent parties. There is often a temptation for companies to cut corners or to act irresponsibly in supply chain management, which can be tempered through verification.[13]

As we have seen in various examples, companies often use third parties to verify and improve their processes. This involves working together with suppliers and partners and using digital technologies such as blockchain and beacons to ensure that systems are robust, risks are minimized and claims can be supported. The value of blockchain is that it provides ongoing verification of a supply chain through an independent, accurate and time-stamped record of each stage in a process. As a blockchain ledger contains all relevant information it delivers consistency, reduces transaction costs and provides confidence.[14] In terms of ensuring social and environmental commitments are adhered to, it plays a vital role. For example, like Tesco, several major European supermarket chains are committed to net zero and to contributing to the UN SDGs, but they can only be confident of publicizing those commitments with resilient supply chains that are robust in tackling deforestation, responsible fishing policies and other issues by a blockchain-based approach. Blockchain's distributed ledgers can be highly valuable in tackling pain points, inefficiencies, opacity and fraud, not only in food but also in integrating diverse data sources in other business areas such as financial services.[15]

[13] Vogel, D. (2019). The false dawn of corporate social responsibility. *California Management Review.* 9 October 2019. https://cmr.berkeley.edu/2019/10/the-false-dawnof-corporate-social-responsibility/.

[14] Werbach, K., (2018). Trust, but verify: Why the blockchain needs the law. *Berkeley Technology Law Journal,* 33,487–550.

[15] Higginson, M., Nadeau M-C., & Rajgopal K. (2019) Blockchain's Occam problem. McKinsey, January 2019. https://www.mckinsey.com/industries/financial-services/ourinsights/blockchains-occam-problem.

'Criticism is good': Inviting Journalists and Activists Inside Rabobank

Chris Kersbergen

After the financial crisis several Dutch journalists and authors painted a dark picture of bankers' morality. Although this was influenced by a book by a Dutch anthropologist on investment bankers in the City of London, the image of greedy bankers without any conscience dominated public perception. At the end of 2017 another Dutch journalist, econometrist and self-proclaimed 'amateur anthropologist', Marcel Canoy, wanted to find out whether anything had changed as a result of the financial crisis and approached all the large banks in the Netherlands, to get access to interview their managers and employees.

As might be expected all banks said 'no'. Except one. When this request reached Rabobank, Leendert Bikker, the head of corporate communications, took a different stance. Although many of his colleagues working in legal, risk and compliance roles (and there are many) were quite vocal in articulating their concerns and why this would be the worst idea ever, Bikker was able to convince CEO Wiebe Draijer to say 'yes'. Moreover, when the journalist was invited in he was allowed to speak to everyone he wanted to, without conditions, without restrictions and without contracts.

Over a period of two years Canoy spoke to around 1500 people: managers, employees, members and clients. And this resulted in the publication in 2019 of a book on Rabobank called *De Bank van Goede Bedoelingen: De ramen open bij de Rabobank (The bank of good intentions; open windows at Rabobank)*.[16] Although the book did make some critical points as to how the bank could be more impactful, the underlying conclusion was that the people working at Rabobank were driven by good intentions and strong co-operative values. This resulted in several stories in leading Dutch newspapers with titles like *'Bankers aren't immoral'* and *'Behind the screens at Rabobank: struggling with strong regulations'*. All in all, this helped to shift a stereotyped banker image of Rabobank employees towards a more nuanced picture of socially engaged people that want to do the right thing for their customers and society—while having to deal with an increasing number of rules, regulations and restrictions from within and outside the bank.

This is what Bikker had hoped for, and expected, and why he had the courage to grant Canoy full access: *'I read the book for the first time after publication'*. This radical transparency approach has guided the way the bank has responded to crises and criticisms. It invests a lot of effort in maintaining an ongoing dialogue with NGOs and activist organizations to enhance mutual understanding. Sometimes activists still choose to pursue publicity by protesting on the doorstep of large organizations, but while many corporates typically respond with calling security and the police to remove them, Rabobank has consistently turned it around and invited them in or stepped out to engage in dialogue. And followed that up with reporting to all employees on the activists' message and explain Rabobank's point of view on the issue. This approach is illustrated by a statement from Wiebe Draijer in an interview on contributing to the energy and food transitions: *'All that criticism is good. (…) A transition is needed. We feel the responsibility to help our clients to make their way through this. We are engaging in dialogue with everyone about this, including Greenpeace. To Greenpeace I say: if you come here to climb our building for a cleaner world, I will join you and hang next to you, because that is what we want too.'*[17]

Chris Kersbergen is Global Head of Brand at Rabobank.

---

[16] Canoy, M. (2019) 'De bank van goede bedoelingen: de ramen open bij de Rabobank'. Prometeus Amsterdam.

[17] https://www.vno-ncw.nl/forum/rabobank-ceo-wiebe-draijer-al-die-kritiek-eigenlijk-goed.

Tell the Story

Having developed insight into how audiences see sustainability issues and then establishing the foundations for issue fluency, the next stage is to explain the story as an expression of the company's conscience in a way that is relevant to people and affects their attitudes and behaviour. The opportunity and the challenge here is that whereas in normal consumer buyer behaviour the focus is on the self, the task here sometimes involves getting people to think longer-term about the needs of others, alongside that of the self. It often takes more time to tell a societal or environmental story, which can be difficult when seeking consumer attention, but the opportunity is that if the story can be explained, it provides a deeper level of meaning as instead of simply being consumers, people begin to think and act as citizens. This point is supported by a comprehensive analysis by Katherine White and colleagues at the University of British Columbia of 320 research articles into the drivers of sustainable consumption. They found that marketing and behavioural science can be very influential in stimulating more sustainable consumption and in overcoming the attitude-behaviour gap.[18] From their analysis, they create an acronym—SHIFT—that illustrates how Social Influence (the presence, behaviours and expectations of others), Habit formation (the changes needed to break repetitive behaviour), Individual self (the desire to maintain positive conceptions of oneself), Feeling and cognition (the roles played by affect and cognitive thinking in decision-making) and Tangibility (the sense of overcoming the distance between actions and outcomes) can be harnessed to stimulate sustainable behaviour that encourages people to think beyond their self-interest. All the elements of SHIFT are relevant to nudge people to act in different ways, but of particular interest is the need to break habits through disruptions and to encourage new behaviours by making sustainable action easy and using prompts, incentives and feedback. We should also note the exhortation to overcome the challenge of the intangibility of sustainable consumption, which can seem 'abstract, vague, and distant from the self' by matching the temporal focus of sustainability, communicating local and proximal impacts, making the consequences of action (or inaction) explicit and promoting dematerialization rather than possession of goods.

The value of SHIFT as a framework is that it helps to provide a structure for developing a communications approach that addresses consumers' lack of

[18] White, K., Habib, R., & Hardisty, D. J. (2019). How to SHIFT consumer behaviors to be more sustainable: A literature review and guiding framework. *Journal of Marketing, 83*(3), 22–49.

knowledge about sustainability and the tactics that can help to overcome the barriers to change. If we take the Dutch chocolate brand, Tony's Chocolonely as an example, we can see the framework in action. This is a brand that truly engages its stakeholders with a cause and uses the data derived from its verification processes to develop a powerful narrative that gives people the opportunity to express their identities through consumption. The story of Tony's is rooted in a cause. It didn't set out to be a commercial brand, rather the brand emerged as a result of a protest. As Arjen Klnkenberg, Brand Guru at Tony's Chocolonely, argues it is not a chocolate company that makes an impact but an impact company that makes chocolate. The company was a result of a Dutch journalist, Maurice Dekkers, reading about the challenge of modern slavery in cocoa farming in West Africa. In spite of the 2001 Harkin-Engel Protocol, which was signed by the leading chocolate producers as a pledge to reduce the worst forms of child labour in the industry, very little seemed to be happening. Together with colleagues, Dekkers decided to highlight the problem by featuring it in their TV programme *Keuringsdienst van Waarde* ('Food Unwrapped'). In one episode, one of the journalists, Teun van de Keuken interviews Nestlé's Head of PR. He asks him directly on film about child slavery, which is refuted, but he then goes on to ask:

So, if you say child slavery is too big a word, do you agree that child labour exists on a large scale in the industry?

The response is surprising;

Yes, let's say slavery exists … because they are so desperately poor.

Van de Keuken responds:

Because they don't get paid enough by Nestlé or by the companies they work for.

Nestlé's Head of PR hangs up.

In 2005, the journalists decided on a new approach: create their own chocolate brand. They knew nothing about building a brand, but they understood very well about how a powerful narrative can engage people. They conducted research into the market and the supply chain and told the story on the TV programme. They then funded the production of 5000 slave-free chocolate bars and sold them through two shops and online under the brand name, Tony's Chocolonely. On the morning of launch, one of the shops at Amsterdam Central Station opened to a queue at 06.30. By 7.00 its 1500 bars were sold out. The entire production was sold on the first day and the nascent brand had orders for 6000 more bars.

A cause such as promoting slave-free chocolate could easily seem 'abstract, vague and distant from the self', but Tony's Chocolonely overcame this by using their journalistic skills to ground the issue in the act of consumption. Initially this was done by using the wrapper itself which featured a broken chain with the message, 'together we'll make chocolate 100% slave free' on the outside and on the inside a narrative about the inequality of cocoa production (Fig. 7.1).

In 2012, Tony's Chocolonely, went one step further and made the bar itself into a message by forming it in a shape that reflects the cocoa producing countries of West Africa (Côte d'Ivoire, Ghana, Togo and Benin, Nigeria and Cameroon). Consumers complained about this—and still do—because the unequal shape, means it is difficult to divide equally, which also gives Tony's the chance to make the point that the chocolate supply chain is also unequal (Fig. 7.2).

Since its launch, the Tony's Chocolonely brand has moved from being a protest to the largest chocolate brand in the Netherlands, and in 2020, it surpassed €100 million in turnover. However, it has never lost its activist focus and sees its route to further success as ensuring the chocolate recipes are appealing and the product of high quality, alongside a robust commitment to its cause of ending slavery in cocoa production that is encapsulated in its slogan: Crazy about chocolate, Serious about people. Again, drawing on the

SHARE OUR CHOCOLATE, SHARE OUR STORY

Right now there is slavery on cocoa farms in West Africa. This is a result of the unequally divided cocoa chain. Tony's Chocolonely exists to change that.

Not just our chocolate, but all chocolate worldwide.

With incredibly tasty chocolate we lead by example and show the world that chocolate can be made differently: in taste, packaging and the way we do business with cocoa farmers.

Alone we make slave-free chocolate but together we'll make all chocolate 100% slave free. So we ask you to join us.

The more people who join our mission and share our story, the sooner 100% slave free becomes the norm in chocolate. The choice is yours. Are you in? Please check www.tonyschocolonely.com

CRAZY ABOUT CHOCOLATE, SERIOUS ABOUT PEOPLE

Fig. 7.1 Tony Chocolonely's wrapper tells the story

Fig. 7.2 The unequal chocolate bar

SHIFT framework, what Tony's does is break existing habits in chocolate consumption. It argues that by making the core message central, once consumers have bought a bar and seen the message on the wrapper, they know about the issue of slavery in chocolate. Also, by providing a high-quality product it makes the switching action easy and, for those who want a deeper engagement, there is the opportunity to be a participant in contributing to the cause and in getting feedback. Tony's does not rely on paid media to build the brand, but instead brings consumers (as citizens) into the process. In particular the network of Serious Friends, as they are called, are active supporters of the slave-free chocolate mission. They help to co-create the Tony's Chocolonely story and extend it through their personal networks as well as taking part in activism to challenge governments and companies. Every year the company gives its stakeholders—consumers, partners and suppliers—feedback with an Annual *Fair* Report that details the successes and the failings of the company in realizing the mission. It shares the progress made in its bean tracker, which uses monitoring systems that are designed to track beans from the farmer to the finished product and thirteen key performance indicators that measure its sustainability performance and which are independently verified by PwC.

Not everyone who consumed one of the 46 million bars of chocolate sold in 2020 reads the *Fair* Report or signs petitions, but Tony's Chocolonely affords the opportunity for consumers to take part in something beyond eating chocolate. Tony's always stresses that its target is not just to ensure fairness in its own supply chain, but through an open approach, to encourage other chocolate companies to act likewise. Consequently, consumers—especially the more activist ones—can feel that they are taking responsibility and making a contribution to meeting the needs of cocoa producing farmers. You can see how Tony Chocolonely has become a catalyst for change and built a successful business by looking at the video (Fig. 7.3).

Fig. 7.3 How Tony's Chocolonely has built a movement for change (see Video 7.1) (▶ https://doi.org/10.1007/000-8kj)

Using Conscience as a Differentiator

Tony's Chocolonely has managed to differentiate itself from competitors by a single-minded and authentic commitment to a conscience that was rooted in the beliefs of the founders and evolved under its current major shareholder, Henk Jan Beltman. The idea that conscience can be used as a brand differentiator would probably have Kant spinning in his grave, but the power of a well-communicated conscience is not only in the way it positions a company or a brand in the mind of its audiences but also in the way that it influences other companies to address their own behaviours. Both these facets of conscience are only viable though if consumers perceive communications as being authentic and truly embedded in the company. The philosopher Peter Singer argues that people attribute greater moral weight to acts that are focused on the welfare of others or a conscientious desire to do what is right above those that are driven by self-interest.[19] If self-interest is too overt, then it is not uncommon to hear people argue that communication of a cause is just marketing. However, consumers can accept companies' use of conscience in communications alongside commercial intent when the motivations are balanced.

---

[19] Singer, P. (2011), *The Expanding Circle: Ethics, Evolution, and Moral Progress*, Princeton NJ: Princeton University Press.

Some energy companies struggle with this, because there is already scepticism as to the probity of their communications—witness the legal action undertaken by the State of Massachusetts against ExxonMobil's environmentally focused advertising, which the State claims is misleading. Law Professor Karen Sokol notes, 'You would think that the company's primary business is saving the world … the legal claim is that's a lie. Because your primary business is oil and gas. It is fossil fuels.'[20] When it comes to oil and gas companies promoting environmental policies in terms of a concern for the environment, people easily doubt the motivations. There needs to be a good alignment between talking and doing—otherwise such companies would tend to be better off by being honest about their self-interest and the economic opportunities of sustainability, rather than talking green.[21] By way of contrast, a brand that has deep customer insight and that demonstrates literacy and fidelity is Dove. Dove can be an advocate for females and commercially oriented at the same time. Some commentators and bloggers have also been critical of Dove and accused it of hypocrisy, but here the 'promise of feminist goals is held simultaneously with the logic of market exchange'.[22] Dove consumers may just be buying the brand for its efficacy, but they can also act politically through consumption and thereby add a layer of meaning to their action.

Companies can communicate conscience in different ways. Some are very explicit in featuring claims or taking activist stances, such as Tony's Chocolonely, Ben & Jerry's and Ecoalf—with its line 'Because there is no Planet B'. For these companies, at the activist end of the spectrum, the cause is core to the way they try to position themselves in the minds of their audiences. Consequently, it makes those who align with the causes that these companies promote, feel more closely connected and willing to pronounce their beliefs explicitly to others.

In contrast to the explicit communicators, Patagonia, virtue signals its conscience in a different way. It does not sloganize its clothing (except as we saw in Chap. 4 with its election label messages), but rather it uses its influential position as an environmental pioneer to make people and other businesses aware of their responsibilities as citizens and companies. This very much aligns with Patagonia's Purpose and Principles and is designed to encourage less

[20] Morris C & Thomas M. (2021) Climate Change: the US state taking on an oil giant for greenwashing. 6 November 2021. BBC News.

[21] De Vries, G., Terwel, B.W., Ellemers, N. & Daamen, D.D. (2015), Sustainability or profitability? How communicated motives for environmental policy affect public perceptions of corporate greenwashing, *Corporate Social Responsibility and Environmental Management*, 22(3), 142–154.

[22] Banet-Weiser, S. (2012), *AuthenticTM: The Politics of Ambivalence in a Brand Culture*, New York: NYU Press. p. 41.

consumption and responsible usage that derives from the founder, Yvon Chouinard's beliefs and the company's culture. Take two illustrations of this motif. First, some years ago on a visit to Ventura to see Patagonia, we saw a simple black-and-white drawing pinned to the wall in the kindergarten for employees' children. It showed a bearded man carrying a surfboard with the line, 'The more you know … the less you need—Yvon Chouinard'. The picture and its message were designed to convey the virtue of a life connected to nature and largely free of consumerism. Second, and building on the theme of Chouinard's drawing, Patagonia produced an advertisement that ran on Friday, November 25, 2011 (Black Friday), in the *New York Times* featuring an image of a fleece with the line, 'Don't Buy this Jacket'. The ad went on to invite the reader to 'take the pledge to reduce consumption'. These examples indicate the counter-intuitive idea of a commercial organization discouraging consumption. This concept of green demarketing does not however advocate stopping consumption in an absolute sense, but rather encourages engagement and the promotion of environmentally responsible consumption.[23]

What should be noted is that the 'Don't Buy this Jacket' ad was a one-off, not a campaign. Patagonia gets its message across primarily through its network of environmentalists and sports enthusiasts who share their stories about the brand online. However, Patagonia does make occasional forays into paid media when it wants to make a point about an issue that it feels is important. Where Patagonia has an outsize influence is in the way it makes an impact on other companies: 'It has an influence … far larger than its size would suggest and serves as a model for how business can have a genuine and positive impact on the environment'.[24]

What connects Patagonia, Tony's Chocolonely and the historical case of the abolition of slavery we featured in Chap. 1, is the sense of building a movement for change. Conscientious communication is not simply about telling the world about corporate achievements, but about inspiring others and persuading them to become contributors to an issue. For the late eighteenth- and early nineteenth-century abolitionists that was about holding meetings, producing pamphlets and encouraging boycotts: estimates suggest that some 300,000 people in Britain abandoned West Indian slave produced sugar, with sales dropping by a third to a half. Today, those pamphlets have been replaced by social media campaigns, but the principles remain the same—of

[23] Soule, C. A.A. & Reich, B. J. (2015). Less is more: is a green demarketing strategy sustainable? *Journal of Marketing Management*, *31*(13–14), 1403–1427.

[24] Ind N. (2001). *Living the Brand: how to transform every member of your organization into a brand champion*. London: Kogan Page, p. 3.

connecting with people's anxieties and moral concerns to influence legislators, the media and other stakeholders—and to effect change together. Often the perception with communications is that companies should follow consumer needs and desires, but as noted by many of our interviewees, sometimes social and environmental issues are not front of mind. In this context companies need to be willing to lead and educate without hectoring by connecting with consumers' deeper needs to find meaning in their lives and to contribute to something outside of themselves.

Conscientious Communication with Financial Audiences

Having looked mostly at consumer, or consumer as citizen, communications, we now turn to the needs of financial audiences. It is clear that there are increasing expectations from investors and others for companies to make real commitments to addressing issues of sustainability and to measure environmental, social and governance factors. In terms of motivations, investors spread across a continuum from those who are more concerned with delivering on societal and environmental needs at one end to those who are focused on the financial returns at the other. Wherever they sit on the continuum, investors want to know the risks and opportunities associated with an investment, but they are often 'baffled by the enormity of the task'.[25] Overall there is a want of trust. For example, Edelman's Trust survey of institutional investors in the US noted that 86% of investors believe that companies frequently overstate or exaggerate their ESG progress, while 72% don't believe that companies will achieve their ESG commitments—even though investors believe that companies that excel at ESG warrant a premium. Interestingly on climate action 94% expect companies to establish and communicate a New Zero plan, while 92% are concerned that companies are not executing on such plans. So, there are expectations. And there is reality. Lex Suvanto of Edelman Financial Communications notes, 'Our research reveals that investors do not trust company ESG disclosures and they do not trust companies to deliver on ESG promises. At the same time, investors now see employee activism as a sign of a healthy corporate culture. These are disruptive forces across the

---

[25] Citi GPS. (2018) United Nations Sustainable Development Goals: Pathways to Success. June 2018, p. 9.

investment community that corporate boards and leaders must embrace to ensure competitive cost of capital and fair valuations.'[26]

Failures of execution and exaggeration of achievements seem like the antithesis of conscience. So, what is going wrong? There are certainly mitigating factors. Before companies can communicate their impacts they need to be able to curate, embed and measure them. As we saw with Unilever, this not only means understanding the emissions of the company and its supply chain (scope 1 and 2), but monitoring and changing the emissions of usage as well (scope 3). Such processes require resources in terms of people and money. There is a notable gap here in terms of expertise, both at board level and below. A study of 301 board members in 2021 showed that while boards believe that addressing climate change is vital to companies' success there is a lack of board expertise and a failure to prioritize climate change in executive performance metrics,[27] while another study of 122 board members by BCG-INSEAD found that 70% of directors reported that they are only moderately or not at all effective in integrating ESG into company strategy and governance—the biggest threat to achieving ESG goals being the inability of the organization to execute.[28] Similarly, PwC noting the lack of talent in the sustainability space announced in the summer of 2021 that it would invest $12 billion over five years to create 100,000 ESG-focused roles. Alongside these challenges is also the lack of consistent standards and different interpretations of 'green'. In a study by PwC into the top barriers facing managers in terms of ESG effectiveness, 37% of respondents cited lack of reporting standards and regulations/complexity.[29] To overcome these challenges, companies need to again use independent verification wherever they can to help ensure that the data presented is robust, but as we saw with consumer markets, they also need to tell their stories in a conscientious way.

Following the example of Rabobank, companies should aim to be open and transparent and critically reflective rather than obfuscating. They should also know the bounds of the truth, in terms of what can be said with confidence. Some of the companies we have talked to such as Oda, Tesco and SAP have stressed the importance of a fact-based approach; in generating data that

---

[26] Edelman (2021) Trust Barometer Special Report: Institutional Investors. https://www.edelman.com/trust/2021-trust-barometer/investor-trust.

[27] https://www.insead.edu/newsroom/2021-boards-are-committed-to-climate-change-but-knowledge-and-experience-gaps-in-boardroom-may-impact-ability-to-drive-future-change.

[28] Soonieus R., Woods W., Young D. & Tatar S. (2022). Directors can up their game on Environmental, Social and Governance Issues. The BCG-INSEAD Board ESG Pulse Check. March 2022.

[29] Gassmann P., Herman C., and Kelly C. (2021). Are you ready for the ESG revolution? *Strategy+business*, 14 June 2021.

enables good choices to be made and the confidence to express impacts and risks. However, the volatility of the debate around sustainability carries with it the problem of uncertainty. The implication of this for financial communications is reporting with accuracy the knowables while avoiding what George Orwell called the language 'of euphemism, question-begging and sheer cloudy vagueness'.[30] This implies a willingness to recognize failures and to be honest about weaknesses and ambiguity. As Ecoalf notes in its reflections on its business, 'We are not afraid to show our weaknesses, frustrations and challenges. We are not perfect and do not claim to be so.'[31] However, we might note that Ecoalf might be rare in this regard. Studies consistently show that in reporting on their sustainability performance, companies dwell on the positives and gloss over the negatives. The quality of reporting on social responsibility and sustainability remains low as companies try to preserve their corporate reputations in spite of their failings.[32] For example, in a study of 23 sustainability reports from the energy and mining sectors that compared the content of reports with significant negative news events involving the companies, there was no mention in more than half of the reports of the events. The author notes that the reports are narcissistic and give emphasis to a firm's positive achievement, while making virtuous statements and commitments and showcasing awards.[33] However, when companies do walk the talk, there are clear benefits. In a study by FCLT Global and the Wharton School of 3000 global companies, there is evidence to show that those businesses that combine strong stakeholder language with strong performance on material ESG measures were able to generate 4% higher revenues over a three-year period in terms of return on invested capital and deliver more stable results. The study notes 'That's not to say that shareholder-centric strategies don't pay off. In the short run, firms focused primarily on their shareholders also perform well', but goes on to argue that results appear to fade over time for those businesses who over-index on a single group of stakeholders and that they are less resilient. Focusing on shareholders therefore, 'is not a winning long-term strategy'.[34]

---

[30] Orwell G (1958) Politics and the English Language in *George Orwell Selected Writings*. London: Heinemann, p. 85.

[31] https://ecoalf.com/en/p/milestones-165.

[32] Hess, D. (2019). The transparency trap: Non-financial disclosure and the responsibility of business to respect human rights. *American Business Law Journal*, 56(1), 5–53.

[33] Boiral, O. (2013). Sustainability reports as simulacra? A counter-account of A and A+ GRI reports. *Accounting, Auditing & Accountability Journal*. 26(7), 1036–1071.

[34] FCLT Global (2022) Walking the talk: valuing a multi-stakeholder strategy. 17 January 2022. https://www.fcltglobal.org/resource/stakeholder-capitalism/.

Conclusion

Conscientious communication is the opposite of greenwashing and woke-washing in that it presents an honest picture of a company and its commitments to environmental and social issues. This requires self-insight and an understanding into the role the company or brand plays in the life of its stakeholders. Mostly stakeholders do not make choices just because a company is 'good', but rather they choose to buy from, work for and invest in a company because it is 'good' and … In some cases, environmental and social issues will be at the front of people's minds and at other times not. A company needs to understand this, if it is to present its conscience in a credible way. However, we should also note that even when conscience is not to the fore in people's minds, a company can be driven by conscience to lead and educate. The problem is that expressions of conscience in the form of environmental and social stories can be complex to narrate, but as we have seen with examples such as Rabobank, Tony's Chocolonely and Patagonia it also affords an opportunity for a company to become closer to its stakeholders and to forge a relationship that enables them to find deeper meaning. In this way conscientious communication provides benefits to the company and enriches the life of people.

8

Leading with Conscience

In the foregoing chapters we discussed how companies with a conscience must be built around a corporate purpose and principles, which then have to be embedded by the organization, properly conveyed to the various stakeholders and reflected in the experience offered. We also covered how such companies foster certain kinds of innovation to transform their business models, creating balanced value for all their stakeholders, boosting social prosperity and promoting sustainability. Like any other kind of organization, companies with a conscience greatly depend on their leaders' philosophy, business vision, leadership style and the role they give other members of the firm. In this chapter, we will focus on the role leaders should play and the features needed for 'leadership with a conscience'.

Ralph Nader, an American lawyer and pioneering consumer rights activist (who also happened to run for US President four times), stated that one of a leader's roles is to train others to follow in his footsteps. From this perspective, when we talk about leadership we not only need to decipher and describe the characteristics of a 'leader with a conscience' but also must grasp how to nurture such leaders. This will help ensure that a new vision of leadership takes root and grows within the company. In a similar vein, this chapter will also discuss the governance models that can help ensure a company with a conscience does not solely depend on the incumbent CEO's commitment. Governance models should help corporate conscience last and thrive.

During the chapter we will extensively rely on John Lewis Partnership and Rabobank as illustrative case studies. Even though they are not conventional businesses, we strongly believe that they are a template that other businesses can follow in order to promote more conscientious approaches to leading.

N. Ind, O. Iglesias, *In Good Conscience*, https://doi.org/10.1007/978-3-031-09338-8_8

Strategic Paradoxes and Leadership Styles

Leaders with a conscience must confront what Wendy Smith (a professor at University of Delaware) and her research partners call leadership-linked 'strategic paradoxes'.[1] This means *both building* a profitable business model in the short term *and* delivering medium and long-term transformation while building IT and sustainability skills to make a firm more competitive. Raising short-term profits means boosting operational efficiency, discipline, consistency and rigorously controlling costs. Transformation in the medium and long term requires experiment, 'opening up' and fast-paced, flexible innovation.

Similarly, companies with a conscience must be able to combine a reasonable investment return and meet the expectations of their stakeholders. The problem lies in squaring short-term business goals with the firm's long-term purpose. Put another way, there is tension between delivering short-term economic-financial value for shareholders and creating economic, social and environmental value for many other stakeholders, including the firm's staff, collaborating companies, society and 'The Planet'. These kinds of strategic binds are called 'obligation paradoxes'.

The bottom line is that these paradoxes call for strategies and deeds that are both contradictory and interdependent.[2] A focus on operational efficiency can clearly work against innovation and *vice versa*. Yet there can be no future growth or efficiency improvements without innovation. Thus, the great challenge for senior executives is that they cannot manage these strategic paradoxes as if they were trade-offs. Indeed, leaders with a conscience must learn to juggle both extremes of these paradoxes at the same time. In a recent interview, Tak Niinami, the CEO of Suntory Holding (one of the world's leading companies in the consumer products field, and which has adopted a responsible business philosophy) said:

> So, the CEO is required to strike a careful balance. [...] It's a constant balancing act, finding ways to meet multiple targets simultaneously. Some shareholder pressure is good in order to make sure you are performing financially but real profitability comes from finding solutions to stakeholder needs. Gaining the trust of our stakeholders is extremely important to keeping our operating license.[3]

---

[1] Smith, W.K.; Lewis, M.W. & Tushman, M. L. (2016) *Harvard Business Review*, May: 2–8. https://hbr.org/2016/05/both-and-leadership.
[2] Smith, W.K.; Lewis, M.W. & Tushman, M. L. (2016) *Harvard Business Review*, May: 2–8. https://hbr.org/2016/05/both-and-leadership.
[3] https://www.ieseinsight.com/doc.aspx?id=2479&ar=17.

How then to do *both* and *and?* First, tackling the innovation paradox calls for a mix of transactional and transformational leadership styles. Transactional leadership theories emerged from the earlier work of sociologist Max Weber who, in 1947, undertook a broad study of leadership styles. Weber identified a leadership style that he called 'bureaucratic' and that he saw as based upon discipline, strict rules and systematic control. The American historian James McGregor Burns drew on Weber's ideas in the late 1970s to propose two political leadership styles: transactional and transformational. Finally, it was Bernard Bass, an American professor, who applied the concepts of transactional and transformational leadership to the management field in the 1990s—specifically to organizational behaviour.

Transactional leadership stresses the transactional relationship forged between a firm's leaders and employees whereby the former set precise goals for the latter. Meeting these goals is linked to staff rewards while failure incurs penalties. Thus, transactional leadership generates processes and rules, with continuous supervision being used to enforce them. This leadership style tends to focus on measurable short-term goals. Transactional leadership is fine for reaching high operational efficiency, which is vital if a firm is to achieve short-term profitability. However, transactional leadership, with its focus on processes, and its rigidity and inflexibility, can neither drive creativity and innovation nor develop a long-term vision for the business.

To transform themselves, companies must develop new skills, and even disrupt their competitive position. This requires leaders who can manage transactional and transformational styles to best effect. According to Burns and Bass, transformational leadership is based on the leader's ability to: influence and inspire, foster corporate change and steer the firm's transformation. Under the transformational leadership paradigm, the leader can wield influence because he draws on a system of deep values based on justice and integrity that elicits staff respect, trust and loyalty. Thus, the transformational leader does not build a solely transactional relationship with his followers but rather seeks to inspire them by building a common identity and a shared strategic vision that is rooted in a value system. This kind of leadership boosts employee empowerment because there is a shared vision of the changes that need to be made. That is why transformational leadership both appreciates and fosters critical thinking, individual creativity and intra-entrepreneurship. Furthermore, the transformational leader promotes change, accepts risks and facilitates experimentation. Recent research shows that the transformational leadership style is best suited to innovation-oriented corporate cultures.[4,5]

---

[4] Khalili, A. (2016), 'Linking transformational leadership, creativity, innovation, and innovation-supportive climate', *Management Decision*, 54(9): 2277–2293. https://doi.org/10.1108/MD-03-2016-0196.

[5] Matzler, N; Schwarz, E.; Deutinger, N. & Harms, R. (2008) The Relationship between Transformational Leadership, Product Innovation and Performance in SMEs, *Journal of Small Business & Entrepreneurship*, 21:2, 139–151, https://doi.org/10.1080/08276331.2008.10593418.

Companies with a conscience also need leaders who can tackle the innovation paradox by judiciously combining transactional and transformational leadership styles. This mix both secures operational efficiency and good short-term returns and acquisition of the new skills needed in socially responsible, sustainable business models.

The two types of leadership are not mutually exclusive. Indeed research shows that both are required to varying degrees[6] while something known as Multi Factor Leadership theory (MLP) affirms that:

> Transactional leadership behaviours and transformational leadership behaviours are necessary to effectively perform as a leader and that transformational leadership adds incremental value to more traditional transactional leadership behaviours.[7]

Second, leaders with a conscience must also be able to manage the obligation paradox. They *both* have to be able to meet investors' expectations, which often focus on short-term returns *and* meet the demands of other stakeholders. The tension created by trying to square this circle overlaps with that created by having to also build a business model based on a long-term vision rooted in the firm's conscience. Maria Besharov at Saïd Business School in Oxford and Rakesh Khurana at Harvard Business School argue that any leader has to strike a balance between meeting demands made from outside the company while maintaining the firm's integrity.[8] In practice, this is tricky because leaders have to satisfy both investors and external stakeholders, reconcile their conflicting interests while acting in ways that do not wound the firm's conscience. Walking this tightrope requires what Philip Selznick, Professor of Sociology and Law at Berkeley terms 'autonomy' and 'responsiveness'.[9]

---

[6] Aarons G. A. (2006). Transformational and transactional leadership: association with attitudes toward evidence-based practice. *Psychiatric services* (Washington, D.C.), 57(8), 1162–1169. https://doi.org/10.1176/ps.2006.57.8.1162.

[7] Piotrowski, C & Watt, J. (2011) Developing Leaders: Examining the Role of Transactional and Transformational Leadership across Business Contexts. *Organization Development Journal*, 29(3): 51–66.

[8] Besharov, M.L. & Khurana, R. (2015), 'Leading Amidst Competing Technical and Institutional Demands: Revisiting Selznick's Conception of Leadership', Institutions and Ideals: Philip Selznick's Legacy for Organizational Studies (Research in the Sociology of Organizations, Vol. 44), Emerald Group Publishing Limited, Bingley, pp. 53–88. https://doi.org/10.1108/S0733-558X20150000044004.

[9] Selznick, P. (1992). The moral commonwealth: Social theory and the promise of community. Berkeley, CA: University of California Press. Selznick, P. (1996). Institutionalism "old" and "new". *Administrative Science Quarterly*, 41(2, 40th Anniversary Issue), 270277.

This need for responsiveness (empathy with the needs and expectations of the firm's sundry stakeholders) calls for a 'servant' leadership style. A servant leader has 'his or her moral responsibility not only to the success of the organisation, but also to his or her subordinates, the organisation's customers, and other organisational stakeholders'.[10] Such a leader's role is thus to serve others and society in general. This approach starkly contrasts with traditional authoritarian models of leadership. Servant leadership is based on empathy and humility, pursues the empowerment of employees and other interest groups and fosters a much more decentralized and collaborative decision-making structure and process. It is also based on the philosophical traditions of Consequentialism and Utilitarianism, which hold that morality involves seeking 'the greatest good for the greatest number'.[11]

The John Lewis Partnership (JLP) has a deep-rooted culture of servant leadership. Director, Purpose and Special Project, Sarah Gillard says:

> (…) leading in the partnership, you basically have to ask where do my people want to go? And then, I will lead them there. So, it's very different and getting leaders to understand that is quite difficult, because normally you get a job as a leader and you're told that you've got all of this experience and expertise to make decisions (…) to lead your team and show them the way forward. Then they'll follow you. Do that humanely and whatever else, but that's your job. And in the partnership, basically what we ask people to do is bring all of their skills and experience and listen really hard to the partners because leaders serve at the pleasure of partners in the partnership. Actually, it's implicit, it's not explicit—but it is servant leadership.

Thus, companies with a conscience need to push servant leadership styles so that they can meet the expectations of all the firm's stakeholders. Yet this needs to be done without compromising either the leader's integrity or that of the firm. Here companies with a conscience need to adopt an 'authentic' leadership style. Such leadership calls for people with strong self-awareness and who thoroughly grasp what their values and principles are and act in accordance with them.[12] These leaders connect with their emotions, are keenly aware of their strengths and weaknesses, and act in a transparent and authentic way without worrying about showing vulnerability. Furthermore, they are

---

[10] Ehrhart, M. G. (2004) Leadership and procedural justice climate as antecedents of unit-level organizational citizenship behavior. *Personnel Psychology*, 57(1): 61–94.

[11] Lemoine, G. J.; Hartnell, C. A. & Leroy, H. (2019) Taking Stock of Moral Approaches to Leadership: An Integrative Review of Ethical, Authentic, and Servant Leadership. *Academy of Management Annals*, 13(1).

[12] https://www.forbes.com/sites/kevinkruse/2013/05/12/what-is-authentic-leadership/?sh=549207fedef7.

committed to the company's purpose and principles and put these before their personal interests.[13] In short, leaders' authenticity and commitment to their own principles and those of the firms they lead let them manage the pressures from outside interest groups without having to compromise.

At John Lewis Partnership, the quest for authentic leadership drives a 5-day leadership development programme that encourages individuals to reflect on themselves and their impact. Sarah Gillard describes the experience as 'an introspective journey around leadership and your sense of it'.

Thus, managing the obligation paradox and striking a delicate balance between responsiveness and autonomy in companies with a conscience means promoting self-aware leaders whose leadership is rooted in service and authenticity.

The Role of the Leader with a Conscience

A leader with a conscience should play three key roles. First of all, she should strengthen the corporate conscience and define a strategic vision. Second, she should promote the alignment of employees and other stakeholders around the strategic vision and organizational conscience. Third, she should nurture the firm's internal talent to ensure that human capital becomes one of its key competitive advantages.

Rabobank's CEO, Wiebe Draijer frames the approach thus:

> We've really thought through [the question] 'What does this bank actually stand for?' What is it that you're after? What makes us tick? Why do we get out of bed in the morning? We've gone through a process—a very decentralised one—then a central formulation of our mission which ended up as: 'Growing a better world together'. So, we built a framework of mission, vision, strategic priorities that we adopted eight years ago.

Rabobank's corporate conscience is articulated through its purpose/mission and corporate principles, which are inspired by the company's unique history and DNA. To uncover the past, Draijer led a process of discovery that involved interviewing former leaders and long-serving employees:

---

[13] https://www.forbes.com/sites/kevinkruse/2013/05/12/what-is-authentic-leadership/?sh=549207fedef7.

There is something there that the company represents and (…) we have tried very hard to feed that conscience. I rekindled what was already there but it was dormant and it was confused. So, I think conscience is essential, but it cannot be new. Don't do something if it's not intrinsically there so to speak.

Along with redefining and revaluing the corporate conscience, the CEO and his top management team also came up with a vision and a set of strategic priorities for the coming years that drew upon the company's self-awareness. Interestingly, both processes were not tackled in a top-down fashion but instead were ones in which many collaborated. This co-operative, co-creative approach to decision-making is a hallmark of Rabobank's corporate culture and also drives employee commitment.

We did that not only with the definition of the mission and vision but also in some massive organisational changes that we went through. [...] We followed the same process of starting with an open invitation, out of which came endless ideas that you could then start to group. So, the process was very open to start with, inviting everyone and thereby making people feel both connected to the end results yet at the same time making them keenly aware that it was impossible to wholly satisfy everybody's needs. That creates an outcome where people say they just own it.

The second role of such a leader is to align employees and other stakeholders with the firm's conscience and strategic vision—something that benefits greatly from a participatory approach. These processes also deliver the servant leadership that any company with a conscience needs to embrace. In this regard, John Lewis echoes the Rabobank approach of participatory decision-making. The thought of involving employees in processes might elicit a groan from some managers, but Gillard argues that it can be more effective because it generates higher levels of engagement and alignment:

It can look like a massive blocker. You basically have to consult 80,000 people before you can make a move—I mean, not officially, but culturally. However, if you approach it in the right way, you genuinely listen and hear what people think. If you do it right, you get 80,000 people behind you. Then the whole thing gets supercharged and there's no friction or if there is it's because each part of the business wants to go even faster.

The third role of a conscientious leader should be to nurture internal talent and empower employees, as well as establish strategies and policies for creating the leaders of the future. This approach stems from their vision of leadership not as an individual, heroic and highly personal task but rather as the articulation of a collaboration network that capitalizes on internal talent. It is therefore a collaborative concept of leadership in which various leaders co-operate, combining their knowledge and skills to achieve goals that a single leader would be unlikely to achieve alone. Collaborative leadership thus exploits systemic processes and relationships to enable a set of individuals to lead change.[14] In the words of Draijer:

> I need to make sure that I create a team that carries out the strategy. So, I invested a lot of time in understanding what it takes to build a top team that can bring about this change. I spent a lot of time in creating a diverse team. When I joined Rabobank, there was just one woman in the top 200; now 35% of the top 200 are women. I made HR and Talent Management a Board position. ... She has freedom to take whatever radical actions are needed to forge the leadership capabilities of the future.

The Traits of Leaders with a Conscience

So far, we have discussed the strategic paradoxes that leaders with a conscience face, the leadership styles they need for resolving these paradoxes and the role they must play. Next, we will outline the traits that characterize leaders with a conscience (Fig. 8.1).

First, leaders with a conscience must act responsibly. This means that regardless of circumstances and role, leaders have to understand how they can meet the challenges of good governance and environmental and social issues. As Fred Kofman, an Executive Coach in the leadership and cultural field, and former Vice-President at LinkedIn and Google, argues, this means being a 'player'.

> You must take unconditional responsibility; you need to see yourself as a 'player', as a central character who has contributed to shape the current situation—and who can thus affect its future. This is the opposite of seeing yourself as a 'victim', subject to forces beyond your control. The player is in the game and can affect the result. The victim is out of the game and can only suffer the consequences of others' actions.[15]

---

[14] Contractor, N. S.; DeChurch, L. A.; Carson, J.; Carter, D. R.; and Keegan, B. (2012) The topology of collective leadership. *The Leadership Quarterly*, 23(6): 994–1011.

[15] Kofman, F. (2006) *Conscious Business. How to Build Value through Values*. Sounds True.

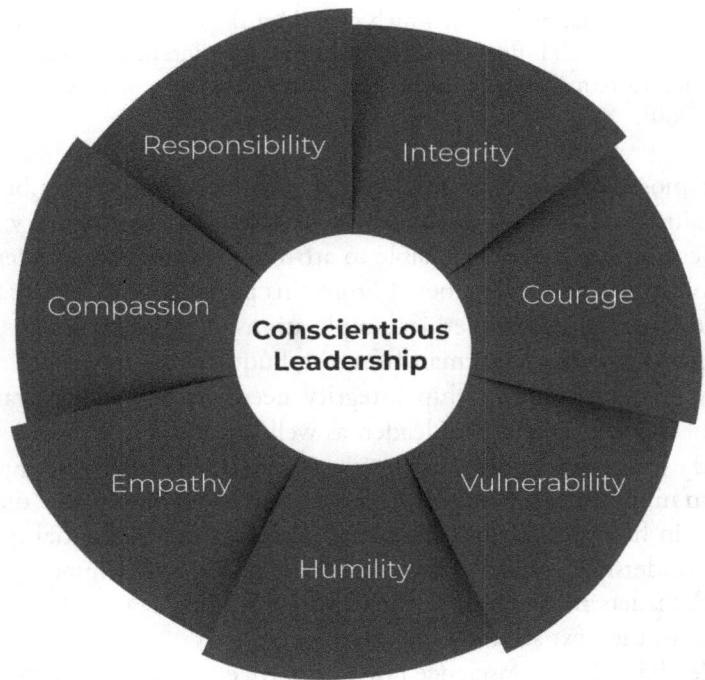

Fig. 8.1 Conscientious leadership traits

Thus, leaders with a conscience, although they may not be to blame for the world's problems, have to be willing to shoulder part of the burden in finding solutions. Such leaders thus assume broader responsibilities that go beyond profit-making by promoting accountability at corporate levels.

Second, leaders with a conscience must have integrity. The word *integrity* has its origins in Sanskrit. *Tag* is the Sanskrit root and means *to touch or handle*. Thus 'Integrity' means touching something. Someone with integrity is a 'whole person' true to himself.[16] From this perspective, integrity has to do with the consistency between words and actions. In this context, writer Ayn Rand argues:

---

[16] Bauman, D. C. (2013) Leadership and the three faces of integrity. *The Leadership Quarterly*, 24(3): 414–426.

Integrity is that quality in Man which gives him the courage to hold his own convictions against all influences, against the opinions and desires of other men; the courage to remain whole, unbroken, untouched, to remain true to himself[17] (p. 260).

Even if most authors agree that integrity requires consistency between a person's values and actions, many others see that this is a necessary but not sufficient condition. It is not possible to attribute integrity to a leader, unless she is committed to ethical values.[18] From this perspective, integrity requires also considering the potential ethical implications of beliefs or actions on others. Professor Christine Moorman from the Fuqua Business School at Duke University argues that leadership integrity needs to be judged against the morality of the values held by a leader, as well as whether the leader behaves consistently with these values.[19] Integrity can thus be defined as acting consistently from moral values.[20] At root, integrity is about following the dictates of conscience in how we lead our lives. Such integrity is an essential quality in authentic leadership styles.[21] Yet in order to nurture this integrity and be 'authentic', leaders must speak to their inner-self. This is a challenge that we will discuss in the next section.

Third, leaders with a conscience must be brave enough to act with integrity and in keeping with their ethical values. One of the first decisions made by Paul Polman when he took over as Unilever's CEO in 2009 was to tell investors that the company would stop publishing quarterly financial reports. At the same time, he also changed the employee wage and bonus system to move the focus from the short-term to the long-term. Both decisions implied shifting existing boundaries notwithstanding major stakeholders' expectations and traditional business practices. Such decisions can only be made by leaders with a conscience who accept their responsibilities and act with integrity and courage—which arises from a tight link between a leader and what reporter Bill Gertz called 'True North', meaning that moral compass within each of us.

---

[17] Harriman D. (1999) *Journals of Ayn Rand.* Penguin.

[18] Graham, J. L. (2002) Does integrity require moral goodness? *RATIO,* 14(3): 234–251.

[19] Moorman, R. H.; Darnold, T. C.; Priesemuth, M.; and Dunn, C. P. (2012) Toward the Measurement of Perceived Leader Integrity: Introducing a Multidimensional Approach, *Journal of Change Management,* 12:4, 383–398, https://doi.org/10.1080/14697017.2012.728746.

[20] Bauman, D. C. (2013) Leadership and the three faces of integrity. *The Leadership Quarterly,* 24(3): 414–426.

[21] Luthans, F. & Avolio, B.J. (2003) Authentic Leadership: A Positive Developmental Approach. In: Cameron, K.S., Dutton, J.E. & Quinn, R.E., Eds., Positive Organizational Scholarship, Barrett-Koehler, San Francisco, 241–261.

This is how Paul Polman describes it:

So, it indeed starts at the top. Just as fish start floating at the top, the same is true of companies. When you see companies buying into value statements but their culture going off track—the Wells Fargos, the Boeings, the GEs—it's because their leaders' behaviour is not living up to their values. That gap actually grows and ultimately you pay the price for that. So, it starts with courageous leaders who have to find their own purpose, which is something that I find tremendously important if one is to withstand the cynics, the sceptics, the shocks, and make you determined to move in a certain direction [...]. That's why I call them courageous leaders—it comes from the French word *coeur* (heart). It starts as much with the heart as it does with the head.[22]

Fourth, leaders with a conscience must accept that they are vulnerable. University of Houston Professor, Brené Brown, in her book *The Power of Vulnerability*, argues that we have a natural tendency to hide our weaknesses. Yet the more we try to shield ourselves from our vulnerability and to hide it, the more fearful and disconnected we become from our true selves and our inner moral compass. Leaders with a conscience acknowledge their vulnerability as something innate and do not strive to conceal it. This lets them relate to the outside world openly, transparently and with integrity. As Draijer says,

You need to be able to be vulnerable when you do not know, or when you actually need others to do something to find an answer. I think I've always been extremely vocal and transparent about my doubts and errors as much as about my convictions.

This ability to connect with one's own vulnerability, as well as to reveal it, is surely the epitome of courage. It contrasts starkly with the notion of perfection and complete control of things—an image many traditional leaders have assiduously sought to project. In his book *Principles*, entrepreneur Ray Dalio argues that leaders should be 'radically open-minded' and promote 'radical transparency'. His idea is that it is only when we accept our mistakes and limitations—frankly admit that we do not know everything and are open about our shortcomings—that we can learn, develop and make better decisions. By acknowledging and revealing our weaknesses, we can forge links with those who have the knowledge and/or skills that we lack. Furthermore, according to Dalio, only by promoting a corporate culture based on 'radical transparency'

---

[22] https://hbr.org/podcast/2021/10/first-he-saved-unilever-now-he-wants-to-save-capitalism?utm_medium=email&utm_source=newsletter_daily&utm_campaign=dailyalert_notactsubs&deliveryName=DM153738

can we build a company in which people ask questions, share, learn and develop. Sarah Gillard adds:

> If you're not embracing vulnerability yourself, you can't ask others to do so, and if you can't do that, then you're not creating an environment where people can share freely, take risks, innovate, collaborate, provide feedback, improve, and grow. It's really difficult because most people have been taught to be invulnerable.

Accepting and embracing vulnerability therefore implies a process of unlearning and of reconnecting with our authentic selves. Research shows that vulnerability lets any leader connect better with their emotions as well as those of others and to be seen as more authentic—something that helps forge more trusting relationships and greater engagement.[23]

Fifth, leaders with a conscience are humble. Humility 'is an interpersonal characteristic that emerges in social contexts that connotes (a) a manifested willingness to view oneself accurately, (b) a displayed appreciation of others' strengths and contributions, and (c) "teachability"'.[24] Thus, humility begins with the ability to recognize one's own shortcomings, as well as the mistakes made. This humility, when combined with vulnerability, is what makes these limitations visible to the outside. Once a leader decides to get off his pedestal and humbly share his vulnerabilities, he can genuinely appreciate others' views and skills.

Jim Whitehurst, the CEO of Red Hat, the world's largest Open Source software provider, whose mission is to bring the power of Linux to solving the biggest problems we face as a society, claims that:

> It's important to be humble. It takes time, effort and a good dose of humility—especially if you're the CEO—to lead an open organisation. If you don't openly allow and encourage your people to tell you you're wrong, you'll never build an organisation that can innovate better than your competitors. People want the opportunity to voice their opinion. They expect to be heard [...]. That's how you remove barriers and quiet the naysayers. Go out and talk to the people with whom you work.[25]

---

[23] Ito, A. & Bligh, M. C. (2017) Feeling Vulnerable? Disclosure of Vulnerability in the Charismatic Leadership Relationship. *Journal of Leadership Studies*, 10(3), 66–70.

[24] http://humaninterop.com/hiwp/wp-content/uploads/2015/04/1526-5455-2013-24-05-15 17-2au.pdf.

[25] https://medium.com/authority-magazine/red-hat-ceo-jim-whitehurst-on-why-its-so-important-for-a-leader-to-be-humble-3128113c3a36.

Humility also implies not only being able to listen but also to develop the ability to incorporate the feedback received, to question one's assumptions and to learn and advance. Last but not least, one should note that humble leaders are not weak, nor do they have to be indecisive. In fact, in his influential book *Good to Great*,[26] Jim Collins showed that the leaders of the best-performing companies worldwide tend to be humble but have great resolve. At the end of the day, humility and courage are not mutually exclusive traits but rather can and should be synergistic.

Sixth, conscientious leaders are empathic. Empathy is the ability to connect with the emotions of others, to put yourself in their shoes, and it is vital for forging deep interpersonal relationships and pursuing a 'servant leadership' approach. According to psychologists Daniel Goleman and Paul Ekman, there are three different kinds of empathy. The first is so-called 'cognitive empathy', which has to do with the ability to perceive and understand the reasoning and feelings of the people around us. Thus, cognitive empathy lets a leader understand different points of view, negotiate and motivate her team. The second is 'emotional empathy', which is the ability to feel and share the emotions felt by others. It is, therefore, a higher level of empathy where the individual not only recognizes the emotions of others but also experiences them from her own perspective, thus forging a much deeper emotional link. Emotional empathy lets leaders build deep interpersonal relationships with their teams and it is also the basis for organizational co-operation. From this perspective, participatory and collective leadership styles have to be rooted in corporate cultures in which empathy plays a central role. In parallel, emotional empathy is also a key trait for any leader who wants to play a coaching role for her staff. Finally, there is 'compassionate empathy', which is what drives people to act and to respond to the other's emotional state.

Developing empathy requires us to: question of our own prejudices; suspend the judgement we normally pass on others' ideas and behaviour and encourage curiosity. Curiosity lets us take an interest in others, in their life experiences and in their inner world (something that takes time and patience). Thus, leaders with a conscience, in addition to developing high levels of self-awareness, must also develop awareness of others. Therefore, management development programmes must be able to work on these two dimensions of awareness.

---

[26] Collins, J. (2001). *Good to great*. Chicago Random House Business Books.

Seventh, leaders with a conscience must be compassionate. While empathy is being able to connect with the emotions of others, compassion goes one step further and is characterized by the active intention to help others. Thus, 'compassion involves not only appraisal of the situation but also includes an active behavioural component'.[27] As Richard Boyatzis and Annie McKee argue in their book *Resonant Leadership*[28] compassion is empathy in action. LinkedIn's CEO Jeff Weiner says that practicing compassion has transformed both his personal and professional life. In an opening speech at Wharton Business School,[29] he stated:

> I decided to change. I vowed that as long as I'd be responsible for managing other people, I would aspire to manage compassionately. That meant pausing, and being a spectator to my own thoughts, especially when getting emotional. It meant walking a mile in the other person's shoes; and understanding their hopes, their fears, their strengths and their weaknesses. And it meant doing everything within my power to set them up to be successful.

According to Weiner, the practice of compassion made him a happier person and helped him build a better company. LinkedIn's vision is to 'Create economic opportunity for every member of the global workforce'. In keeping with this vision, the company launched a new service that allows any of its members to apply for a job by asking a contact in their network on LinkedIn for a recommendation. The new service was an immediate success. However, Meg Garlinghouse, its Head of Social Impact, in line with the compassionate leadership style that Weiner tries to apply to the company, pointed out that this new service would surely not help those people with lots of talent but who do not have the money to study at university and lack a good contact network. This led LinkedIn to act and develop its Career Advice Service for all those lacking training, experience and contacts with people with such resources. Nearly a million LinkedIn members are already part of this mentoring programme.

---

[27] Shuck, B; Alagaraja, M; Immekus, J.; and Cumberland, D.; and Honeycutt-Elliott, M. (2019) *Human Resource Development Quarterly*, 30(4): 537–564.

[28] Boyatzis, R. and McKee, A. (2005) *Resonant Leadership: Renewing Yourself and Connecting with Others Through Mindfulness, Hope, and Compassion*. Harvard Business Review Press.

[29] https://knowledge.wharton.upenn.edu/article/linkedin-ceo-how-compassion-can-build-a-better-company/.

Last but not least, one should note that compassionate leaders must first work on self-compassion before they can have compassion for others. Although compassion is often seen as a virtue, self-compassion is often thought of as a vice, with connotations of self-indulgence or complacency.[30] Yet academic research shows that managers with great self-compassion also score highly on conscience, optimism, happiness and initiative scales.[31] Likewise, leaders with greater self-compassion tend to have strong commitment to the goals they set.[32] These results reveal the wisdom of The Dalai Lama's reflections in his book *The Art of Happiness*, where he states:

> If you want others to be happy, practice compassion. If you want to be happy, practice compassion.

How Can One Develop Leaders with a Conscience?

The previous section discussed the traits of leaders with a conscience. While it is important to grasp what these traits are, it is even more important to understand how they can be developed. Thus, leaders with a conscience must foster leadership development strategies that boost the firm's social capital. Leadership development is about:

> (…) expanding the collective ability of organisational members to engage effectively in leadership roles and processes.[33]

Any such leadership development strategy must achieve two complementary goals. First, it must promote higher levels of self-awareness in the organization's leaders so that they can connect with and monitor their inner world. In a Harvard Business Review article, organizational psychologist, Tasha Eurich, showed that while most leaders believe they are self-aware, less than

---

[30] Wasylyshyn, K. M. & Masterpasqua, F. (2018) Developing self-compassion in leadership development coaching: A practice model and case study analysis. *International Coaching Psychology Review*, 13 (1) Spring.

[31] Neff, K.D. & Pommier, E. (2013). The relationship between self-compassion and other-focused concern among college undergraduates, community adults, and practicing meditators. *Self and Identity*, 12(2), 1–17.

[32] Neff, K.D., Hsieh, Y.P. & Dejitterat, K. (2005). Self-compassion, achievement goals, and coping with academic failure. *Self and Identity*, 4(3), 263–287.

[33] Day, D. V. (2000) Leadership development: A review in context. *The Leadership Quarterly*, 11(4): 581–613.

15% of those studied actually met the criteria.[34] As ESADE Professor, Josep Maria Lozano stresses, business schools bear a lot of the blame for this sorry state of affairs. The reason is that they have tended to focus on furnishing their students with technical tools through a purely instrumental approach to training that overlooks any sense of purpose—what might be called 'the being component'. Thus, fostering greater self-awareness cannot be achieved only through horizontal development. Technical learning is necessary but insufficient. This is why vertical development must also take place so that leaders can advance their understanding of their inner selves and in the process, enrich their interpretations of the world.[35] These intrapersonal skills (vital for attaining high levels of self-awareness) are the key to fostering more authentic leadership styles. While leadership development programmes work on self-awareness, it should also be possible to forge leaders who are more responsible, upright, vulnerable, courageous and humble.

Second, such a development strategy must also promote high awareness of others and society at large. This requires observing and listening and demonstrating the ability to empathize with others' feelings. Such social awareness calls for a deep commitment to caring and 'attention, solicitation and active involvement with others'.[36] The challenge for leaders is to understand how to respond to this caring instinct. At certain times, caring will require a given top-down response to employee or corporate needs. That said, a caring leader must have more in his tool box than paternalistic answers to life's problems. Caring leadership is about inspiring and empowering others and about helping them grow:

> In practice, it [caring] can be directive and transactional, as well as emancipating and inspirational. It demands a balancing of stepping in, with standing back; gauging whether and how to remove power from, or grant power to, others; and bearing responsibility for what emerges through both emphatic and vaguer modes of knowing.[37]

Raising social awareness also helps leaders realize what they do not know, whetting their curiosity and boosting creativity. This dimension of leadership development stresses the need to hone interpersonal skills, which are vital for

---

[34] https://hbr.org/2018/01/what-self-awareness-really-is-and-how-to-cultivate-it.

[35] Petrie, N. (2014) Future Trends in Leadership Development. White Paper. Center for Creative Leadership. https://leanconstruction.org/media/learning_laboratory/Leadership/Future_Trends_in_Leadership_Development.pdf.

[36] Ciulla, J.B. (2009) Leadership and the Ethics of Care. *Journal of Business Ethics* 88: 3–4. https://doi.org/10.1007/s10551-009-0105-1.

[37] Tomkins, L., & Simpson, P. (2015). Caring Leadership: A Heideggerian Perspective. *Organization Studies*, 36(8): 1013–1031.

Fig. 8.2   Two dimensions of awareness

forging understanding, respect and mutual trust. While leadership development programmes work on social awareness, it should also be possible to train more empathetic, compassionate leaders.

Figure 8.2 links the two dimensions of awareness (self and social) that leaders need to develop, along with the leadership style and associated traits that each fosters. The figure also shows two tools that are valuable for each of the awareness dimensions that leaders need to operate in.

First, coaching is a key tool to develop higher levels of self-awareness. Leading business coach, Myles Downing, who defines his craft as 'The art of facilitating the performance, learning and development of another',[38] emphasizes the importance of self-awareness. The main principle of coaching is dialogue between the coach and the learner. This dialogue begins with the coach's questions and the learner's answers to them. Thus, coaching embodies an almost Socratic dialogue to delve into the nature of ethical, virtuous behaviour. Socrates believed that the best way to find the truth and make decisions was to discover what is right through discussion and dialogue rather than through self-contemplation.

By formulating (mostly open-ended) questions, the coach encourages the leader to reflect. This process of dialogue and reflection usually leads the

[38] Downey, M. (2003). *Effective coaching: Lessons from the coach's coach* (2nd ed.). New York: Thomson/Texere.

learner to become more aware of her values and beliefs and more open to new perspectives.[39] Step-by-step, the leader is able to steadily draw her own conclusions and to end up making her own decisions. Wiebe Draijer stresses that he has always tried to foster an approach to leadership in which he acts more like a coach than as 'the big boss', by inspiring his team to reflect, draw their own conclusions and reach their goals. In his words:

> I've always worked with the conviction that the only thing that I can get done is what other people will see by themselves. So I've organised many conversations and dialogues to inspire them. Just a micro illustration ... there is a nice company in the country whose name is *Tony's Chocolonely.* ... So, I brought account managers who I know are influential in the bank. I took them to Tony's and we had a conversation about chocolate and child labour. From the conversation I knew I had two more allies on the path to be a leader in sustainability and food ... so, I bring people to places where I know they can be inspired.

Coaching is an extraordinarily powerful tool for fostering greater levels of self-awareness and for promoting more authentic leadership styles. For coaching to be effective it must be personalized, letting the learner also take part in deciding the focus and goals to be covered. In addition, the coach must play the role of thinking partner but never that of expert or authority giving answers.[40] Although coaching spurs personal reflection, asking too many 'why' questions can be ineffective. Research in this field has shown that we do not have direct access to most of the motives, feelings or beliefs that we want to tap into during the coaching process. That is because all these things lie in our unconscious.[41] This leads us to come up with answers which in many cases are mental constructions that we want be true, but that are actually wrong and far-removed from our inner world. So, instead of asking too many 'why' questions, coaching should focus on asking more 'what' questions. The reason is that questions starting with 'what' spur reflection in a context that steadily lets more precise, reliable answers emerge. For example, instead of asking 'Why do you feel realised at work?', the coach might ask 'What are the situations in which you feel unrealised at work? What do they have in common?' The research carried out by the Tasha Eurich team also shows that

---

[39] Neenan, M. (2009) Using Socratic Questioning in Coaching. *Journal of Rational-Emotive and Cognitive-Behaviour,* 27: 49–264. https://doi.org/10.1007/s10942-007-0076-z.

[40] Petrie, N. (2014) Future Trends in Leadership Development. White Paper. Center for Creative Leadership. https://leanconstruction.org/media/learning_laboratory/Leadership/Future_Trends_in_Leadership_Development.pdf.

[41] https://hbr.org/2018/01/what-self-awareness-really-is-and-how-to-cultivate-it.

coaching is more effective when leaders are able to connect with two kinds of self-awareness. The first is internal self-awareness, which has to do with one's values, beliefs, expectations or desires and is what we have mostly referred to so far. The second is external self-awareness and it refers to understanding how other people see us with respect to these same dimensions.

Academic research[42] also suggests a need to go beyond traditional coaching based on the dyadic relationship between coach and learner. These studies point to group-type coaching being especially effective for fostering authentic leadership styles. This is because the participants also learn about themselves through the impressions of others. In parallel, the experiences and reflections of others also shape one's own reflections on oneself. According to the sociological theory of Symbolic Interactionism proposed by George Mead, the self is not fixed but is dynamically constructed in a social context and thus emerges through interpersonal relationships. From this standpoint, if our self develops through comparison with others, then group coaching provides an excellent context for change and personal growth. This is, for example, why John Lewis Partnership's management development programme included prominent spaces for group reflection. As Sarah Gillard argues:

> You need to give these people an opportunity to think for themselves and collectively about what they believe great leadership is, what the purpose of the organisation is, what it means for them, how they're going to connect their own purpose, the purpose of the organisation, what that means for how they make decisions, all the rest of it.

Second, when it comes to encouraging social awareness, service-learning is an effective tool. Service-learning is a type of experiential training through which participants try to grasp the needs of a given community and to help meet them. The whole process takes time and involves a great deal of commitment by participants but it also enhances their development as human beings and pricks their conscience to shoulder their moral duties as individuals.[43]

Deepa Krishnan is an entrepreneur, educator and social worker in India, who co-ordinates a service-learning experiential course at the S P Jain Institute of Management and Research (SPJIMR) in Bombay, India. In this course,

---

[42] Fusco, T.; O'Riordan, S.; and Palmer, S. (2015) Conscious, Competent, Confident, and Congruent: A Grounded Theory of Group Coaching and Authentic Leadership Development. *International Coaching Psychology Review*, 10(2): 131–146.

[43] Sabbaghi, O., Cavanagh S. J., G.F. and Hipskind S. J., T. (2013) Service-Learning and Leadership: Evidence from Teaching Financial Literacy. *Journal of Business Ethics*, 118: 127–137. https://doi.org/10.1007/s10551-012-1545-6.

MBA students mentor schoolchildren in slums. By spending time together and gradually immersing themselves in the lives of these children and the slum community, the students steadily forge stronger ties with the children. They share in the highs and lows of slum life and as a result of this immersive experience, they stop seeing the slum as a distant, unknown setting and instead begin to understand the community almost as if they were insiders. The whole process helps them become more empathetic.

As Deepa[44] puts it,

> Poverty is a complex, multi-dimensional phenomenon. One cannot teach it in a classroom; it needs an immersion in the cauldron of real life. [...] Empathy is innate among humans but it often takes an immersive real-life experience to bring it to the surface. The world needs business managers who have this sort of empathy—people with courage and the ability to fight battles on behalf of the weak.

ESADE, the business school where one of the two co-authors of this book works, is also an entity that has been promoting service-learning for almost 20 years. ESADE has a unit (SUD—University Development Service) that offers students the opportunity to engage in initiatives and communities around the world. The goal is to make participants observe, reflect on and act to drive fairer development for all. Throughout the programme's 19 editions, 916 students have taken part in 530 projects in countries in Europe, North and South America, Africa and Asia, giving over 300,000 hours to community service. These initiatives boost students' compassion because they work hand in hand with the community to drive change.

Research shows that service-learning helps participants develop empathy and compassion and hone their interpersonal skills. It also heightens participants' sense of their own responsibility.[45] In short, service-learning is a powerful tool for fostering social awareness and for developing servant leadership styles. For service-learning to be effective, it must combine experiential immersion in a certain community, with spaces for reflection, both individually and in groups. Oddly enough, while this methodology is increasingly being applied in business schools, it is generally poorly incorporated into management development programmes in the business world.

---

[44] https://www.strategy-business.com/author/Deepa+Krishnan.

[45] Lester, S. W. (2015). Melding Service Learning and Leadership Skills Development: Keys to Effective Course Design. *Journal of Experimental Education*, 38(3), 280–295. https://doi.org/10.1177/1053825915576196.

Rabobank aims to stimulate servant leadership by offering the opportunity to its entire staff to contribute personally to the work of the Rabo Foundation in rural areas. Rabo Foundation invests significantly (€36.2 million in 2020) in impact funding to achieve continuous positive economic, social and ecological change. Employees can add value to one of the Foundation's many projects in rural Africa, Asia and Latin America (where they are encouraged to take temporary assignments). This makes employees identify with the bank's mission and helps boost personal leadership skills, such as responsibility, empathy and compassion.

Going Beyond the Leader of the Moment

Another of the key challenges for any company with a conscience is to ensure an ongoing commitment to the organizational conscience, while maintaining high leadership standards. The only way to achieve this is through governance systems that go beyond the individual and collective characteristics of the people leading the company at any given moment and consolidate a certain identity and leadership style.

For example, Rabobank merged its network of highly autonomous local co-op banks with the central co-op *Rabobank Nederland* into one co-op bank operating with just one banking licence and one consolidated financial statement (first published in 2016). One of the requirements of the merger was that the bank's co-operative nature had to be firmly anchored in the new structure. This meant developing a corporate governance mechanism that could systematically preserve and nurture Rabobank's unique co-operative company identity and its singular perspective on the role of leaders.

Therefore, each local bank kept its own Members Council. This council elects the local Supervisory Board, which ultimately approves the bank's strategy through bottom-up decision-making. At the local level, each Members Council is involved in monitoring the banking business as well as the co-operative role in local communities. Each Members Council is thus Rabobank's 'eyes and ears', maintaining valuable networks and connections with society. This constitutes the bank's precious social capital. Each Members Council has its own special budget termed 'Co-operative Dividend' and decides how this should be distributed to benefit the local communities that the bank operates in. Internal rules and the Articles of Association were redrafted to grant powers and duties to supervisory bodies and directors at the local level. So, despite Rabobank's merger, the co-op kept many of its local, decentralized features.

Rabobank's most important decision-making body is the General Members' Council (GMC), on which Member Representatives sit (i.e. the chairs of the local Supervisory Boards). The GMC sets the strategy for the Rabobank Group and safeguards its co-operative identity. It is charged with important formal tasks and responsibilities. The bank's Managing Board and the Supervisory Board are accountable to the GMC.[46]

One should also note that the largest part of Rabobank's capital still consists of retained earnings (i.e. net surpluses that members have left in the bank since its establishment, as laid down in the Articles of Association approved by those members). That is why the GMC now acts as owner of Rabobank. Rabobank Certificates constitute another valuable source of core capital and were originally Member Certificates (they could only be bought by members after 2000). In 2013, Member Certificates were converted into Rabobank Certificates, which are publicly listed.

Overall, Rabobank's governance system is strongly linked to its 'co-operative' nature. Co-ops follow certain key principles and values that have guided and served them well over the years. The European Association of Co-operative Banks describes the hallmarks of such entities thus:

> Democracy—materialised by the co-operative share, a strong commitment to social values and the proximity offered by the network of many bank branches to its customers.

Many other corporations based on different principles are also promoting new governance structures to foster more conscience-based approaches to business and to meet the main challenges facing mankind. Another interesting example of this trend is furnished by BBVA, a major Spanish bank. BBVA's governing bodies have defined and promoted a corporate strategy that takes in sustainability, the fight against climate change, and fostering responsible business as key priorities. In addition, the key feature of this corporate strategy is integration of sustainability and a responsible approach to business— principles that now lie at the heart of all the group's activities. In 2021, BBVA created its Global Sustainability Division (GSD), to which the bank's business units report. This reporting structure is a bold and innovative step in the financial sector that will help transform the business model. The GSD leads all the BBVA Group's sustainability initiatives, fostering innovative financial solutions to spur a sustainable transition in all of the bank's activities, setting

---

[46] H. Groeneveld et al.: National Initiatives to Drive the Evolution of the Cooperative Banking Sector, 2018; p. 109, 110 in: M. Migliorelli et al.; New Cooperative Banking in Europe. Palgrave Macmillan, 2018.

and applying the principles on which responsible management of the business is based.

The BBVA Board is helped by four committees. The Executive Committee provides support for the integration of sustainability in all the group's business processes and activities. The Risk and Compliance Committee helps integrate sustainability in the analysis, planning and management of the group's risks. The Audit Committee supervises the information on sustainability that is publicly reported to the markets. Finally, the Remuneration Committee provides support in the incorporation of sustainability indicators, which are linked to the group's variable remuneration models.

The Changing Face of Leadership

Liz Sweigart

A smartphone user captures a video of an individual's racist, homophobic tirade in a public park and posts it on social media. Within hours, the video goes viral and internet users quickly discover not only the identity of the person involved but their employer and other organizational affiliations as well. Almost instantaneously, internet commentators begin bombarding the employer's corporate accounts on Twitter, LinkedIn, Facebook, and Instagram demanding a response for the employee's behaviour. The news media wants a statement. Investors are calling wanting to know how the incident will affect the launch of the company's new product. How is the CEO to respond?

Elsewhere in the world, a government's belligerent acts prompt an outcry from the public. Simple internet searches reveal the names of companies doing business in the offending jurisdiction. Rapidly, users flood social media channels with calls for boycotts unless the identified organizations, particularly the more iconic brands, denounce the territory's actions and cease local operations immediately. Simultaneously, companies' employees in the local country are reaching out to headquarters wanting to know what will happen to their jobs and whether their companies will help protect them and their families amidst the geopolitical violence and instability. What should the affected businesses' executives and boards do?

Meanwhile, a company's founder and CEO recognizes an opportunity to take a stand on income inequality, an issue of personal importance to her. She announces new mandatory minimum salaries for entry-level personnel and pledges to cut her own pay by 90%. The action receives a mixed response. Employees and advocacy groups applaud the move as tangible and meaningful. Caught off guard and now under scrutiny from their own workers, other industry executives denounce the action as unsustainable and public relations theater. Political pundits also weigh in, accusing the CEO of trying to promote a radical agenda that will be punished by investors and quickly forgotten by the public. Should the CEO be making business decisions based on her personal values and beliefs?

(continued)

(continued)

Although all three scenarios are anonymized representations of actual events, none of them were imagined when these corporate leaders were climbing the corporate ladder or appeared as case studies in business school textbooks. What were previously distant hypotheticals are now stark reality for many corporate leaders. How should CEOs tackle this brave new world?

Increasingly, business leaders are facing calls from stakeholders—ranging from customers, employees and suppliers to regulators, social media influencers and the public—to speak out and take immediate action when it comes to moral and ethical issues both in their organizations and in society. These leaders are also recognizing that they have opportunities to make change in their organizations and even in society more broadly based on their own purpose, values and ethics. Unlike the financial accounting scandals of the early 2000s, these new challenges and opportunities for business leadership are equity- and justice-oriented. As a result, business leaders must fundamentally reassess and re-evaluate how they understand and practice leadership.

Leaders face a difficult balancing act, simultaneously trying to drive financial returns that please shareholders while building trust with stakeholders who perceive an obligation on the part of business to contribute to just and equitable outcomes in society. In this dynamic and often polarized environment, conscientious firms need conscientious leaders who can act as moral integrators: people who recognize the conflict between shareholder primacy and stakeholder expectations and who possess the skills necessary to bridge these seemingly competing positions.

As Warren Bennis wrote, leadership is simultaneously one of the most studied and least understood subjects in the realm of human knowledge.[47] Although leaders have existed for millennia, the academic study of leadership is a relatively recent phenomenon. Starting in the mid-nineteenth century with the conceptualization of the 'Great Man',[48] our understanding of leadership has evolved over the years. The focus has shifted, away from an entitative view of leadership that emphasized leaders' individual traits and characteristics towards the study of the complex relationships between leaders, followers and their environments.[49] This change demonstrates a growing appreciation for the importance of context in leaders' decision-making.[50] It has also put significant pressure on current conceptualizations of what it means to be an ethical leader.

(continued)

---

[47] Bennis, W. G. (1959). Leadership theory and administrative behavior: The problem of authority. *Administrative Science Quarterly*, 4(3), 259–301. https://doi.org/10.2307/2390911.

[48] Carlyle, T. (1841). *Heroes and hero worship*. Adams.

[49] Uhl-Bien, M., & Arena, M. (2017). Complexity leadership: Enabling people and organizations for adaptability. *Organizational Dynamics*, 46(1), 9–20. https://doi.org/10.1016/j.orgdyn.2016.12.001.

[50] Antonakis, J., Avolio, B. J., & Sivasubramaniam, N. (2003). Context and leadership: An examination of the nine-factor full-range leadership theory using the Multifactor Leadership Questionnaire. *The Leadership Quarterly*, 14(3), 261–295. https://doi.org/10.1016/S1048-9843(03)00030-4; Avolio, B. J., Wernsing, T., & Gardner, W. L. (2018). Revisiting the development and validation of the Authentic Leadership Questionnaire: Analytical clarifications. *Journal of Management*, 44(2), 399–411. https://doi.org/10.1177/0149206317739960; King, A. S. (1990). Evolution of leadership theory. Vikalpa, 15(2), 43–56; Kimura, T., & Nishikawa, M. (2018). Ethical leadership and its cultural and institutional context: An empirical study in Japan. *Journal of Business Ethics*, 151(3), 707–724. https://doi.org/10.1007/s10551-016-3268-6.

(continued)

Traditionally, ethical leadership is defined as, *'The demonstration of normatively appropriate conduct through personal actions and interpersonal relationships, and the promotion of such conduct to followers through two-way communication, reinforcement, and decision-making'* (emphasis in original).[51] In this view, ethical leaders both act morally (as 'moral persons') and cultivate an environment that encourages or induces others to behave morally (as 'moral managers').[52]

Although this description of ethical leadership dominates the literature, recently scholars and practitioners have begun to question its completeness. Muel Kaptein proposed expanding the definition to include the dimension of moral entrepreneurship, reflecting the role corporate leaders play outside of their organizations in helping to innovate new ethical norms in society.[53] In my own doctoral work, I posited that the definition of ethical leadership should also encompass the growing demands for organizational leaders to integrate calls for ethical action from various groups within society (e.g. the public, socially conscious investors) into the enterprise.[54] I argued that, as presently constituted, none of the aspects of ethical leadership (or corporate social responsibility practices for that matter) adequately capture the dimension of the moral integrator. While the moral entrepreneur applies ethical leadership to transmit a new moral standard to society, the moral integrator must synthesize internal and external stakeholders' expectations for ethical business conduct with the organization's values. Moreover, I asserted that the role of the moral integrator is only growing more critical as organizational leaders face increasingly complex ethical situations, such as when a member of the public documents and shares evidence of an employee violating an organizational ethical norm in their private life. The last few years have seen a dramatic increase in the need for corporate leaders to effectively practice moral integration.

Across the spectrum of business, from closely held domestic family companies to publicly traded multinational enterprises, corporate leaders must effectively practice moral integration whether they are responding to viral videos showing employees engaged in racist behaviour, addressing controversial new laws, assessing organizational responsibilities in the face of geopolitical conflict or any other of the numerous instances of value judgements leaders must make every day. Although leadership exists and is important at every level of an organization, for companies to truly behave as conscientious, executives must set the tone and lead by example.

(continued)

---

[51] Brown, M. E., Treviño, L. K., & Harrison, D. A. (2005). Ethical leadership: A social learning perspective for construct development and testing. *Organizational Behavior and Human Decision Processes*, 97(2), 117–134. https://doi.org/10.1016/j.obhdp.2005.03.002, p. 120.

[52] Barnard, C. J. (1938). *The functions of the executive*. Harvard University Press; Treviño, L. K., Hartman, L. P., & Brown, M. (2000). Moral person and moral manager: How executives develop a reputation for ethical leadership. *California Management Review*, 42(4), 128–142. https://doi.org/10.2307/41166057.

[53] Kaptein, M. (2019). The moral entrepreneur: A new component of ethical leadership. *Journal of Business Ethics*, 156(4), 1135–1150. https://doi.org/10.1007/s10551-017-3641-0.

[54] Sweigart, E. A. (2021). The moral integrator: How for-profit organizations in the United States apply ethical leadership in response to publicized incidents of anti-Black racism (Publication Number 28497513) [PhD, The Chicago School of Professional Psychology]. ProQuest Dissertations & Theses Global. Ann Arbor, MI.

(continued)

There are several approaches for leaders looking to embrace the role of moral integrator. Learning how better to foster communication through dialogue can help leaders have more productive conversations with shareholders and stakeholders. Rather than being performative, dialogue should create dynamic exchanges and build mutual understanding between groups with seemingly opposing priorities.[55]

Creating spaces for effective dialogue requires a leader to be intellectually curious, seeking to advance knowledge and understanding of complex topics for themselves and those around them.[56] Leaders can nurture an open and inquisitive mindset through asking open-ended questions that evoke awareness and surface insights.[57] Powerful questions most often begin with words like *what* and *how*, that invite reflection and the infusion of context. Words like *why* or leading questions frequently come across as judgmental and may create defensiveness rather than encourage open sharing.

The response of Starbucks' executives to a widely reported incident of anti-Black racism that took place at one of the company's Philadelphia area cafés in 2018, exemplifies this approach. In a live, nationally televised interview, CEO Kevin Johnson explained why he felt it was important to connect with the two Black men who were targeted by the store manager.[58] He said, 'I'd like to have a dialogue with them so that I can ensure that that we have the opportunity to really understand the situation and show some compassion and empathy for the experience they went through'. Moreover, he indicated that he wanted to invite the men to join his team as they worked to address the larger issue of unconscious bias. In addition to travelling to Philadelphia to meet with the men in person, Johnson and other key executives also engaged with civic leaders, community members, customers and employees to hear and seek to understand their perspectives and expectations.

Leaders can also develop their own emotional intelligence, enhancing their self-awareness, situational awareness and ability to self-regulate. Self-aware leaders are more likely to behave in alignment with their values. Enhancing situational awareness puts leaders in closer touch with those around them and helps to contextualize decisions. Leaders who can self-regulate better manage their emotions and act in accordance with situational demands. All these elements are critical to practicing ethical leadership successfully.

(continued)

---

[55] Leahy, M. J. (2001). The heart of dialogue (Publication Number 3022121) [PhD, Fielding Graduate Institute]. ProQuest Dissertations & Theses Global. Ann Arbor, MI.

[56] Hosking, D.-M., Shamir, B., Ospina, S., & Uhl-Bien, M. (2012). Exploring the prospects for dialogue across perspectives. In M. Uhl-Bien & S. Ospina (Eds.), Advancing relational leadership research: A dialogue among perspectives (pp. 501–535). Information Age Publishing.

[57] Whitmore, J. (2017). *Coaching for performance: The principles and practice of coaching leadership* (5th ed.). Nicholas Brealey.

[58] Roberts, R., Johnson, K., Stephanopoulos, G., & Robach, A. (2018, April 16). Starbucks CEO speaks out after Black men arrested. ABC News. https://www.youtube.com/watch?v=-YPZ2FhVFGA.

(continued)

Although often considered an innate trait, individuals can learn and increase their emotional intelligence over the course of their lives.[59] Research shows that coaching focused on developing emotional and social competencies supports leaders in developing their own emotional intelligence.[60] For coaching to be effective, however, individuals must be willing to be humble and acknowledge what they do not yet know, along with potential blind spots.

Responding to a viral video showing one of her employees engaged in a racist rant, Franklin Resources CEO, Jennifer Johnson admitted that she recognized gaps in her understanding of the prevalence and insidiousness of the racism often encountered by her Black employees. 'I thought I was probably much more aware than I was', she told *Bloomberg*'s Scarlet Fu. Johnson described how she increased her understanding and empathy through listening and dialogue as well as examination of how and why her own experiences differed from others.[61] Although challenging, self-reflection and introspection are important technique leaders can use to develop their emotional intelligence.

With business executives facing these complex events and issues seemingly daily, the need for the development of moral integration capabilities has never been greater. By adopting these approaches and building this new skills set, organizational leaders can deliver outcomes that build trust with stakeholders and produce sustainable value for shareholders.

Liz Sweigart is Chief Product and Strategy Officer at Safe Kids AI. Formerly she was a Partner in PwC's Global Structuring Practice.

Conclusion

Leadership is an increasingly complex activity. There are two main reasons for this. One is that leaders have to face strategic paradoxes that can only be tackled by combining different leader styles. The other is that we live in an unstable, extremely dynamic and uncertain world, as shown by the COVID pandemic and geopolitical crises. In this context, it is hard for a leader to play a 'heroic' visionary role and come up with the right answers to ever more frequent disruptive changes. Additionally, such settings call for leaders who can combine different leader styles but this is easier said than done and not all

---

[59] Bradberry, T., & Greaves, J. (2009). *Emotional intelligence 2.0.* TalentSmart.

[60] Van Oosten, E. B., McBride-Walker, S. M., & Taylor, S. N. (2019). Investing in what matters: The impact of emotional and social competency development and executive coaching on leader outcomes. *Consulting Psychology Journal: Practice and Research*, 71(4), 249–269. https://doi.org/10.1037/cpb0000141.

[61] Fu, S., & Johnson, J. (2020, August 28). Front row: Jenny Johnson, Franklin Templeton President & CEO full show [Video]. Bloomberg Markets and Finance. https://www.youtube.com/watch?v=M05Sgsm4T3M.

managers can pull it off. From this standpoint, there is a pressing need to foster much more collective leadership.[62] Thus, a key CEO role is nurturing a team of leaders who bring complementary skills and leader styles. In addition, such a CEO must also empower this team and give its members reasonable latitude in making decisions. Last but not least, she must also foster deep, ongoing dialogue between the team members so that each person's complementary skills generate the desired synergies.

This collective approach to leadership calls for great self-awareness on the part of all members of the management team so that they can grasp what their strengths and weaknesses are and how they can best draw on their colleagues' complementary skills. This requires the courage to acknowledge one's own vulnerabilities and listen carefully to others. One of the benefits of collective approaches to leadership is that it greatly speeds up decision-making by being better able to gauge stakeholders' needs and expectations. Finally, collective leadership greatly boosts commitment to the firm's strategic vision.

---

[62] Contractor, N. S.; DeChurch, L. A.; Carson, J.; Carter, D. R.; and Keegan, B. (2012) The topology of collective leadership. *The Leadership Quarterly*, 23(6): 994–1011.

9

It's Up to You

In an essay about Charles Dickens, George Orwell wrote 'For you can only create if you can care'. This reflects Orwell's own belief as a social observer and writer,[1] but it also sets a challenge to managers, employees, investors and citizens, because it argues that to create the solutions that can tackle such problems as climate change, biodiversity loss and inequality, we need to care. A commitment to caring helps people to listen to their conscience and to have the courage to act in line with their purpose and principles. This is a difficult process and indeed Orwell acknowledged it himself, because it is all too easy to become alienated from the reality of the things around us. We care in the moment, but we then forget. In his book, *The Road to Wigan Pier* (1937), Orwell describes the experience of visiting coal mines—at a time in Britain when nearly a million people were miners. In the style of an ethnographer, he writes about the noise, the intense heat and near-naked miners, the dust and the claustrophobic conditions, with the men always stooping, and sometimes crawling, as they cover long distances underground. Then Orwell is back at home and writing in front of a coal fire and he forgets where coal comes from and the conditions of the miners: 'It is only very rarely, when I make a definite mental effort, that I connect this coal with that far-off labour in the mines. It is just "coal"—something that I have got to have.'[2]

Coal might seem remote to many people in certain parts of the world, but a similar argument can be made about our mobile phones. Mobiles too are something we have got to have. They have become an integrated part of people's lifestyles and are seen to be a necessary ingredient to function in a

---

[1] Orwell, G. (1981) *A Collection of Essays*. New York: Harvest Books.
[2] Orwell G (1958) Down the Mine in *George Orwell Selected Writings*. London: Heinemann, p. 44.

© The Author(s), under exclusive license to Springer Nature Switzerland AG 2022
N. Ind, O. Iglesias, *In Good Conscience*, https://doi.org/10.1007/978-3-031-09338-8_9

social context. Yet, we rarely give pause to think about the consequences of consumption and the desire to update ourselves with the latest models. Richard Herrington, Head of Earth Science at the Natural History Museum in London, observes that the business and environmental practices where the raw materials are sourced isn't always good and includes exploitation of workers, dangerous conditions and the use of child labour. A raw material such as Cobalt, 70% of which comes from the Democratic Republic of Congo, is particularly susceptible, not least because mining it, is so hazardous in the first place.[3] Herrington's hope is that by understanding 'the environmental (and human) cost of cheap electronics' that people will 'reduce their own waste and make choices that in turn force manufacturers to lift their standards'.[4]

What Herrington, and indeed Orwell, push us towards is a recognition that as individuals and as the people who populate organizations, we have a responsibility to think about the consequences of our actions beyond ourselves—especially when the impacts can seem remote to us in terms of time and place—and to recognize the role conscience can play in guiding us and businesses to do the right thing. This concerns creating value in new ways (as we saw in Chap. 6), educating consumers as to good consumption practices and building movements for change in a way that recognizes people's needs and desires (as we saw in Chap. 7). To be clear this is not about telling consumers what to do but rather taking a conscientious perspective that is both human- and planet-centric while being cognizant of the needs of a business.

In this chapter, we zero in on four inter-dependent themes, which align with environmental, social and governance factors and create the opportunity to build deeper and more enduring relationships with stakeholders. *First* is about taking responsibility for making people's lives better. *Second* is the ability to think critically. *Third* is the promotion of an open and transparent philosophy that stimulates trust and sharing. *Fourth* is the adoption of a human-centric focus to decision-making that is empathetic and energizing and makes the organizations that practice it, better places to work at, invest in and buy from.

Each of the opportunities is something that organizations should address, but these are also opportunities that each of us, as individuals, can seize. As you will read later in this chapter, the people that populate organizations are

---

[3] Baumann-Pauly D (2020) Why Cobalt mining in the DRC needs urgent attention. 29 October 2020. Council on Foreign Relations. https://www.cfr.org/blog/why-cobalt-mining-drc-needs-urgent-attention.
[4] Lotzok K (2020) Your mobile phone is powered by precious metals and minerals. 7 October 2020. https://www.nhm.ac.uk/discover/your-mobile-phone-is-powered-by-precious-metals-and-minerals.html.

increasingly activist and make demands as a condition of employment. Just as they expect their employers to be conscientious, so they too want to exercise their conscience and to do the right thing. Employees can be passive or, worse, disinterested, but to realize meaning at work requires a more active approach where people help to enact, and sometimes challenge, the organizational conscience by stretching out and helping to find solutions to the environmental and social ills of the world. This means encouraging managers, employees and partners, to take the time to reflect on situations, to doubt, to listen to alternative perspectives and to weigh up the impacts of different choices. The barrier here is that often businesses valorize speed and want fast, safe decisions that endorse existing practices, not discussion, reflection and the uncertainty of the new.[5] However, as the philosopher Michael Anker notes, there is no place of certainty, 'Every decision reorganizes the fabric of life, but each move in itself does not lead to a conclusive point of certainty; it leads to a new, uncertain, undecidable, and aporetic space from which once again we must decide and act.'[6] Managers and employees need to accept uncertainty and risk as facets of organizational life. This encouraging people to question is not about trying to overturn well-founded truths that are rooted in thorough analysis, but it is about recognizing the nuances involved in making conscientious decisions and considering together with others, 'the dialectic between our judgments about particular situations and the principles we affirm on reflection'.[7]

Taking Responsibility

As members of organizations or as entrepreneurs, we can use our conscience to seize opportunities to effect change. This recognizes that we don't only want to perform well in terms of meeting sales targets, increasing margins or being efficient, we also want more intrinsic rewards related to making a contribution to the wider world. This way of thinking shifts us away from the idea that the meaning of something is defined by the organization to a recognition that meaning is developed through shared experiences of 'interacting, communicating and collaborating' together.[8] Organizations can of course make it more or less easy for individuals to express their conscience—for

[5] Matthing, J., Sandén, B., & Edvardsson, B. (2004). "New service development: learning from and with customers", *International Journal of Service Industry Management*, 15(5),479–498.

[6] Anker M. (2009). *The Ethics of Uncertainty: Aporetic Openings*. New York: Atropos Press, p. 61.

[7] Sandel M (2010) *op cit.*, p. 28.

[8] Magala S (2009) *The Management of Meaning in Organizations*. Basingstoke: Palgrave Macmillan, p. 50.

example, by encouraging individuals to think through their own purpose (Unilever) or by building a democratically oriented culture (John Lewis Partnership) or by promoting participation in innovation and sustainability processes (Patagonia). Yet it is also the case that individuals can influence organizations to be more conscientious by challenging existing ways of thinking, engaging in dialogue and taking initiatives. By taking such actions, we embark on a journey of self-discovery that is not so much concerned with finding something that is hidden from us but is more about the making of oneself in the act of searching.[9]

Research endorses this belief that employees want their work to be meaningful and that they are also willing to become activists to realize their aims. A 2021 study of 7000 employees in seven countries showed that COVID-19 had changed values and made employees more belief-driven in selecting and staying with a company. Personal empowerment (77%) and social impact (71%) are almost equivalent with career advancement (82%) in deciding where to work and there is an expectation that companies will take a stand on issues. Half the respondents agree with the statement 'A large group of employees exerting strong pressure within our organization can get it to change almost anything about itself', while some 60% think employees have more power and leverage than before the pandemic to create change and 76% of employees see themselves as activists. Employees are willing to take action to produce change either by working within the system (58%) or taking it public (40%) through whistleblowing, use of social media, strikes, leaking documents and emails and protesting outside offices or factories.[10]

Companies don't always find such activism to their liking. It can be disruptive and polarizing and runs counter to the desire for control. Sometimes, a company will even undermine its own stated belief systems in the desire to have things its own way. For example, in 2021, Amazon attempted to stop its workers from voting in favour of unionizing by reminding them of their benefits and advising them, 'it won't be easy to be as helpful and social with each other'. Ranged against them though were 70 of Amazon's institutional investors, who noted that the attempts to sway workers appeared to be against

[9] Rousseau J-J (2008) *Confessions*. Trans Angela Scholar. Oxford: Oxford University Press.

[10] Edelman (2021) Edelman Trust Barometer. Special Report: The Belief-Driven Employee. https://www.edelman.com/sites/g/files/aatuss191/files/2021-09/2021%20Edelman%20Trust%20Barometer%20Special%20Report%20The%20Belief-Driven%20Employee%20Global%20Report%20Full%20w%20Talk%20Track.pdf.

Amazon's own human rights principles and that the company should remain neutral in the vote.[11]

Activism within organizations is no longer something for the few. It has become something for each of us. Employees who care and take responsibility and enact power *with* can create transformative change that brings a conscience to life. Let's meet Kené Umeasiegbu, Campaigns Director at Tesco again. During his time at Tesco, the commitment to sustainability has waxed and waned. In 2009, Tesco had made a zero carbon commitment, but when Umeasiegbu joined in 2013 as Head of Climate Change, there was no plan in place to deliver it. Undeterred, he asked an external expert body—Carbon Trust—to provide validation and recommendations as to the actions necessary to reach zero carbon by 2050. While Tesco had been making some progress in terms of energy efficiency, there was a need for a transformative change—key to which was a switch to renewable energy. Yet, the switching cost was prohibitive—the argument was that the money could be better used elsewhere. Umeasiegbu got round the problem by creating a long-term renewables transition plan and entering power purchase agreements to fund the transition. Having used the gambit once, he used a similar approach by partnering with Volkswagen and Podpoint to roll out electric vehicles charging points at Tesco supermarkets. In both cases the 'how' is important. Umeasiegbu didn't accept internal funding constraints, but instead used external validation to make a business case for change and tied it into the strategic commitment to net zero and then found long-term partners to help finance the transition. Once the initiatives were up and running, telling the stories behind them both engendered pride among employees and unleashed creativity in other parts of the business. As the changes took effect, support from the Board increased. Now the date for zero carbon for Tesco's own operations is 2035.

In a similar vein, Umeasiegbu has spurred Tesco to think about food production and waste reduction: 'when I joined Tesco, I'd hear people say, "wouldn't it be great if we had an alternative to soya; wouldn't it be great if we found a way to reduce emissions from livestock"'. And I remember thinking, this is Tesco, the UK's biggest food retailer and we are just wishing and hoping. Who else is going to act, if not us?' The result was Tesco established a sustainability innovation fund with WWF to hunt for late-stage innovations within the food sector where the 'science was proven, the technology is conceivable and the economics still need to be figured out'. The rationale here is to innovate in such a way that the company is ahead of the market. Within

---

[11] Lee D. (2021) Amazon must not interfere with US union effort, say investors. *Financial Times*. 9 February 2021.

Tesco such initiatives can generate some tension and lots of discussion, but Umeasiegbu argues that a key learning from working with sustainability is to plan well and take a long-term view, with pragmatic intermediate steps. He notes, 'if we have to jump at the last moment, then it's almost never good for business'.

Taking responsibility, as Umeasiegbu demonstrates, is akin to thinking of oneself as a citizen, using freedom to effect positive change. The idea of citizenship as 'individual behaviour, not directly or explicitly recognized by the formal reward system, and that in the aggregate promotes the effective functioning of the organisation' is rooted in participation. Citizenship encourages individuals (a) to become autonomous, lively and responsive; (b) to be committed and purposeful, thus influencing their colleagues to be committed and purposeful; (c) open to others, which helps to integrate diverse views.[12] If we can think of ourselves as citizens as well as managers, employees or entrepreneurs, we can take a broader view of our role that goes beyond a specific work mandate to effect positive change.

Thinking Critically

Whenever we make difficult decisions, we have to assess the known facts and accept uncertainty. To do this we need accurate and timely information with which to evaluate, challenge and act on the issues that confront us. Without this we are in a world of myths and half-truths. The value of compiling data and using it to make well-informed decisions comes through in many of the discussions we have had with companies. 'Doing the right thing' sounds like an emotive exhortation; to do the right thing for people or the planet, come what may. Yet, while there may indeed be emotion involved, in most cases decisions should be based on the data derived from consumer insights, materiality analyses and verification from independent bodies. Without insight, thinking is uncritical and is just opinion. This leads to gestures that sometimes might sound impressive, but either have unintended negative consequences or fail to really deliver significant impacts.

For example, imagine yourself, employed as a manager responsible for deciding the policy on carbon offsets. Since the Kyoto Protocol of 2005, which requires wealthy countries to reduce their greenhouse gas emissions, there has been a burgeoning business in companies trading their emissions for projects that avoid or remove carbon. This is a valuable process, but one that

---

[12] Gratton, L. (2004) *The Democratic Enterprise*. London: Pearson Education.

is beset by a lack of good data and lack of transparency. Critics argue that carbon offsetting diverts companies away from decarbonization by giving them a palliative for pollution and that there is a questionable quality in many of the projects. In a review of 65 certified carbon offset projects for BrewDog, only 5 were found to be 'good'. Mike Berners-Lee, a professor and carbon emissions consultant, whose team conducted the review, notes that the problem of carbon offsets is that 'for a long time nobody was asking hard enough questions'.[13] This lack of critical thinking is also reflected in the problem that offsets used by companies to fund protection of forests can end up being used to protect forests that aren't under threat: 'the problem of empty offsets has dogged the global climate mission for decades … about two-thirds of offset projects allowed into this market [buying and selling carbon offsets] don't represent true emissions reductions, say academics studying the projects'.[14]

Whatever the company policy, you, as a conscientious manager, would have to ensure that the carbon offset policy is not an excuse for inaction in other environmental areas and would need to ask the hard questions of certification bodies to ensure that the offsets are being used in an authentic way to tackle climate change. You would need to build the data to make the case for your choices both internally and externally—and ought to have the confidence to be open in reporting the successes and failures of the programme, rather than simply touting the positives. Here the hope would be that the organizational conscience and yours align. However, it might be the case that there are different agendas and that the organization might choose to hide inconvenient truths about carbon offsets or trumpet what they have done without proper substantiation. Then you have to decide how to act. You could be passive and just go with the flow or you can think in a critical way and challenge the corporate conscience—something as we saw above in the Edelman research that employees are increasingly willing to do.

From the corporate perspective, encouraging critical thinking might sound like a recipe for discordancy as employees challenge existing norms. Yet, if individuals have a deep connection with the purpose and principles, they can use them as a framework for thought. This is particularly important in a sector, such as financial services where customer needs and societal expectations are changing at such a rapid pace that there is often little in the way of precedent to draw on and legislation and regulation lags behind innovation. As a

---

[13] Hodgson C & Nauman B. (2021) Carbon offsets: a licence to pollute or a path to net zero emissions? *Financial Times* 31 August 2021. https://www.ft.com/content/cfaa16bf-ce5d-4543-ac9c-9d9234e10e9d ?emailId=617294fec8f9e800048301af&segmentId=a8cbd258-1d42-1845-7b82-00376a04c08f.

[14] Elgin B. (2020) These trees are not what they seem. 9 December 2020. Bloomberg. https://www.bloomberg.com/features/2020-nature-conservancy-carbon-offsets-trees/.

consequence, banks are becoming instrumental in shaping new social, environmental and governance norms and employees are becoming more involved in having to make judgements as to the right course of action. This is easier when there is clarity as to what a bank stands for. For example, we have seen that Rabobank's mission and moral compass is deeply embedded within the way people think and act. This creates a structure within which employees can manage risk, but also think critically and have conversations with colleagues, to determine better ways to deliver systemic change.

Practising Transparency

Before we consider the value that transparency provides, we should perhaps consider the scenario when companies, through a lack of balance in their approach to stakeholders, intellectual property concerns or having something embarrassing to hide, keep secret their intentions and activities. Worrying over intellectual property and the consequences for competitive advantage is a genuine strategic reason for discretion, but stakeholder imbalance is rather the result of giving too much weight to one group (e.g. Boeing and shareholders as we saw in Chap. 3) and then covering up the consequences from other groups. Overall, too much secrecy undermines the working of ecosystems and relationships as it diminishes trust and disempowers stakeholders. At worst, it makes people suspicious that there is something underhand going on. As the philosopher Spinoza argues, people can only truly participate if they are properly informed rather than what often happens, which is 'the supreme folly to wish to transact everything behind the backs of citizens'.[15]

Without transparency, employees cannot be certain that what a company tells them is true and consequently they lack the ability to interact with confidence with each other and with partners. Employees may believe that they have only part of a story and are therefore unable to think in a critical way and to contribute to processes. Similarly, customers cannot be certain that they are making good choices, if the company is withholding information about the product or service and the way it has been produced or delivered. By holding back unpalatable information or simply being very selective in what is shared, a company not only undermines its own integrity, but that of its employees and customers as well. Investors also want timely and accurate information about the uses their money is put to. A company that lacks transparency in its

---

[15] Spinoza, Benedict de. (1998) *Tractatus Politicus*. Rendered into HTML and Text by Jon Roland of the Constitution Society. Available: http://www.constitution.org/bs/poltreat.txt. VII, 27.

approach to the environment or its policies towards people and society creates tangible and reputational risk for itself and for those individuals and institutions that finance and own it. This is why non-financial reporting is growing fast and 'companies that are not prepared will lack access to capital, sacrifice value, suffer damage to their reputation and ultimately end up falling foul of the law. Transparency leaders, on the other hand, will build trust among all stakeholders, differentiate themselves, enhance the effectiveness of capital markets and help society advance.'[16] Overall, an absence of trust increases transaction costs, while 'trust acts like a lubricant that makes any group or organization run more efficiently'.[17]

We would argue that transparency is good in itself, because it demonstrates faith in the probity of others to judge a company's conscience and its actions, but it also confers business benefits. As we have seen, companies such as Patagonia, Oda and Asket are very explicit about their processes and their impacts and this not only makes them distinctive but also creates a sense of closeness between them and their stakeholders. Similarly, Rabobank lives transparency in its use of buildings. For example, in the head office in Utrecht in the Netherlands, the office is designed to be accessible to anyone passing by who wants to have a coffee, view the art collection or meet friends or colleagues. The idea of sharing is baked into the culture by the bank's co-operative roots. The researchers, Oana Brindusa Albu and Mikkel Flyverbom, in a review of the academic literature on transparency, also note that alongside its value as a means of verifying what organizations say and do, there is a second aspect, which is performativity. This views transparency as a process that induces social action by focusing on the discussions and tensions that arise from making things visible; it talks new ways of thinking and behaving into existence. As they argue performativity, 'helps us understand issues of power, discipline, secrecy, and unintended consequences of disclosing information'.[18]

To enable transparency, we have to shift perspective from seeing the outside world as something separate, to one that sees others—consumers, lead users, experts—as partners in the development of value. This co-creative philosophy implies a willingness to share knowledge and to be receptive to new insights and ideas developed with people (as Sandro Kaulartz argued in Chap. 6). This is about encouraging power *with* and inviting relevant stakeholders to

---

[16] Chalmers J & Picard N. (2021) Learning to love transparency. *strategy+business*. Spring 2021. https://digitaledition.strategybusiness.com.

[17] Fukuyama, F. (2000) *Social Capital* in Culture Matters. How Values Shape Human Progress. Ed. L, E Harrison and S. P Huntington. Basic Books, p. 98.

[18] Albu, O. B., & Flyverbom, M. (2019). Organizational transparency: Conceptualizations, conditions, and consequences. *Business & Society*, 58(2), p. 289.

influence and shape new ways of working. In a previous article about conscientious corporate brands, we wrote that 'this demands a genuine will and an absolute commitment to listening to different stakeholders' needs, expectations and desires', and a willingness to 'engage them in strategic decision-making processes'.[19] In this view, transparency is a sign of good governance that delivers efficiency and effectiveness.[20]

Does this mean individuals and organizations should practice total transparency? Probably not, but instead of seeing the default as secrecy and admitting of exceptions where things can be more open, the default should be set to transparent. If you are attentive to the company conscience, then there is less to fear when criticism comes—because you can draw on the purpose and principles in your defence. The alternative is hiding embarrassing facts and then having them winkled out by others. Our argument then is that conscience is better served by sharing, wherever possible—using reports, social media, web sites, on-product QR codes and even till receipts (like Oda and Asket) to convey ideas and impacts, and build, co-creatively, movements of change together with stakeholders.

Focusing on People

When you seek to be more efficient and to meet targets, do you just see numbers or do you also see people? Ever since Frederick Taylor's 1911 book, *The Principles of Scientific Management*, the quest for efficiency in business has focused on control through measurement. This has helped companies to define strategies and working policies and to manage their processes, but at a cost. As Charlie Chaplin aptly parodied in his film *Modern Times* (1936), it also leads to dehumanizing work practices. We use data to justify decisions without remembering that facts are 'but an adaptation of the real to the interests of practice and to the exigencies of social life'[21] and we easily ignore the consequences of our actions on the lives of others. Consequently, employees become assets to be used and consumers become revenue generating units. This objectification means companies can outsource processes and industrialize craft-based work without worrying overly much about the wellbeing of

---

[19] Iglesias, O., & Ind, N. (2020). Towards a theory of conscientious corporate brand co-creation: the next key challenge in brand management. *Journal of Brand Management*, 27(6), 710–720.

[20] Albu, O. B., & Flyverbom, M. (2019). Organizational transparency: Conceptualizations, conditions, and consequences. *Business & Society*, 58(2), 268–297.

[21] Bergson H (2005). *Matter and Memory*. Trans by N M Paul and W S Palmer. New York: Zone Books, p. 183.

employees—especially if they are far away from the home market: out-of-sight, out-of-mind. We might argue this is the reality of modern business, whereby companies seek to reduce costs by shifting production or services to places where labour is cheaper than home markets and resisting the unionization of work forces.

A failure to pay attention to—and help develop—the knowledge and skills of employees though undermines the potential of organizations. When the dominant element in the valuation of companies is intellectual capital, it makes sense for managers to focus on people. This matters for the wellbeing of employees and for business performance—something that is increasingly recognized by investors who are also wary of the risks of toxic work cultures and mechanisms designed to silence workplace criticism. In Edelman's 2019 Trust Barometer study of Institutional Investors, 74% of global investors agreed that companies with activist employees were less attractive investments. By 2021 the mood was different, with 74% agreeing that employee activism within a company is indicative of a healthy workplace culture, good leadership and/or highly engaged workforce. Also, 85% of investors think that a workplace culture that fosters employee empowerment is important for building trust.[22] Putting aside the irony that we have questioned the emphasis on numbers and then used them to make a point, what Edelman's research demonstrates is the way business is having to change to meet the reality of stakeholder expectations.

If companies want to attract and keep the most able and committed people who align with their purpose and principles and to attract investors, then they will have to be conscientious and build processes that are human-centric and cultures that are empathetic. Drawing on Kant, managers should view employees as an end in themselves and not as merely a means, honour their self-respect, provide them with the freedom to satisfy certain of their desires and pay them sufficiently well that they have an independent existence.[23] These Kantian principles come through in many of the companies we have described in this book and remind managers of the need to think through the implications of their actions and to try to influence the organizations that they work for. This is sometimes easier said than done. Some organizations have a tendency to see people as a means to something else. However, others have the capability and confidence to nurture the skills and knowledge of their people. As an example of the latter, the Italian fashion entrepreneur,

[22] Edelman (2021) Edelman Trust Barometer Special Report: Institutional Investors. https://www.edelman.com/sites/g/files/aatuss191/files/2021-11/2021%20Investor%20Trust%20Report_FINAL.pdf.

[23] Bowie, N. E. (1998). A Kantian theory of meaningful work. *Journal of Business Ethics*, 1083–1092.

Brunello Cucinelli, has structured a business around the ideals of what he calls humanistic capitalism that ensures employees are well-paid (around 20% above market rate) and have opportunities for personal development. When the company floated on the Milan Stock Exchange, Cucinelli made it clear that his aim was to grow in a 'gracious way' that recognized the needs of suppliers, artisans and employees to grow as well.[24] Addressing the G20 in Rome in 2021, Cucinelli said, 'I decided that the dream of my life would be to live and work for the moral and economic dignity of the human being. I wanted a company that made healthy profits, but did so with ethics, dignity and morals. … I wanted human beings to work in slightly better places, earn a little more in wages and feel like thinking souls at work.'[25] In his creed, Cucinelli states specifically, that 'human dignity is restored solely through the rediscovery of conscience'.

We might all wish that we worked for a company like Brunello Cucinelli, but of course the reality for most is somewhat different. However, even if we work for a company that is not overtly conscientious, we can still seize the opportunity to use our own conscience in everyday work by looking beyond abstract ideals and think about the needs of the people one works with and builds relationships with. When human centricity is forgotten, the damage can be significant, both to a company and to the individuals that populate it. Although it can be intimidating to take on the power of the organization and its norms, we should try to build coalitions of change. This is the way to make our own working lives meaningful, as well as those around us. As the political philosopher, Todd May suggests, 'One of the elements of a meaningful life is the ability to contribute to creating it. … First if one cannot contribute to creating one's own life, it may turn out that the life one lives is not the life one would have chosen. … Second, if one cannot contribute to creating one's life, then in some sense it isn't *one's own* life that is being created.'[26]

How to Think Different

As you come to the end of this book, you should think critically about what you have read and to think about what you might do as a result. It's tempting for us to pre-judge what your conscience might tell you to do. After all, as

---

[24] Gino F and Pisano G. (2019). Humanistic Capitalism at Brunello Cucinelli. *Harvard Business School Case* 9-920-007. 27 August 2019.

[25] https://www.brunellocucinelli.com/en/g20.htmlq.

[26] May, T. (2008) *The Political Thought of Jacques Rancière: Creating equality.* Edinburgh: Edinburgh University Press, p. 90.

humanity we are faced with significant environmental and social challenges and surely we can agree on that. Yet the relative weight of those challenges and the way that we understand and choose to tackle them will vary, depending on context, culture and prejudice. Our message is not that there is a universal miracle cure, but rather that we should exercise our conscience whenever we encounter a dilemma; to think through what is the right thing to do as individuals and for the organizations that we work for, invest in and buy from. This means doing two things that derive from the formula: **conscience = critical thought + acting together to effect change**. First, it means assembling with an open mind, the best insight we can find on a given issue and reflecting critically on it. Given the volume of information we are bombarded with and the need often to have data mediated by experts, this is a complex process. It requires the ability to distinguish fact from opinion and to use good judgement to valorize what we see and hear. Second—and linked to the first part of the formula—is an awareness of the world and our common humanity that should enable us to step over narrow interests and to understand, empathize and work with others to create meaningful change. As theorist Maurice Blanchot writes, 'If I want my life to have meaning for myself, it must have meaning *for someone else*'.[27]

Our motivation in writing '*In Good Conscience*' is to encourage managers to think differently about business and the way it can contribute to the world. Of course, we see organizations who pay little or no attention to this—that are fixated on shareholder returns above all else—and managers who are narcissistic and self-aggrandizing—that are interested in their own wellbeing. And we see businesses that make grandiose claims backed by little substance. Yet, we hope we have offered sufficient and varied examples to illustrate what can be. This does not mean that all the companies that are cited in the book are virtuous through and through, but rather that they are committed to positive change. Our hope is that through the book and the online and face-to-face programmes that we run for undergraduates, graduates and executives at ESADE Business School in Barcelona and other Universities that we can transform the attitudes and behaviour of current managers and those that will run the businesses of the future.

---

[27] Blanchot, M. (1988) *The Unavowable Community*. (La Communauté Inavouable, 1983, Les Editions de Minuit). Trans. Pierre Joris. Barrytown, New York: Station Hill, p. 22.

Index[1]

---

[1] Note: Page numbers followed by 'n' refer to notes.

Printed in the USA
CPSIA information can be obtained
at www.ICGtesting.com
CBHW062126241024
16148CB00029B/584

9 783031 093371